Study Guide

Dea K. DeWolff

Children

Robert V. Kail
Purdue University

Upper Saddle River, New Jersey, 07458

Upper Saddle River, New Jersey 07458

10 9 8 7 6 5 4 3 2 1

ISBN 0-13-093323-6

Printed in the United States of America

Contents

Chapter 1
The Science of Child Development

This chapter gives you tips on how to use your text, describes the theories of child development, and the themes that guide child-development research.

USING THIS BOOK

MODULE 1.1

Using This Book

- *Organization of Chapters*
- *How to Use These Features to Learn About Children*
- *Terminology*
- *A Final Word*

If you did not read this module in your textbook, **STOP**, go to your text, and read this module.

This Study Guide has been written to accompany *Children* by Robert Kail. The purpose of this study guide is to help **YOU**, the student, learn the text material by actively testing your knowledge of the material. The first step in learning the material in the textbook is to keep up with your assigned readings. You will find that learning this material is **much** easier if you do not try to learn everything the night before the exam. The following is a guide for using this study guide with your textbook.

✔ Skim each chapter paying attention to module learning objectives, outlines, and headings.

✔ Before reading each module, read the learning objectives at the beginning of the module.

✔ After reading each module, answer the *Check Your Learning* questions at the end of the module. If you don't know the answer to a question, go back and find the answer in the module.

✔ Now turn to the Study Guide.

✔ Read the module **outline** and try to remember some of the information that was presented under each heading.

✔ Read the **learning objectives** and mentally answer these questions.

✔ Now see what you need to know to **master the learning objectives**. Notice that each mastery objective is linked to the following sections in the study guide.

✔ Complete each section of the study guide. On matching sections, try to figure out the answers before looking at your choices in the boxes.

✔ At the end of each chapter, test yourself using the short **multiple-choice** tests.

✔ Try to integrate the information and apply it by answering the **essay** questions at the end of each chapter.

MODULE
1.2

Theories of Child Development

- *The Biological Perspective*
- *The Psychodynamic Perspective*
- *The Learning Perspective*
- *The Cognitive-Developmental Perspective*
- *The Contextual Perspective*
- *The Big Picture*

THEORIES OF CHILD DEVELOPMENT

Textbook Learning Objectives

- **What are the major tenets of the biological perspective?**
- **How do psychodynamic theories account for development?**
- **What is the focus of learning theories?**
- **How do cognitive-developmental theories explain changes in children's thinking?**
- **What are the main points of the contextual approach?**

TO MASTER THESE LEARNING OBJECTIVES:

1. Describe each theory
2. Know how each theory accounts for developmental changes
3. Know the terms associated with each theory
4. Know the details of the theories

Description of Each Theory: Match the description to the correct theory

Bronfenbrenner's contextual	Maturational
Cognitive-developmental	Operant conditioning
Contextual	Psychodynamic
Ethological	Psychosocial
Information-processing	Social cognitive

1. This theory suggests that development reflects a natural unfolding of specific and prearranged biological plans within the body. ____________
2. This theory emphasizes the adaptive nature of behavior and the importance of experience during critical periods of development. ____________
3. This theory suggests that development is determined by how well people resolve the conflicts they face at different ages. ____________

4. This theory emphasizes the unique challenges or crises posed during different stages of development. ____________
5. This theory emphasizes that the consequences of a behavior determine whether a behavior is repeated in the future. ____________
6. This theory emphasizes children's efforts to understand their world, using punishment, reinforcement, and imitation. ____________
7. This theory focuses on children's thinking and how it changes over time. In trying to make sense of their world, children create theories about the world that they test. ____________
8. This theory proposes that human cognition consists of mental hardware and software. ____________
9. This theory suggests that child development should be considered against the backdrop of one's cultural beliefs, customs, and skills.
10. The theory of child development that is illustrated by the diagram below.__________

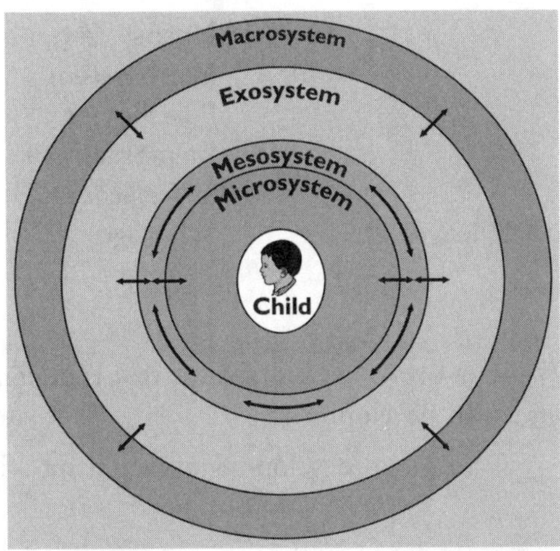

How Does the Theory Account for Developmental Change? Match each key assumption with the correct theory

Cognitive-developmental
Contextual
Ethological
Information-processing
Maturational
Operant conditioning
Psychodynamic
Psychosocial
Social cognitive

1. Development is determined primarily by how a child resolves psychological and social crises.____________
2. The rewards and punishments in one's environment direct one's development.____________
3. Development is determined by how a child resolves conflicts between his biological drives and society's standards for right and wrong.____________

4. Development is influenced by immediate and more distant environments that influence each other.____________

5. Development is the result of a natural unfolding of biological plans and experience is relatively unimportant.____________

6. Development is the result of improvements in mental software and mental hardware.____________

7. Development is the result of adaptive behaviors and behaviors that are learned during critical periods of development.____________

8. Development is directed by the reinforcements, punishments, and imitation of other's behavior that children encounter in their environments as they try to understand their world.____________

9. Development is the result of children's efforts to understand their environments by creating theories about the physical and social worlds. When their predicted theories are not supported they must revise their theories. These revisions lead to developmental changes.____________

Know the Terms: Match the terms with the definition

Critical period
Culture
Ego
Exosystem
Id
Imitation (observational learning)
Imprinting
Macrosystem
Mesosystem
Microsystem
Punishment
Reinforcement
Self-efficacy
Superego
Theory

1. A ____________ is an organized set of ideas that is designed to explain and make predictions about development.

2. A ____________ is a time in development when a specific type of learning can take place.

3. Creating an emotional bond with a mother or mother figure is called ____________.

4. In psychodynamic theory, the ____________ is the component of personality where primitive instincts and drives reside and it presses for immediate gratification of bodily needs and wants.

5. According to psychodynamic theory, the ____________ is the practical, rational component of personality.

6. The third component of personality in psychodynamic theory is the ____________ that internalizes adult standards of right and wrong.

7. A consequence that increases the future likelihood of the behavior it follows is called a ____________.

8. A consequence that decreases the future likelihood of the behavior it follows is called a ____________.

9. Learning by watching others is called ____________.

10. ____________ refers to children's beliefs about their own abilities and talents.

11. ____________ is the knowledge, attitudes, and behavior associated with a group of people.
12. The people and objects in an individual's immediate environment make up one's ____________.
13. Connected microsystems create an individual's ____________.
14. The ____________ refers to social settings that a person may not experience first hand but that influence development.
15. The broadest environmental context, the ____________, includes the subcultures and cultures in which the other systems are embedded.

Know the Details of the Theories

1. T F Jean Jacques Rousseau believed that the child was born a *tabula rasa*, or blank slate.
2. T F Theories do *not* lead to predictions that can be tested in research.
3. T F According to Maturational Theory, parents should carefully construct their children's environments so that behaviors like speech, play, and reasoning all emerge.
4. T F Learning a behavior before or after a critical period is very difficult.
5. T F According to Ethological Theory, experience is necessary for triggering programmed, adaptive behavior.
6. T F According to maturational theorists, creating an emotional bond with a mother or mother figure is called bonding.
7. T F Freud believed that early experiences established patterns of behavior that endure throughout a person's life.
8. T F According to Freud, the id is the component of personality that internalizes society's standards for right and wrong.
9. T F The ego, one of Freud's components of personality, tries to resolve the conflict between one's biological desires and socially acceptable behavior.
10. T F The superego emerges during the preschool years.
11. T F Each of Freud's stages of psychosexual development is focused on pleasure in different parts of the body.
12. T F According to Freud, the task of parents is to over-indulge their children so that they are sure that their children's needs will be met at each stage of development.
13. T F According to Erikson, the challenge during adolescence is to develop a sense of trust in the world.
14. T F According to Erikson, the challenge during infancy is to develop a sense of identity.
15. T F According to Erikson, the earlier stages of psychosocial development provide the foundation for the later stages.
16. T F According to John Watson, experience is the most important determinant of the course of development.
17. T F Giving a child a candy bar after he cleans his room is an example of negative reinforcement.

18. T F A punishment decreases the future likelihood of the behavior that it follows.

19. T F According to Bandura, self-efficacy beliefs help determine when children will imitate others.

20. T F During Piaget's preoperational period, knowledge of the world is based on an infant's sensory and motor skills.

21. T F Abstract thinking characterizes thought during Piaget's stage of formal operational thinking.

22. T F According to information-processing theory, mental hardware refers to cognitive structures such as different memories where information is stored.

23. T F According to information-processing theory, cognitive development occurs in abrupt stages.

24. T F According to Vygotsky, a child's development must be considered against the backdrop of his culture's beliefs, customs, and skills.

25. T F According to Bronfenbrenner's contextual theory, only a child's immediate environment influences her development.

ANSWERS

Describe the Theories

1. Maturational (11)
2. Ethological (11)
3. Psychodynamic (12)
4. Psychosocial (13)
5. Learning (15)
6. Social cognitive (15)
7. Cognitive-developmental (15)
8. Information-processing (16)
9. Contextual (17)
10. Bronfenbrenner's contextual (17)

Assumptions About Development

1. Psychosocial (13)
2. Operant conditioning (14)
3. Psychodynamic (12)
4. Contextual (17)
5. Maturational (11)
6. Information-processing (16)
7. Ethological (11)
8. Social cognitive (15)
9. Cognitive-developmental (15)

Key Terms

1. theory (10)
2. critical period (11)
3. imprinting (11)
4. id (12)
5. ego (12)
6. superego (12)
7. reinforcement (14)
8. punishment (14)
9. imitation or observational learning (14)
10. Self-efficacy (15)
11. Culture (18)
12. microsystem (18)
13. mesosystem (18)
14. exosystem (18)
15. macrosystem (18)

Know the Details

1. false (10)
2. false (10)
3. false (11)
4. true (11)
5. true (11)
6. false (11)
7. true (12)
8. false (12)
9. true (12)
10. true (12)
11. true (12)
12. false (12)
13. false (13)
14. false (13)
15. true (13)
16. true (14)
17. false (14)
18. true (14)
19. true (15)
20. false (16)
21. true (16)
22. true (16)
23. false (17)
24. true (18)
25. false (18)

THEMES IN CHILD-DEVELOPMENT RESEARCH

MODULE
1.3

Themes in Child-Development Research

- *Early Development is Related to Later Development but Not Perfectly*
- *Development is Always Jointly Influenced by Heredity and Environment*
- *Children Help Determine Their Own Development*
- *Development in Different Domains is Connected*

Textbook Learning Objectives

- **How well can developmental outcomes be predicted from early life?**
- **How do heredity and environment influence development?**
- **What role do children have in their own development?**
- **Is development in different domains connected?**

TO MASTER THESE LEARNING OBJECTIVES:

1. Describe the 4 themes in child-development research
2. Know the details of each theme

Description of Each Theme: Match the description with the correct theme

Active-passive child	Connection of domains
Continuity-discontinuity	Nature-nurture

1. Development is jointly influenced by heredity and environment.__________
2. Development in one domain is connected to development in other domains.__________
3. Early development is related to later development, but not perfectly.__________
4. Children help determine their own development.__________

Know the Details of Each Theme

1. T F The belief that outgoing 5-year-olds become outgoing adults is consistent with the belief that development is discontinuous.
2. T F Later development can be predicted perfectly from earlier aspects of development.

3. T F Development is shaped by the interaction of nature and nurture.
4. T F The effects of heredity and environment are equal in all areas of development.
5. T F The view that children are passive in their development corresponds to Locke's view that children are blank slates.
6. T F The view that children are active in their development means that children are simply at the mercy of their environments.
7. T F Cognitive and social development are independent from each other.

ANSWERS

Describe the Themes

1. Nature-nurture (23)
2. Connection of domains (24)
3. Continuity-discontinuity (22)
4. Active-passive child (24)

Know the Details

1. false (22)
2. false (23)
3. true (23)
4. false (23)
5. true (24)
6. false (24)
7. false (24)

SUMMARY

MODULE 1.1: USING THIS BOOK

learning

Organization of Chapters. Each chapter includes three or four modules that begin with learning objectives, a vignette, and a mini-outline. In the text, key terms and their definitions appear in boldface type. Each module includes a special feature that examines a specific topic in depth. The module ends with questions that allow you to check your __________. Each chapter ends with several elements that should encourage you to think about the information in the chapter as well as a summary like the one you're reading now.

summarize

How to Use These Features to Learn About Children. Preview the entire chapter, then read one module daily. As you read, try to __________ the main ideas; ask yourself questions. When you've finished the chapter, review each module and use the study aids at the end of the chapter.

preschooler; adolescent

African; European

Terminology. In your text people of different ages are referred to using specific terms: newborn, infant, toddler, __________, school-age child, __________, and adult. Also, terms that identify the unique cultural heritage of different ethnic groups are used: __________ American, Asian American, __________ American, and Native American.

A Final Word. Enjoy the book!

MODULE 1.2: THEORIES OF CHILD DEVELOPMENT

Theories are important because they provide the __________ for development and provide __________ for research. Traditionally, five broad theoretical perspectives have guided researchers.

explanations
hypotheses

The Biological Perspective. According to this perspective, biological factors are critical in shaping development. In maturational theory, child development reflects a natural unfolding of a pre-arranged __________. Ethological theory emphasizes that children's behavior is often __________–it has survival value.

biological plan
adaptive

The Psychodynamic Perspective. This perspective emphasizes the role of __________ or crises in development. Freud proposed a theory of personality that included the id, __________, and superego; he also proposed a theory of psychosexual development in which the focus of physical __________ shifts to different parts of the body. Erikson proposed a life-span theory of psychosocial development, consisting of eight universal stages, each characterized by a different struggle.

conflict
ego
pleasure

The Learning Perspective. Learning theory focuses on the development of observable behavior. Operant conditioning is based on the notions of reinforcement, __________, and environmental control of behavior. Social learning theory proposes that people learn by __________ others. Social cognitive theory emphasizes that children actively interpret the events they observe.

punishment
observing

Cognitive-Developmental Theory. Cognitive-developmental theory focuses on thought processes. Piaget proposed a four-stage universal sequence based on the notion that, throughout development, people create their own __________ to explain how the world works. According to information-processing theory, people deal with information like a computer does; development consists of increased __________ in handling information.

theories
efficiency

The Contextual Perspective. Vygotsky emphasized the role of __________ in children's development and Bronfenbrenner proposed that development occurs in the context of interconnected systems. These range from the microsystem (people and objects in the child's immediate environment) to the macrosystem (the cultures and subcultures in which all other __________ are embedded).

culture
systems

MODULE 1.3: THEMES IN CHILD-DEVELOPMENT RESEARCH

Four themes help unify the findings from child-development research that are presented throughout this book.

Early Development is Related to Later Development, But Not Perfectly. According to the view that development is continuous, children stay on the same pathway throughout development; according to the view that development is discontinuous, children can __________ paths at virtually any point in development. Research supports an intermediate view: Development is not completely __________ as in the continuous view, nor is it completely flexible as in the discontinuous view.

change
rigid

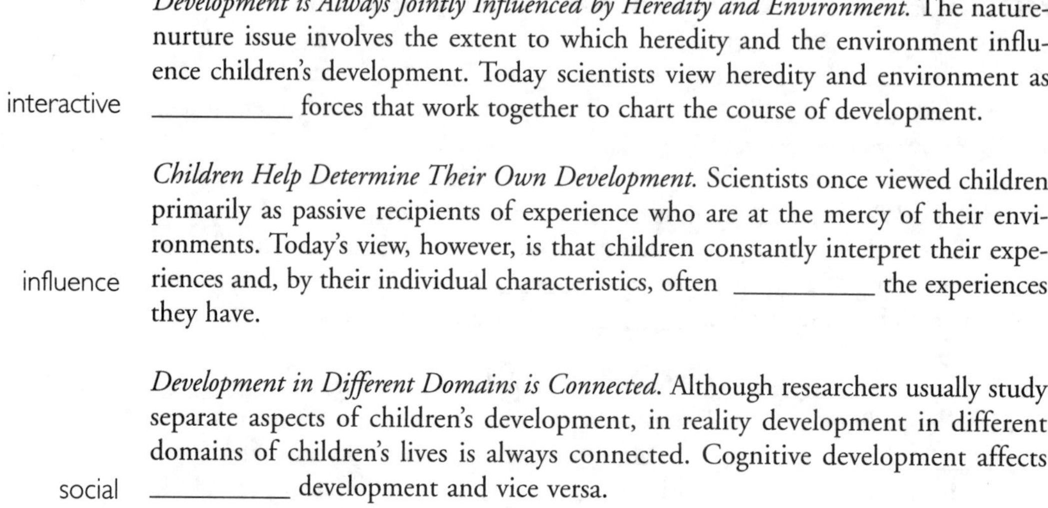

Development is Always Jointly Influenced by Heredity and Environment. The nature-nurture issue involves the extent to which heredity and the environment influence children's development. Today scientists view heredity and environment as __________ forces that work together to chart the course of development.

interactive

Children Help Determine Their Own Development. Scientists once viewed children primarily as passive recipients of experience who are at the mercy of their environments. Today's view, however, is that children constantly interpret their experiences and, by their individual characteristics, often __________ the experiences they have.

influence

Development in Different Domains is Connected. Although researchers usually study separate aspects of children's development, in reality development in different domains of children's lives is always connected. Cognitive development affects __________ development and vice versa.

social

CHAPTER 1 THE SCIENCE OF CHILD DEVELOPMENT

TEST YOURSELF

1. The idea that the mind of the human infant is a *tabula rasa* at birth reflects the belief that
   a. experience molds each person into a unique individual.
   b. children should be left alone so that their good natures can unfold.
   c. heredity plays a major role in an individual's development.
   d. infants cannot think because their minds are blank.
2. The French philosopher, Jean Jacques Rousseau, believed that
   a. the human infant is born a *tabula rasa.*
   b. infants were born with an innate sense of justice and morality.
   c. experience molds each human into a unique individual.
   d. parents should teach their children rationality and self-control.
3. The idea of continuity in development
   a. is consistent with the view that behavior during the preschool years is not related to behavior during later childhood.
   b. means that development in one domain is related to development in other domains.
   c. is consistent with the view that early development is related to later development.
   d. means that development is jointly influenced by heredity and environment.

4. Michael and Lisa are new parents and they believe that their actions will influence their new son. They don't think that their son's behavior will influence their parenting. Michael and Lisa's views of parenting are consistent with the __________ position of the __________ issue.
   a. nature; nature-nurture
   b. passive; active-passive child
   c. connection; connection of domains
   d. continuity; continuity-discontinuity

5. Ximena and Chris believe that they don't need to worry about parenting their new son, Brant, because he was born with a good nature and his good nature will determine his outcomes in life. Chris and Ximena's views of parenting are consistent with the __________ position of the __________ issue.
   a. nature; nature-nurture
   b. passive; active-passive child
   c. connection; connection of domains
   d. continuity; continuity-discontinuity

6. The view that development is a result of the unfolding of a specific and prearranged scheme or plan within the body is characteristic of
   a. Konrad Lorenz's ethological theory.
   b. Sigmund Freud's psychodynamic theory.
   c. Erik Erikson's psychosocial theory.
   d. Arnold Gesell's maturational theory.

7. According to ethologists, some behaviors can only be learned
   a. when the behavior is reinforced and opposing behaviors are punished.
   b. through observational learning.
   c. during a critical period when the organism is biologically programmed to learn that behavior.
   d. when the conflict between biological drives and society's standards is resolved.

8. Freud's psychodynamic theory contributed to the field of child development by suggesting that
   a. learning is more important than maturation.
   b. early experiences establish patterns that endure throughout a person's life.
   c. learned, adaptive behaviors influence later development.
   d. children's cognitive development influences later behavior.

9. According to Freud, psychosexual development is determined by
   a. how a child satisfies the need for pleasure that is focused on various areas of the body.
   b. improvements in mental hardware and mental software.
   c. children's efforts to understand their physical and social worlds.
   d. the reinforcements and punishments in one's environment.

10. According to Erikson's theory of psychosocial development, development
    a. is the result of a natural unfolding of biological plans.
    b. is determined by the resolution of conflicts between one's biological drives and society's standards of right and wrong.
    c. is the result of children's attempts to understand their worlds.
    d. is determined by children's resolution of psychological and social crises.

11. Carol begged her father for some candy when they were in the grocery store. Eventually, Carol's father gave in and bought Carol some candy. According to operant conditioning, what is likely to happen the next time Carol and her father go to the grocery store?
a. Carol will not beg for candy because her father punished her begging the last time that they were in the store.
b. Carol will not beg for candy because her father reinforced her begging the last time that they were in the store.
c. Carol will beg for candy because her father reinforced her begging the last time they were in the store.
d. Carol will beg for candy because her father punished her begging the last time they were in the store.

12. Frank was watching a Saturday morning cartoon in which the main character kicked someone and took away a toy. Frank then walked across the room and kicked his brother Joe and took away Joe's toy just as a cartoon character had done on the TV show. According to social cognitive theory, Frank has just demonstrated
a. observational learning or imitation.
b. punishment for aggressive behavior.
c. reinforcement for sharing toys.
d. imprinting.

13. Jean Piaget's theory of cognitive development focused on
a. the resolution of psychological crises.
b. improvements in mental hardware and software.
c. children's creation of "theories" that help them understand their worlds.
d. adaptive behaviors that are learned during critical periods.

14. According to information-processing theory, mental hardware
a. does not change with development.
b. refers to cognitive structures.
c. includes organized sets of cognitive processes.
d. becomes less sophisticated with age.

15. According to Lev Vygotsky, development
a. should be considered within the context of the child's culture.
b. occurs within contexts that are embedded within each other.
c. occurs when children create "theories" that help them understand their worlds.
d. is the result of resolving psychological and social crises.

16. According to Bronfenbrenner's contextual theory,
a. events that happen in one microsystem do not influence other microsystems.
b. only one's immediate environment influences development.
c. individuals experience exosystems first hand.
d. the macrosystem is the broadest environmental context.

17. Heidi lives with her mother, father, sister, and brother. According to Bronfenbrenner's contextual theory, Heidi's immediate family are part of her
a. mesosystem.
b. exosystem.
c. macrosystem.
d. microsystem.

ESSAY QUESTIONS

1. One day you and a friend are talking and your friend states, "Development is the result of the genes that you inherit, and those genes put you on a developmental path that stays the same throughout your life." What can you tell your friend about the issues of nature versus nurture and continuity versus discontinuity?
2. Your friends have a new baby girl named Kaycee and they have told you that they can't wait to raise her because they will create a wonderful environment that Kaycee will love. For example, they will never let Kaycee watch worthless shows on televison and she will love to read because they will read to her all the time when she is a baby. What can you tell your friends about the issue of the child being active versus passive in her development?
3. Your sister Kumi is having problems with her 2-year-old daughter. Your niece, Kayla, has been throwing tantrums to get her own way. As you watch Kumi and Kayla interact, you see that Kumi will say "no" to Kayla, Kayla will scream and cry, and then Kumi will give in to her. What can you tell Kumi about the principles of operant conditioning that might help her deal with the situation?

ANSWERS

Multiple Choice

1. a (10)
2. b (10)
3. c (22)
4. b (23)
5. a (23)
6. d (11)
7. c (11)
8. b (12)
9. a (12)
10. d (13)
11. c (14)
12. a (14)
13. c (15)
14. b (16)
15. a (18)
16. d (18)
17. d (18)

Essay

1. You can tell your friend that both nature and nurture interact with each other to influence development. So, your friend's idea that genes are the only important influence on development is wrong. Almost all aspects of development are shaped by both heredity and environment. Also, the developmental path that one is on is not completely rigid and fixed as your friend thinks. Early behavior does not predict later behavior perfectly so a child who is a brat may actually grow up to be a nice adult. (23)
2. According to John Locke, a child is a blank slate on which experiences in the environment are written. Locke's view is consistent with the view of the child who is passive in her development. Your friends also seem to be taking the view that Kaycee will be the passive recipient of the environment that they structure for her. In reality, children often are active in influencing and interpreting their worlds. For example, Kaycee may not sit still when they read to her so they will eventually stop trying. Also, Kaycee may prefer playing catch and kicking a soccer ball to sitting and reading. (10; 23-24)

3. You should tell Kumi that reinforcement is a consequence that increases the future likelihood of the behavior that it follows. Reinforcers can include food, candy, toys, or getting your way. By giving in to Kayla, Kumi is reinforcing her tantrums and increasing the likelihood that Kayla will throw another tantrum. Instead Kumi should be punishing Kayla's tantrums because punishment decreases the likelihood that a behavior will be repeated. Punishments can include things such as being sent to one's room, having privileges taken away, or having a toy taken away. So, Kumi should stop reinforcing Kayla's tantrums by giving in to her. (14)

Chapter 2
Research in Child Development

Module 2.1 *Doing Child-Development Research*

Module 2.2 *Child-Development Research and Family Policy*

This chapter explains the techniques that researchers use to study children and their development.

DOING CHILD-DEVELOPMENT RESEARCH

MODULE
2.1

Doing Child-Development Research

- *Measurement in Child-Development Research*
- *General Designs for Research*
- *Designs for Studying Development*
- *Ethical Responsibilities*
- *Communicating Research Results*

Textbook Learning Objectives

- **How do scientists measure topics of interest in children's development?**
- **What general research designs are used in child-development research? What designs are unique to child-development research?**
- **What ethical procedures must researchers follow?**
- **How do researchers communicate results to other scientists?**

TO MASTER THESE LEARNING OBJECTIVES:

1. Describe each type of measurement
2. Know the strengths and weaknesses of each type of measurement
3. Give an example of each type of measurement
4. Know why it is important that measures be both reliable and valid
5. Know the general and developmental research designs including the terms associated with each
6. Know the strengths and weaknesses associated with each type of research design
7. Know the details of doing developmental research

Describe Each Type of Measurement: Match the description with the correct term

Naturalistic observation
Structured observation
Self-report
Systematic observation

1. Children's answers to questions about a topic of interest.____________
2. Watching children and carefully recording what they do or say.____________
3. Observing children as they behave spontaneously in a real-life situation.____________
4. Creating a setting that is likely to elicit a behavior that is of interest to a researcher.____________

Know the Strengths and Weaknesses of Each Measure: Match each strength or weakness with the correct measure

Naturalistic observation
Structured observation
Self-report

1. The strength of this measure is that it can be used to study behaviors that are rare or that occur in private.____________
2. The strength of this measure is that it is relatively convenient, particularly when administered in groups.____________
3. The weakness of this measure is that the results may be invalid if the structured setting changes children's behavior.____________
4. The strength of this measure is that it captures children's behavior in its natural setting.____________
5. The weakness of this measure is that it is difficult to use to study behaviors that occur infrequently or that occur in private settings.____________
6. The weakness of this measure is that the results may be invalid because children answer incorrectly because of forgetting or response bias.____________

Give an Example of Each Type of Measure: Match the example with the correct measure

Naturalistic observation
Structured observation
Self-report

1. A researcher who is interested in seeing if boys and girls play in same-sex or mixed-sex groups might observe children playing on a school playground at recess. This is an example of ____________.
2. A researcher who is interested in cooperation between children might observe children in the lab while they play a game that requires cooperation. This is an example of ____________.
3. A researcher who is interested in the characteristics of children's friendships might ask children a number of questions about friendship. This is an example of ____________.

Know the Terms Associated with Each Type of Measure: Match the term with the correct definition

Populations
Valid

Reliable
Sample

Variables

1. The factors that are subject to change during an experiment are the ____________ .
2. A measure is ____________ if it really measures what researchers think it measures.
3. A measure is ____________ if the results are consistent over time.
4. Broad groups of children are called ____________.
5. A ____________ is a subset of a population.

Describe the Research Designs and the Terms Associated with Each: Match the description with the correct term

Cohort effects
Correlation coefficient
Correlational study
Cross-sectional study
Dependent variable

Experiment
Field experiment
Independent variable
Longitudinal study
Microgenetic study

1. This research design is a systematic way of manipulating key factors that an investigator thinks causes a particular behavior.__________
2. This research design involves looking at relations between variables as they exist naturally in the world.__________
3. This expresses the strength and the direction of a relation between 2 variables in a correlational study.__________
4. The factor that is manipulated by an investigator in an experimental study.__________
5. The behavior of interest that is observed by an investigator in an experimental study.__________
6. This type of research design involves observing or testing the same group of individuals repeatedly at different points in their lives.__________
7. This type of research design involves identifying developmental changes by looking for differences between children of different ages. These children are tested at the same point in time.__________
8. These are differences between different age groups that are the result of environmental events rather than developmental processes.__________
9. In this type of research, the experimenter manipulates independent variables in a natural setting. ____________
10. This type of research involves testing children repeatedly over a span of days or weeks to observe change as it occurs. ____________

Know the Details

1. T F A strength of correlational studies is that they can be used to determine cause and effect.
2. T F A strength of correlational studies is that investigators can examine relations between variables as they exist naturally in the world.

3. T F A strength of experimental studies is that investigators can control the different treatments that children may experience.

4. T F A weakness of experimental studies is that one can draw conclusions about cause and effect because the manipulation of independent variables occurs under controlled conditions.

5. T F A weakness of experimental studies is that the behavior of interest is not studied in its natural setting.

6. T F A strength of field experiments is that the results are more likely to be representative of behavior in real-world settings than results obtained in the laboratory.

7. T F When a correlation coefficient equals 0, two variables are inversely related (e.g., children who watch many violent television shows are less aggressive).

8. T F When a correlation coefficient is greater than 0, two variables are positively related (e.g., children who watch many violent television shows are more aggressive).

9. T F When a correlation coefficient is less than 0, two variables are not related (e.g., the number of violent television shows viewed is not related to aggressive behavior).

10. T F Random assignment to different treatment conditions is not important in experimental studies.

11. T F Longitudinal studies involve testing children of different ages at the same time.

12. T F One strength of longitudinal studies is that they allow researchers to chart an individual's development.

13. T F One disadvantage of cross-sectional studies is that repeated testing may change participants' behavior.

14. T F One disadvantage of longitudinal studies is cohort effects.

15. T F A weakness of microgenetic studies is that researchers cannot observe change as it occurs.

16. T F Researchers should use methods that minimize potential harm or stress for participants in their studies.

17. T F Researchers do not need to describe the research to people before they participate.

18. T F Research participants do not need to be told if deception is a part of the experiment.

19. T F Children's names should be linked with their data so that they are easy to identify.

20. T F Converging evidence from many research studies leads to increased confidence in research findings.

ANSWERS

Descriptions of the Measures

1. self-report (32)
2. systematic observation (30)
3. naturalistic observation (30)
4. structured observation (31)

Strengths and Weaknesses of the Measures

1. structured observation (31)
2. self-report (32)
3. structured observation (31)
4. naturalistic observation (30)
5. naturalistic observation (30)
6. self-report (31)

Examples of the Measures

1. naturalistic observation (30)
2. structured observation (31)
3. self-report (32)

Key Terms

1. variables (31)
2. valid (33)
3. reliable (33)
4. populations (33)
5. sample (33)

Describe the Research Designs and Terms

1. experiment (35)
2. correlational study (34)
3. correlation coefficient (34)
4. independent variable (35)
5. dependent variable (35)
6. longitudinal study (37)
7. cross-sectional study (38)
8. cohort effects (38)
9. field experiment (36)
10. microgenetic study (37)

Know the Details

1. false (34)
2. true (34)
3. true (35)
4. false (36)
5. true (36)
6. true (36)
7. false (34)
8. true (34)
9. false (34)
10. false (35)
11. false (37)
12. true (37)
13. false (37)
14. false (38)
15. false (37)
16. true (39)
17. false (39)
18. false (39)
19. false (40)
20. true (40)

CHILD-DEVELOPMENT RESEARCH AND FAMILY POLICY

MODULE
2.2

Child-Development Research and Family Policy

- *Background*
- *Ways to Influence Social Policy*
- *An Emphasis on Policy Implications Improves Research*

Textbook Learning Objectives

- **Why have child-development researchers recently become more involved in designing social policy?**
- **How do child-development researchers influence family policy?**
- **How has concern for family policy improved child-development research?**

TO MASTER THESE LEARNING OBJECTIVES:

1. Know the terms associated with child-development research and family policy
2. Know the details of child-development research and family policy

Know the Terms: Match the terms with the definition

Family policy | Quasi-experimental design

1. The laws and regulations that directly or indirectly affect families with children.____________

2. A research design that includes multiple groups that were not formed by random assignment. ____________

Know the Details of Research and Family Policy

1. T F Links between child development and family policy have become much weaker in recent years.

2. T F Research on child development may influence policies on day care and custody arrangements in the case of divorcing parents.

3. T F The Index of Social Health for Children and Youth assesses the well-being of children in the United States.

4. T F The Index of Social Health for Children and Youth includes information on teenage suicide and drug use.

5. T F Effective policy-making should be based on stereotypes.

6. T F Most children are able to represent their own interests.

7. T F Family policies can be evaluated by using existing theories and research in child development.

8. T F Child-development researchers can influence family policy by developing a model program that is designed to attack a particular problem.

9. T F The School of the 21st Century focused only on children's academic success.

10. T F While child-development research can improve social policy, social policy implications should not influence child-development research.

11. T F Random assignment of children to different experimental groups is an important aspect of quasi-experimental research designs.

12. T F Researchers who have a focus on family policy usually take a very narrow approach to child-development research.

ANSWERS

Key Terms

1. family policy (42) **2.** quasi-experimental design (46)

Know the Details

1. false (43)	**5.** false (44)	**9.** false (45)
2. true (44)	**6.** false (44)	**10.** false (46)
3. true (43)	**7.** true (44)	**11.** false (46)
4. true (43)	**8.** true (45)	**12.** false (46)

SUMMARY

MODULE 2.1: DOING CHILD-DEVELOPMENT RESEARCH

Measurement in Child-Development Research. Research typically begins by determining how to __________ the topic of interest. __________ involves recording children's behavior as it takes place, either in a natural environment (__________ observation) or a structured setting (__________ observation). Researchers sometimes create tasks to obtain samples of children's behavior. In __________, children answer questions posed by the experimenter. Researchers must also obtain a sample that is __________ of some larger population.

measure; Systematic observation
naturalistic
structured
self-reports
representative

General Designs for Research. In __________ studies, investigators examine relations among variables as they occur naturally. This relation is often measured by a __________, r, which can vary from -1 (strong negative relation) to 0 (no relation) to +1 (strong positive relation). Correlational studies __________ determine cause and effect, so researchers do experimental studies in which an __________ variable is manipulated and the impact of this manipulation on a __________ variable is recorded. __________ studies allow conclusions about cause and effect but the strict control of other variables that is required often makes the situation artificial. The best approach is to use both experimental and correlational studies to provide converging evidence.

correlational
correlation coefficient
cannot
independent
dependent
Experimental

Designs for Studying Development. To study development, some researchers use a __________ design in which the same children are observed repeatedly as they grow. This approach provides evidence concerning actual patterns of individual growth but has several shortcomings as well: it is time-consuming, some children __________ of the project, and repeated testing can affect performance. The __________ design involves testing children in different age groups. This design avoids the problems of the longitudinal design but provides no information about __________ growth. Also, what appear to be age differences may be __________ effects. Because neither design is problem-free, the best approach is to use both to provide converging evidence.

longitudinal
drop out
cross-sectional
individual, cohort

Ethical Responsibilities. Planning research also involves selecting methods that preserve the __________ of research participants. Experimenters must minimize the __________ to potential research participants, describe the research so that potential participants can decide if they want to participate, avoid __________, and keep results anonymous or confidential.

rights
risks
deception

Communicating Research Results. Once research results are collected and analyzed, investigators __________ the results in scientific journals where they are read and criticized by others. Such results form the foundation of __________ knowledge about child development.

publish
scientific

MODULE 2.2: CHILD-DEVELOPMENT RESEARCH AND FAMILY POLICY

Background. Child-development researchers have become __________ interested in applying the results of their work to family policy because of many changes in the American family and because changes in infant mortality, child abuse, and

increasingly

other variables indicate that American children and youth face many challenges to healthy development.

Ways to Influence Social Policy. Child-development researchers help to shape family
knowledge policy by providing useful __________ about children and their development so
that policies can be based on accurate information about children. They also con-
advocates tribute by serving as __________ for children, by evaluating the impact of pro-
programs grams on families and children, and by developing effective __________ that can
be implemented elsewhere.

An Emphasis on Policy Implications Improves Research. Focusing on public policy
broader implications improves research because researchers must take a __________ perspective on children's development than they would otherwise. Also, policy-related
research has produced more sophisticated research methods, such as the quasi-
experimental design.

CHAPTER 2 RESEARCH IN CHILD DEVELOPMENT

TEST YOURSELF

1. Which of the following is *true* of naturalistic observation?
   a. Researchers usually record all of a child's behaviors.
   b. Because children are being observed in their natural settings, the behavior of interest is less likely to be disturbed.
   c. This method is useful for studying phenomena that occur rarely.
   d. This method is useful for studying behaviors that occur in private settings.

2. Which of the following is a problem with the use of self-report?
   a. Answers do not lead directly to information on the topic of interest.
   b. Children may provide answers that are socially acceptable.
   c. The collection of information is not convenient.
   d. Children have very accurate memories so their answers regarding past events can be trusted.

3. Which of the following is *true* of sampling behavior with tasks?
   a. Sampling behavior with tasks may not really sample the behavior of interest.
   b. Sampling behavior with tasks can be used to observe behavior directly.
   c. Sampling behavior with tasks isn't a popular method because it isn't convenient to use.
   d. Sampling behavior with tasks might lead some children to provide socially acceptable answers.

4. If Mohammed took the same achievement test at 3 different times and received scores of 100, 75, and 85, the test would have low levels of
   a. validity.
   b. representativeness.
   c. sampling behavior.
   d. reliability.

5. A correlation coefficient of 0.0 indicates what about the relation between two variables?
   a. The two variables are directly related.
   b. The two variables are inversely related.
   c. The two variables are completely unrelated.
   d. This coefficient indicates which variable was the "cause" and which the "effect."

6. A researcher is interested in how the scores that children receive on a spelling test are affected by the amount of food that they eat for lunch. The independent variable is
   a. the age of the children.
   b. the scores on the spelling test.
   c. the words on the spelling test.
   d. the amount of food eaten for lunch.

7. Field experiments
   a. involve manipulation of independent variables.
   b. occur in a laboratory setting.
   c. do not allow investigators to draw conclusions about cause and effect.
   d. are usually fairly easy to conduct.

8. Which of the following is a disadvantage of longitudinal studies?
   a. The development of "test-wise" subjects.
   b. The problem of cohort effects.
   c. The sample of subjects over the course of the research stays the same.
   d. The cost of conducting a longitudinal study is relatively low.

9. The fact that differences between age groups in a cross-sectional study may result as easily from chance environmental events as from significant developmental processes
   a. is an example of the sample constancy problem.
   b. is a major problem of longitudinal studies.
   c. is a problem with a random sample from a population of interest.
   d. is a major disadvantage of the cross-sectional approach.

10. Which of the following is an ethical responsibility that researchers have to the participants in their research?
   a. Researchers do not need to explain the use of deception in their studies.
   b. Children's data should be linked with their names so that they can be identified easily.
   c. Researchers should minimize the potential for harm or stress to their participants.
   d. Researchers do not need to describe the research to participants before they decide to participate.

11. Which of the following is *not true* of the relation between child-development research and family policy?
   a. The links between child-development research and family policy have become weaker in recent years.
   b. Existing theory and child-development research can be used to evaluate how policies may affect children and their families.
   c. Child-development researchers have many methods to assess how families

and children are affected by social policies.
d. A focus on social policies can improve child-development research.

12. The Index of Social Health for Children and Youth (ISHCY)
   a. does *not* include measures of teenage suicide and drug use.
   b. is a barometer of the nation's economic health.
   c. assesses the well-being of children and youth in the United States.
   d. shows that American children and youth faced fewer challenges at the end of the 20th century than ever before.

ESSAY QUESTIONS

1. A researcher wants to see if watching a violent movie leads to more aggressive behavior in preschool children. How should the researcher proceed? Be sure to discuss sampling, assignment to conditions, and choice of independent and dependent variables.
2. A researcher wants to examine the changes in the stability of friendship between first- and third-grade children. Should the researcher use a cross-sectional or a longitudinal research design? Give the advantages and disadvantages of each design.
3. Using examples from everyday life, explain why a correlation between two variables does not prove a cause-and-effect relation between the variables.
4. Do you believe that the potential benefits to research justify the use of deception by the researcher? Support your answer.
5. Your friend is a child-development researcher who believes that her research and social policy are completely independent and should remain that way. What can you tell your friend about the benefits to both social policy and child-development research when the two are closely linked?

ANSWERS

Multiple Choice

1. b (30)	**5.** c (34)	**9.** d (38)
2. b (32)	**6.** d (35)	**10.** c (39)
3. a (32)	**7.** a (36)	**11.** a (44)
4. d (33)	**8.** a (37)	**12.** c (43)

Essay

1. The researcher could use an experimental design. The participants should be a sample of preschool children who are similar in social class, IQ, etc., to the population of interest (representative sampling). These children would be assigned randomly to one of two experimental conditions. In one condition, children would see a movie that contained many violent acts. In the other condition, children would see a movie about sharing that contained no violent acts. The type of movie that the children watched is the independent variable. After watching the movie, the children would be allowed to play in a room with toys. Structured observation would be used to determine if the amount of aggressive behavior while playing was related to the type of movie

that the children had watched. Aggressive behavior while playing (e.g., hitting, kicking, punching) is the dependent variable. (35-36)

2. A longitudinal study would involve looking at children's friendships in first grade. Later, when the same children were in third grade, researchers could see how many friendships still existed. A cross-sectional study might involve asking a group of first graders and a group of third graders questions about the stability of their friendships. The main advantage of a cross-sectional research design is that it can be done in a relatively short period of time and at a much lower cost than a longitudinal study. The major disadvantage is that cohort effects may be present which make if difficult to draw conclusions about developmental change. The main advantage of longitudinal research designs is that cohort effects are eliminated and actual change can be studied. The major disadvantages of longitudinal studies are that they are expensive, the sample may not remain constant as participants drop out of the study, and participants might become "test-wise." (37-38)

3. There is a positive correlation between the number of fire trucks at a fire and the number of deaths in the fire. In other words, the more fire trucks at a fire the more people who will die in the fire. However, it doesn't make sense to say that the fire trucks cause the deaths or that the number of deaths cause the presence of more fire trucks. In this case, a third variable, the size of the fire, leads to more fire trucks at the fire and more deaths in the fire. So, while the number of fire trucks and the number of deaths are correlated there is no cause-effect relation between the two variables. Try to figure out this next example. The number of drowning deaths is positively correlated with the number of ice cream cones sold on a given day. Does buying ice cream lead to drowning? (34-35)

4. Here are some possible arguments for and against the use of deception in research.

   Against--People who are deceived may not trust another researcher and they may be unwilling to participate in future research projects.

   Against--If participants find out that they were deceived their data may be distorted.

   For--Deception is okay if any false information given to participants is corrected and a rationale for the deception is given.

   For--Sometimes deception is necessary. For example, studies that examine honesty, sharing, and aggression may need to use deception because full knowledge of the purpose of the study may change participants' behaviors. (39-40)

5. Social policy and child-development research both benefit when there are close links between the two. Social policy benefits from research on child development in a number of ways. First, research on child development can provide factual information, rather than stereotypes, about children and adolescents so that effective, informed policies can be formulated. Second, child-development researchers can serve as advocates for children and can argue for policies that address children's needs. Third, child-development researchers often have the information, theories, and methods to evaluate policies that may affect children and their families. Fourth, researchers with

knowledge of child development may be able to develop model programs that effectively meet children's needs such as the need for better schools and quality child care. Child-development research also can benefit from social policy. Research that is focused on social policy implications usually has a broader emphasis and is more likely to examine connections between various aspects of development than research that is not focused on social policy. (43-46)

Chapter 3
Genetic Bases of Child Development

Module 3.1 *Mechanisms of Heredity*

Module 3.2 *Genetic Disorders*

Module 3.3 *Heredity Is Not Destiny*

This chapter deals with the basic mechanisms of heredity, disorders that some children inherit, and the role of the environment in determining how heredity influences development.

MECHANISMS OF HEREDITY

MODULE
3.1

Mechanisms of Heredity

- *The Biology of Heredity*
- *Single Gene Inheritance*
- *Behavioral Genetics*

Textbook Learning Objectives

- **What are chromosomes and genes?**
- **What are dominant and recessive traits? How are they inherited?**
- **How does heredity influence behavioral and psychological development?**

TO MASTER THESE LEARNING OBJECTIVES:

1. Know the terms associated with genetic inheritance
2. Know the details of genetic inheritance

Know the Terms: Match the terms with the correct definition

Alleles	Heterozygous
Autosomes	Homozygous
Chromosomes	In vitro fertilization
Codominance	Monozygotic
Deoxyribonucleic acid	Phenotype
Depression	Polygenic inheritance
Dizygotic	Recessive

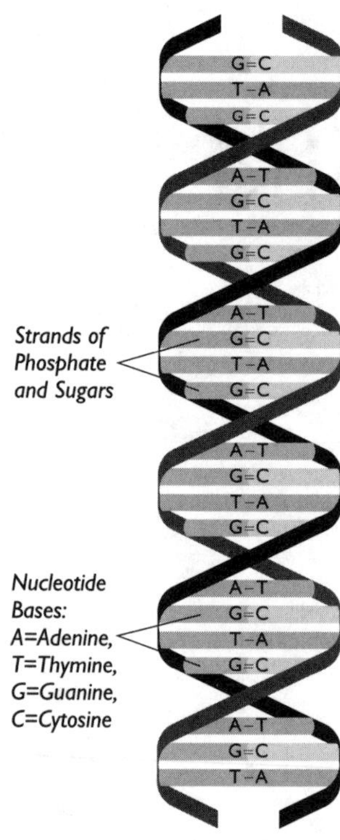

Dominant
Gene
Genotype
Schizophrenia
Sex chromosomes
Sickle-cell trait

1. Tiny structures in the nucleus of sperm and eggs that contain genetic material.__________
2. Mixing sperm and egg together in a laboratory dish.__________
3. The first 22 pairs of chromosomes.__________
4. The 23rd pair of chromosomes that determines the sex of the child.__________
5. This is found in each chromosome and it looks like the diagram at left.__________
6. A group of nucleotide bases that provides a specific set of biochemical instructions.__________
7. The complete set of genes that makes up a person's heredity.__________
8. An individual's physical, behavioral, and psychological features.__________
9. The different forms of genes.__________
10. This refers to alleles in pairs of chromosomes that are the same.__________
11. This refers to alleles in pairs of chromosomes that differ.__________
12. This refers to an allele whose chemical instructions are followed.__________
13. This refers to an allele whose chemical instructions are ignored when it is paired with a dominant allele.__________
14. This occurs when one allele does not completely dominate another.__________
15. Individuals with one dominant and one recessive allele for sickle-cell anemia have this.__________
16. The branch of genetics that deals with the inheritance of behavioral and psychological traits. __________
17. The pattern of inheritance that occurs when phenotypes reflect the combined activity of many separate genes.__________
18. This refers to twins who come from a single fertilized egg that splits in two.__________
19. This refers to twins who come from two separate eggs fertilized by two separate sperm.__________
20. This occurs when individuals have pervasive feelings of sadness, irritability, and low self-esteem.__________
21. This occurs when individuals hallucinate, have confused language and thought, and often behave bizarrely.__________

Know the Details of Genetic Inheritance

1. T F Each sperm and egg contains 46 chromosomes.
2. T F *In vitro* fertilization involves combining sperm and egg in a laboratory dish.

3. T F About 80% of attempts at *in vitro* fertilization succeed.

4. T F Women who become pregnant by means of *in vitro* fertilization are more likely to have twins or triplets than other women.

5. T F The autosomes determine the sex of the child.

6. T F A male is the product of an X-carrying sperm and an X-carrying egg.

7. T F Chromosomes consist of deoxyribonucleic acid (DNA).

8. T F Genes are made up of groups of nucleotide bases.

9. T F An individual's complete set of genes makes up one's phenotype.

10. T F A homozygous individual has 2 alleles that are the same.

11. T F If a person is heterozygous for a trait, the chemical instructions of the recessive allele are followed and those of the dominant allele are ignored.

12. T F Incomplete dominance occurs when one allele does not dominate another allele completely.

13. T F Individuals with sickle-cell trait have a severe form of anemia.

14. T F Individuals with the sickle-cell allele are more resistant to malaria.

15. T F The sickle-cell allele is becoming less common in African Americans.

16. T F Most behavioral and psychological traits are polygenic traits.

17. T F Dizygotic twins are the result of two separate eggs fertilized by two separate sperm.

18. T F Monozygotic twins commonly are known as identical twins.

19. T F In twin studies, it is assumed that heredity influences a characteristic if fraternal twins are more alike than identical twins.

20. T F Adoption studies are based on the assumption that an adopted child's biological parents provide the child's environment and the adoptive parents provide the child's heredity.

21. T F In adoption studies, if a behavior has genetic roots, adopted children should be more similar to their biological parents than to their adoptive parents.

22. T F One problem with twin studies is that the experiences of identical twins may be more similar than the experiences of fraternal twins so that heredity may appear to have a greater influence than it really does.

23. T F One problem with adoption studies is that a child's adoptive parents may be very different from a child's biological parents.

24. T F If twin and adoption studies produce similar results one should not trust those results.

25. T F If one identical twin is depressed, the other twin has a 25% chance of becoming depressed.

26. T F Plomin and Rowe's study of sociability in twin toddlers indicated that sociability is influenced by heredity.

ANSWERS

Key Terms

1. chromosomes (52)
2. *in vitro* fertilization (53)
3. autosomes (53)
4. sex chromosomes (54)
5. deoxyribonucleic acid (54)
6. gene (54)
7. genotype (54)
8. phenotype (54)
9. alleles (54)
10. homozygous (54)
11. heterozygous (54)
12. dominant (54)
13. recessive (54)
14. incomplete dominance (55)
15. sickle-cell trait (55)
16. behavioral genetics (56)
17. polygenic inheritance (56)
18. monozygotic (58)
19. dizygotic (58)
20. depression (60)
21. schizophrenia (60)

Know the Details

1. false (52)
2. true (53)
3. false (53)
4. true (53)
5. false (53)
6. false (54)
7. true (54)
8. true (54)
9. false (54)
10. true (54)
11. false (54)
12. true (55)
13. false (55)
14. true (55)
15. true (55)
16. true (56)
17. true (58)
18. true (58)
19. false (58)
20. false (58)
21. true (58)
22. true (59)
23. false (59)
24. false (59)
25. false (60)
26. true (61)

MODULE 3.2

Genetic Disorders
- *Inherited Disorders*
- *Abnormal Chromosomes*

GENETIC DISORDERS

Textbook Learning Objectives

- **What disorders are inherited?**
- **What disorders are caused by too many or too few chromosomes?**

TO MASTER THESE LEARNING OBJECTIVES:

1. Know the causes and symptoms of each inherited and chromosomal disorder
2. Know the details of the inherited and chromosomal disorders and genetic counseling

Know the Causes and Symptoms of Each Disorder: Match the cause or symptom with the correct inherited disorder

Down syndrome
Huntington's disease
Turner's syndrome
XXX syndrome

Klinefelter's syndrome XYY complement
Phenylketonuria (PKU)

1. This disorder is caused by a dominant allele found on chromosome 4.__________
2. This disorder usually is caused by an extra 21st chromosome.__________
3. This disorder occurs when a male receives an extra X chromosome.__________
4. This disorder occurs when a male receives an extra Y chromosome.__________
5. This disorder occurs when a female receives only one X chromosome.__________
6. This disorder occurs when a female receives an extra X chromosome.__________
7. Males with this disorder are tall and sometimes have below-normal intelligence.__________
8. Females with this disorder are short, have limited development of secondary sex characteristics, and have problems perceiving spatial relations.__________
9. Males with this disorder are tall, have small testicles, are sterile, and have below-normal intelligence.__________
10. Females with this disorder have delayed motor and language development.__________
11. Individuals with this disorder cannot break down phenylalanine which then accumulates and leads to mental retardation.__________
12. Individuals with this disorder suffer from a progressive degeneration of the nervous system beginning in middle age.__________
13. Individuals with this disorder have small heads and are mentally retarded.__________

Know the Details of the Inherited and Chromosomal Disorders and Genetic Counseling

1. T F If an allele for a disorder is dominant, then every person who receives the allele will have the disorder.
2. T F Most people with Huntington's disease die before they pass the allele for Huntington's on to their children.
3. T F Genetic counselors construct detailed family trees to determine the likelihood that someone is carrying an allele for a particular disorder.
4. T F During genetic counseling, if family trees indicate that someone probably carries an allele for a particular disorder no other tests are conducted.
5. T F Development usually is normal even if someone receives extra, missing, or damaged chromosomes.
6. T F During the first few months of life, babies with Down syndrome appear to be developing normally.
7. T F Mainstreaming involves putting children with Down syndrome in special classes away from other children.

8. T F The extra 21st chromosome that often is found in Down syndrome usually comes from the father's sperm.

9. T F The risk of having a baby with Down syndrome decreases as the mother gets older.

10. T F A woman's eggs exist in her ovaries since her own prenatal development.

11. T F The presence of abnormal autosomes is a major cause for spontaneous abortions (miscarriages) in the first 2 weeks of pregnancy.

12. T F The presence of a Y chromosome appears to be necessary for life.

ANSWERS

Causes and Symptoms

1. Huntington's disease (63)
2. Down syndrome (62)
3. Klinefelter's syndrome (65)
4. XYY complement (65)
5. Turner's syndrome (65)
6. XXX syndrome (65)
7. XYY complement (65)
8. Turner's syndrome (65)
9. Klinefelter's syndrome (65)
10. XXX syndrome (65)
11. phenylketonuria (PKU) (63)
12. Huntington's disease (64)
13. Down syndrome (64)

Know the Details

1. true (63)
2. false (63)
3. true (64)
4. false (64)
5. false (64)
6. true (64)
7. false (64)
8. false (64)
9. false (65)
10. true (65)
11. true (65)
12. false (65)

MODULE
3.3

Heredity Is Not Destiny

- *Paths From Genes to Behavior*
- *Reaction Range*
- *Changing Relations Between Nature and Nurture*
- *The Nature of Nurture*

HEREDITY IS NOT DESTINY

Textbook Learning Objectives

- **How do genes affect behavior?**
- **Does a genotype always lead to the same phenotype?**
- **How does the relation between heredity and environment change as children develop?**
- **How do family environments influence children's development?**

TO MASTER THESE OBJECTIVES:

1. Know the terms associated with the interaction of genes and environment
2. Know the details of the interaction of genes and environment

Know the Terms Associated with the Interaction of Genes and Environment: Match each definition with the correct term

Active gene-environment relation	Nonshared environmental influences
Evocative gene-environment relation	Passive gene-environment relation
Niche-picking	Reaction range

1. The concept that the same genotype can lead to a range of phenotypes depending upon the environment where development takes place.__________
2. Parents pass on genotypes and provide much of the early environment for their young children.__________
3. Different genotypes evoke different responses from the environment.__________
4. Individuals actively seek environments related to their genetic makeup.__________
5. Deliberately seeking environments that fit one's heredity.__________
6. The forces within a family that make children different from one another. __________

Know the Details

1. T F Reaction range means that phenotypes are fixed by one's genotype.
2. T F An individual with PKU who is not exposed to phenylalanine will have normal intelligence.
3. T F Most newborns in the United States are *not* screened for PKU even though the screening is simple to perform.
4. T F A child who receives genes for high levels of intelligence, asks many relevant questions in class and, in turn, receives much positive attention from teachers and, therefore, excels intellectually is demonstrating a passive gene-environment relation.
5. T F Passive gene-environment relations are most common with infants and young children.
6. T F A child who has inherited some musical ability and who joins the band and listens to music constantly is an example of an active gene-environment relation.
7. T F Choosing an environment that fits one's heredity is known as niche-picking.
8. T F Most siblings are very similar in terms of cognitive and social development.
9. T F Parents showing more affection to one child than another is an example of nonshared environmental influences.
10. T F Parents provide the same family environment for all of their children.

ANSWERS

Key Terms

1. reaction range (68)
2. passive gene-environment relation (68)
3. evocative gene-environment relation (69)
4. active gene-environment relation (69)
5. niche-picking (69)
6. nonshared environmental influences (70)

Know the Details

1. false (68)
2. true (67)
3. false (67)
4. false (69)
5. true (69)
6. true (69)
7. true (69)
8. false (70)
9. true (70)
10. false (70)

SUMMARY

MODULE 3.1: MECHANISMS OF HEREDITY

23
autosomes
nucleotides
gene
genotype; phenotype
environment

The Biology of Heredity. At conception, the __________ chromosomes in the sperm merge with the 23 chromosomes in the egg. The 46 chromosomes that result include 22 pairs of __________ plus two sex chromosomes. Each chromosome is one molecule of DNA, which consists of __________ organized in a structure that resembles a spiral staircase. A section of DNA that provides specific biochemical instructions is called a __________. All of a person's genes make up a __________; the __________ refers to the physical, behavioral, and psychological characteristics that develop when the genotype is exposed to a specific __________.

alleles
homozygous
heterozygous
recessive
incomplete dominance

Single Gene Inheritance. Different forms of the same gene are called __________. A person who inherits the same allele on a pair of chromosomes is __________; in this case, the biochemical instructions on the allele are followed. A person who inherits different alleles is __________; in this case, the instructions of the dominant allele are followed whereas those of the __________ allele are ignored. In __________, the person is heterozygous but the phenotype is midway between the dominant and recessive phenotypes.

polygenic inheritance
twins
personality

Behavioral Genetics. Behavioral and psychological phenotypes that reflect an underlying continuum (such as intelligence) often involve __________. In polygenic inheritance, the phenotype reflects the combined activity of many distinct genes. Polygenic inheritance is often examined by studying __________ and adopted children. These studies indicate substantial influence of heredity on intelligence, psychological disorders, and __________.

MODULE 3.2: GENETIC DISORDERS

Inherited Disorders. Most inherited disorders are carried by __________ alleles. Examples include sickle-cell anemia, albinism, cystic fibrosis, Tay-Sachs, and __________. Inherited disorders are rarely carried by __________ alleles because individuals with such a disorder would not survive to have children. An exception is __________ disease, a disorder in which nerve cells begin to deteriorate during middle age.

recessive
phenylketonuria; dominant
Huntington's

Abnormal Chromosomes. Most fertilized eggs that do not have 46 chromosomes are aborted spontaneously soon after conception. One exception is __________ syndrome, in which individuals usually have an extra 21st chromosome. Down-syndrome individuals have a distinctive appearance and are __________. Disorders of the sex chromosomes, which are __________ common because these chromosomes contain less genetic material than autosomes, include Klinefelter's syndrome, XYY complement, __________ syndrome, and XXX syndrome.

Down
mentally retarded
more
Turner's

MODULE 3.3: HEREDITY IS NOT DESTINY

Paths from Genes to Behavior. Genes __________ influence behavior directly. Instead, they affect behavior indirectly by increasing the odds that a child will behave in a particular way. Also, the impact of a gene on behavior depends on the __________ in which the genetic instructions are carried out.

never
environment

Reaction Range. PKU does not lead to mental retardation when individuals with the disorder maintain a diet low in __________. This demonstrates the concept of __________-- same genotype can lead to different phenotypes. The outcome of heredity depends upon the __________ in which development occurs.

phenylalanine
reaction range
environment

Changing Relations between Nature and Nurture. Common in infants and young children is a __________ gene-environment relation, in which parents pass on genotypes to their children and provide much of the early environment for their young children. Also common in children is an __________ gene-environment relation, in which different genotypes evoke different responses from the environment. Common in older children and adolescents is an __________ gene-environment relation, in which individuals actively seek environments related to their genetic makeup.

passive
evocative
active

The Nature of Nurture. Family environments affect siblings __________, which is known as nonshared environmental influences. Parents provide a __________ environment for each child in the family as well as providing a unique genotype for each child.

differently
unique

CHAPTER 3 GENETIC BASES OF CHILD DEVELOPMENT

TEST YOURSELF

1. Each sperm and egg contains __________ chromosomes.
   a. 23
   b. 26
   c. 46
   d. a variable number of

2. *In vitro* fertilization
   a. usually is accompanied by surrogate motherhood.
   b. is successful about 80% of the time.
   c. is less likely to result in the birth of twins or triplets.
   d. sometimes involves the use of egg and sperm from donors.

3. The first 22 pairs of chromosomes
   a. contain either X or Y chromosomes.
   b. determine the sex of the individual.
   c. are called autosomes.
   d. do not vary in size.

4. An individual's physical, behavioral, and psychological features are known as one's
   a. phenotype.
   b. deoxyribonucleic acid.
   c. genotype.
   d. genes.

5. An individual who is heterozygous for eye color would have
   a. two alleles for brown eyes.
   b. one allele for brown eyes and one for blue eyes.
   c. two alleles for blue eyes.
   d. blue eyes.

6. If the allele for brown eyes is dominant and the allele for blue eyes is recessive, which genotype produces a person with blue eyes?
   a. A blue-eyed person is homozygous with 2 alleles for brown eyes.
   b. A blue-eyed person is homozygous with 2 alleles for blue eyes.
   c. A blue-eyed person is heterozygous with 1 allele for blue eyes and 1 allele for brown eyes.
   d. The alleles for eye color are demonstrating incomplete dominance.

7. Sickle-cell anemia
   a. occurs in individuals who have 1 allele for normal blood cells and 1 allele for sickle-shaped cells.
   b. is not an inherited disorder.
   c. is not a serious health problem because it is easily cured.
   d. is becoming less common in successive generations of African Americans.

8. Polygenic inheritance
  a. reflects the influence of a single gene.
  b. determines "either-or" traits such as eye color.
  c. cannot be studied because its influence is too broad.
  d. influences behavioral and psychological traits such as intelligence.

9. Twin studies
  a. cannot be used to study polygenic traits such as intelligence.
  b. are based on the assumption that monozygotic twins are *not* more similar genetically than dizygotic twins.
  c. are based on the assumption that heredity influences a trait if identical twins are more alike than fraternal twins.
  d. often underestimate the influence of heredity because identical twins may have more similar environments than fraternal twins.

10. In adoption studies,
  a. the results may be biased because biological and adoptive parents may be similar.
  b. adoptive parents are assumed to provide genetic influence.
  c. biological parents are assumed to provide environmental influence.
  d. the greater similarity of adoptees to biological than to adoptive parents on a trait would indicate that the trait is influenced by the environment.

11. In Plomin and Rowe's study of sociability in twins,
  a. there was no evidence that sociability is inherited.
  b. identical twins showed more similar levels of sociability than fraternal twins.
  c. fraternal twins showed more similar levels of sociability than identical twins.
  d. there was considerable evidence that sociability was influenced primarily by the environment.

12. Individuals with Down syndrome show which of the following characteristics?
  a. Mental retardation
  b. Aggression
  c. An extra X chromosome
  d. A lack of sexual development

13. Phenylketonuria
  a. is caused by a dominant allele.
  b. does not affect one's intelligence.
  c. does not show any symptoms until someone is middle-aged.
  d. involves the accumulation of an amino acid.

14. Huntington's disease
  a. is caused by 2 recessive alleles.
  b. can lead to depression and changes in personality.
  c. is apparent in young babies.
  d. usually is not fatal.

15. An XYY complement of sex chromosomes is associated with which of the following characteristics?
  a. Problems perceiving spatial relations

b. Short stature
c. Below-normal intelligence
d. Susceptibility to heart defects

16. A female who is short, has limited development of secondary sex characteristics, and who has problems with spatial relations would have which of the following disorders?
a. Klinefelter's syndrome
b. XYY complement
c. Turner's syndrome
d. XXX syndrome

17. A female who has normal stature but delayed language and motor development would have which of the following disorders?
a. Klinefelter's syndrome
b. XYY complement
c. Turner's syndrome
d. XXX syndrome

18. Phenylketonuria (PKU) is an example of
a. the interaction between genes and environment.
b. a disorder caused by a dominant allele.
c. a chromosomal abnormality caused by an extra chromosome.
d. a disorder whose effects cannot be changed by the environment.

19. Which of the following is an example of a passive gene-environment relation?
a. Parents give their child "good reader" genes and provide many books and opportunities for reading.
b. Parents give their child "good reader" genes but the child will not sit still when the parents read to her so they stop trying.
c. A child who inherits "good reader" genes frequently goes to the library and to bookstores to get reading material.
d. A child who inherits "good reader" genes chooses to play video games rather than read books.

20. Which of the following is an example of niche-picking? An example of niche-picking is
a. parents enrolling their active child in many structured, sedentary activities in hopes that he will calm down.
b. parents enrolling their active child in many athletic activities in hopes that he will burn off some steam.
c. an active child choosing to participate in many athletic events.
d. an uncoordinated child choosing to participate in athletic events in hopes of becoming more coordinated.

21. The concept of nonshared environmental influences means that
a. parents provide the same environment for all of their children.
b. siblings will be very similar to each other because they shared the same home environment.
c. children's genes do *not* influence their experiences.
d. parents may have higher expectations for school achievement for one child than another.

ESSAY QUESTIONS

1. Your friends Fox and Dana are expecting a baby. Both Dana and Fox are farsighted and have cheek dimples. Dana and Fox have said that they hope that their baby won't need to wear glasses or have cheek dimples because they both hate their glasses and dimples. Using the table below, what can you tell Fox and Dana about genetic inheritance and the likelihood that they will get their wish?

Some Common Phenotypes Associated with Single Pairs of Genes

Dominant Phenotype	Recessive Phenotype
Curly hair	Straght hair
Normal hair	Pattern baldness (men)
Dark hair	Blond hair
Thick lips	Thin lips
Cheek dimples	No dimples
Normal hearing	Some type of deafness
Normal vision	Nearsightedness
Farsightedness	Normal vision
Normal color vision	Red-green color blindness
Type A blood	Type O blood
Type B blood	Type O blood
Rh-positive blood	Rh-negative blood

Source: McKusick, 1995.

2. You and a friend were talking about the role of heredity and environment and your friend said, "Heredity is destiny. When someone inherits genes for bad diseases there is nothing about the environment that can change the negative effects." What can you tell your friend about the interaction of heredity and environment in cases such as those involving individuals with phenylketonuria?
3. You and a friend are talking and she says that when her infant son grows up he will be musically talented because she has passed along musical genes and she will provide an environment that stimulates musical talent. Which gene-environment relation is your friend stating? Why? What can you tell your friend about the other 2 gene-environment relations that might foil her plans?
4. Your friend Vladimir has two grown children who are very different from each other. He can't figure out how his two children could be so different since they had the same parents and were raised in the same home. What can you tell Vladimir about nonshared environmental influences that might explain why his children are so different?

ANSWERS

Multiple-Choice

1. a (52)
2. d (53)
3. c (53)
4. a (54)
5. b (54)
6. b (54)
7. d (55)
8. d (56)
9. c (58)
10. a (59)
11. b (60)
12. a (62)
13. d (63)
14. b (63)
15. c (65)
16. c (65)
17. d (65)
18. a (67)
19. a (69)
20. c (69)
21. d (70)

Essays

1. You can tell Fox and Dana that both farsightedness and cheek dimples are dominant traits. That means that an individual who is heterozygous with one dominant allele and one recessive allele will still show the dominant trait. Given that both Fox and Dana show the dominant traits, they both must have at least one allele for the dominant trait so the likelihood that their baby will NOT have the dominant traits of farsightedness and cheek dimples is small. (54-56)

2. You can tell your friend that heredity is not destiny. One can inherit a particular genotype but that genotype can interact with a particular environment to change the phenotype. In the case of phenylketonuria (PKU), an individual may inherit the gene for PKU. Typically, the individual lacks an enzyme that breaks down phenylalanine. Phenylalanine is found in many foods such as breads and dairy products. When the phenylalanine is not broken down it builds up and produces toxins that damage the nervous system which leads to mental retardation. However, if the environment is changed so that the amount of phenylalanine in a child's diet is reduced, then the damage to the nervous system does not occur and normal intelligence occurs. In other words, the same genotype for PKU can interact with 2 different environments (either a regular diet or a low-phenylalanine diet) to lead to 2 very different outcomes (either normal intelligence or mental retardation). So, even in the case of a negative, inherited disorder the environment can still play an important role in shaping development. (67-68)

3. You can tell your friend that she is arguing for a passive gene-environment relation. She is assuming that her child will passively receive musical genes and will passively receive the musical stimulation from the environment. This may work while the child is an infant or young child but other gene-environment relations may become more important when the child is older. An evocative gene-environment relation also might occur. For example, if the child has inherited no musical talent, all of his music instructors might stop giving him lessons because he is a hopeless case. An active gene-environment relation also might occur where the child does not have any musical genes and is not interested in taking music lessons or joining the band. The active gene-environment relation becomes more common as children grow older and can pick the niches that fit their heredity. (68-69)

4. In fact, many siblings are not very much alike in their cognitive and social development. Even though siblings may have the same parents and may grow up in the same home, parents provide unique genes and unique family environments for each of their children. Nonshared environmental influences means that parents create a unique environment for each of their children. For example, they may be more affectionate with one than another, they might have higher expectations for school achievement for one child than another, etc. These varying influences affect the children in the family in different ways so that the children develop in different ways. So, because of different genes and nonshared environmental influences, Vladimir shouldn't be surprised by how different his children are from each other. (70)

Chapter 4
Prenatal Development and Birth

This chapter covers the events of normal prenatal development, some developmental problems that can occur before birth, and the process of labor and delivery.

MODULE
4.1

From Conception to Birth

- *Period of the Zygote (Weeks 1-2)*
- *Period of the Embryo (Weeks 3-8)*
- *Period of the Fetus (Weeks 9-38)*

FROM CONCEPTION TO BIRTH

Textbook Learning Objectives

- **What happens to a fertilized egg in the first 2 weeks after conception?**
- **When do body structures and internal organs emerge in prenatal development?**
- **When do body systems begin to function well enough to support life?**

TO MASTER THESE LEARNING OBJECTIVES:

1. Know the terms associated with prenatal development
2. Know the major events that are associated with each period of prenatal development
3. Know the details of prenatal development

Know the Terms Associated with Prenatal Development: Match the terms with the correct definition

Age of viability	Implantation
Amnion	Mesoderm

Amniotic fluid
Cephalocaudal
Cerebral cortex
Differentiation
Ectoderm
Endoderm
Embryo
Germ disc
Period of the fetus
Placenta
Prenatal development
Proximodistal
Umbilical cord
Vernix
Zygote

1. Changes that transform the fertilized egg into a newborn human.__________
2. The fertilized egg.__________
3. The process by which the zygote burrows into the lining of the uterine wall and establishes connections with the mother's blood vessels.__________
4. A small cluster of cells near the center of the zygote that will develop into the baby.__________
5. This is what the zygote is called after it is completely embedded in the uterine wall.__________
6. The outer layer of the embryo that will become hair, the outer layer of skin, and the nervous system.__________
7. The middle layer of the embryo that will become muscles, bones, and the circulatory system.__________
8. The inner layer of the embryo that will form the digestive system and lungs.__________
9. The sac that surrounds the embryo as illustrated by #1 in the diagram below.__________
10. The fluid in the sac that cushions the embryo and helps maintain a constant temperature for the embryo (see #2 in the diagram below).__________

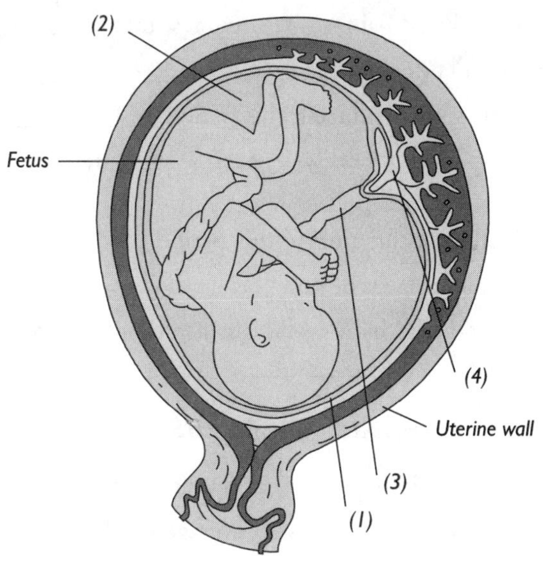

11. The structure that contains blood vessels and connects the embryo to the placenta (see #3 in the preceeding diagram).__________
12. The structure where the blood vessels from the umbilical cord and the mother's blood vessels exchange nutrients, oxygen, vitamins, and waste products (see #4 in the preceeding diagram).__________
13. The principle that states that growth occurs from the head to the base of the spine.__________
14. The principle that states that growth occurs near the center of the body before it occurs in the extremities.__________
15. The final and longest phase of prenatal development.__________
16. This occurs around 7 months when most systems are functioning well enough that the fetus has a reasonable chance to survive.__________
17. The thick, greasy substance that protects the fetus during its long bath in amniotic fluid. __________
18. The wrinkled surface of the brain that regulates many important human behaviors. __________

Know the Events Associated with Each Period of Prenatal Development: Match the events with the correct period of prenatal development

Period of the embryo | Period of the zygote
Period of the fetus

1. This begins with fertilization and ends when the zygote implants in the lining of the uterine wall.__________
2. This period begins the third week after conception and lasts until the end of the eighth week.__________
3. The final and longest phase of prenatal development.__________
4. During this period, body structures and internal organs develop.__________
5. During this period, differentiation of cells occurs.__________
6. During this period, the baby-to-be becomes much larger.__________
7. Implantation occurs during this period.__________
8. Rapid cell division occurs during this period.__________
9. During this period, bodily systems are refined and begin to work.__________
10. The age of viability occurs during this period.__________
11. During this period, a layer of body fat develops.__________
12. During this period, the baby-to-be can hear, and will react to, sounds that occur outside the uterus.__________

Know the Details of Prenatal Development

1. T F There are 5 periods of prenatal development.
2. T F Prenatal development takes an average of 38 weeks.

3. T F The period of the zygote is the longest period of prenatal development.

4. T F The period of the zygote ends when the zygote implants in the lining of the wall of the uterus.

5. T F Fraternal twins result when the zygote separates into two clusters of cells.

6. T F Implantation takes about a week to complete.

7. T F Cell differentiation begins in the period of the fetus.

8. T F By the end of the period of the embryo, most bodily organs are in place, in some form.

9. T F During the period of the fetus, the brain begins to function.

10. T F The lungs of babies who are born at 7 months are as mature as the lungs of full-term babies.

11. T F Premature babies often have difficulty regulating their body temperature.

12. T F There is no evidence that babies can recognize sounds that they hear during prenatal development.

13. T F A more active fetus is more likely to be a fussy baby.

14. T F A pregnant woman should visit her doctor weekly throughout her pregnancy.

15. T F Women should not exercise during pregnancy.

16. T F Smoking during pregnancy is not a problem.

ANSWERS

Key Terms

1. prenatal development (76)
2. zygote (76)
3. implantation (76)
4. germ disc (77)
5. embryo (77)
6. ectoderm (77)
7. mesoderm (77)
8. endoderm (77)
9. amnion (78)
10. amniotic fluid (78)
11. umbilical cord (78)
12. placenta (77)
13. cephalocaudal (79)
14. proximodistal (79)
15. period of the fetus (79)
16. age of viability (80)
17. vernix (79)
18. cerebral cortex (80)

Periods of Prenatal Development

1. period of the zygote (76)
2. period of the embryo (77)
3. period of the fetus (79)
4. period of the embryo (77)
5. period of the zygote (76)
6. period of the fetus (79)
7. period of the zygote (76)
8. period of the zygote (76)
9. period of the fetus (79)
10. period of the fetus (79)
11. period of the fetus (79)
12. period of the fetus (79)

Know the Details

1. false (76)
2. true (76)
3. false (76)
4. true (76)
5. false (76)
6. true (76)
7. false (77)
8. true (79)
9. true (80)
10. false (80)
11. true (80)
12. false (81)
13. true (81)
14. false (82)
15. false (82)
16. false (82)

MODULE 4.2

Influences on Prenatal Development

- *General Risk Factors*
- *Teratogens: Diseases, Drugs, and Environmental Hazards*
- *How Teratogens Influence Prenatal Development*
- *Prenatal Diagnosis and Treatment*

INFLUENCES ON PRENATAL DEVELOPMENT

Textbook Learning Objectives

- **How is prenatal development influenced by a pregnant woman's nutrition, the stress she experiences while pregnant, and her age?**
- **What is a teratogen, and what specific diseases, drugs, and environmental hazards can be teratogens?**
- **How exactly do teratogens affect prenatal development?**
- **How can prenatal development be monitored? Can abnormal prenatal development be corrected?**

TO MASTER THESE LEARNING OBJECTIVES:

1. Know the effects associated with each of the general risk factors and the teratogens mentioned in the book
2. Know the prenatal procedures and uses of each
3. Know the details of the influences on prenatal development and prenatal procedures

Know the Effects Associated with the General Risk Factors and Teratogens: Match each effect with the correct risk factor or teratogen associated with it

AIDS
Alcohol
Aspirin
Caffeine
Cocaine/heroin
Cytomegalovirus
Fetal Alcohol Syndrome
Genital herpes
Inadequate nourishment
Lead
Low levels of folic acid
Marijuana
Mercury
Mother in her 40s
Nicotine
PCB
Rubella
Stress
Syphilis
Thalidomide
X-rays

1. Spina bifida, a disorder in which the neural tube does not close properly during prenatal development, is associated with this.__________

2. A weakened immune system in the pregnant woman is more likely as a result of this.__________
3. An increased risk of having a baby with Down syndrome.__________
4. Babies who were born with deformed arms, legs, hands, or fingers were the result.__________
5. Frequent infections, neurological disorders, and death occur in children with this disease.__________
6. Children who are exposed to this disease have damaged central nervous systems, teeth, and bones.__________
7. Children with this disorder have heart problems, retarded growth, and misshapen faces.__________
8. Prenatal exposure to this environmental teratogen can lead to mental retardation.__________
9. This can lead to prematurity, lower birth weight, damage to the nervous system, and increased vulnerability to illness.__________
10. This can lead to a secretion of hormones that reduce the flow of oxygen to the fetus while increasing its heart rate and activity level.__________
11. Babies who are exposed to this disease may develop encephalitis, an enlarged spleen, and improper blood clotting.__________
12. Prenatal exposure to this drug can result in a lower birth weight and less motor control.__________
13. Moderate exposure to this is related to lower scores on tests of attention, memory, and intelligence.__________
14. Exposure to these drugs can lead to retarded growth and irritability in newborns.__________
15. Exposure to this environmental teratogen is related to retarded growth, mental retardation, and cerebral palsy.__________
16. Prenatal exposure to this disease is related to deafness, blindness, and abnormally small head, and mental retardation.__________
17. Exposure to this drug is related to deficits in intelligence, attention, and motor skill.__________
18. Exposure to this environmental teratogen is related to impaired verbal ability and impaired memory skill.__________
19. Exposure to this disease can result in mental retardation and damage to the eyes, ears, and heart.__________
20. Exposure to this drug is related to retarded growth and possible cognitive impairments.__________
21. Exposure to this environmental teratogen is related to retarded growth, leukemia, and mental retardation.__________
22. Exposure to this drug is related to lower birth weight and decreased muscle tone.__________

Know the Prenatal Procedures and Their Uses: Match the descriptions of the procedures and their uses with the correct procedure

Amniocentesis	Fetal surgery
Chorionic villus sampling	Gene therapy
Fetal medicine	Ultrasound

1. This procedure involves inserting a needle through the mother's abdomen to obtain a sample of the amniotic fluid.__________
2. This procedure involves taking a sample of tissue from the part of the placenta called the chorion.__________
3. This procedure uses sound waves to generate a picture of the developing child.__________
4. This procedure involves treating prenatal problems before birth.__________
5. This could be used to treat defects in the fetal diaphragm, heart, or urinary tract.__________
6. This procedure could be used to detect a genetic disorder but it can't be done until 16 weeks after conception.__________
7. This procedure can detect multiple pregnancies, sex of the fetus, physical deformities, and the position of the fetus and placenta.__________
8. This procedure could detect a genetic disorder within 8 or 9 weeks after conception.__________
9. This procedure involves replacing defective genes with synthetic normal genes.__________

Know the Details of the Influences on Prenatal Development and Prenatal Procedures

1. T F Pregnant women should double their caloric intake because they are eating for two.
2. T F Women should not gain more than 15 pounds during pregnancy.
3. T F The majority of the weight that a woman gains during pregnancy is the weight of the baby.
4. T F Low levels of folic acid can result in spina bifida.
5. T F Inadequate nourishment during pregnancy can lead to prematurity and low birth weight.
6. T F Very little brain growth occurs during the last few months of pregnancy so good nutrition during this time is not important.
7. T F When pregnant nonhuman females are exposed to constant stress, they give birth to offspring that are smaller than average and that are more likely to have other physical and behavioral problems.
8. T F The babies of women who report greater stress and anxiety during pregnancy do not differ from those whose mothers report low levels of stress and anxiety.
9. T F Pregnant women under stress are more likely to smoke or drink alcohol and less likely to rest, exercise, and eat properly.

10. T F Even occasional, mild anxiety has negative effects on the developing child.

11. T F Teenage mothers are more likely to have problems with pregnancy, labor, and delivery even when they get good prenatal care.

12. T F Children of teenage mothers generally do less well in school and are more likely to have behavioral problems.

13. T F Women in their 30s who are in good health are more risk prone during pregnancy, labor, and delivery than women in their 20s.

14. T F Women in their 40s are more likely to give birth to babies with Down syndrome.

15. T F Rubella, syphilis, and cytomegalovirus cross the placenta to attack the fetus or embryo.

16. T F Babies may be infected with genital herpes as they pass through the birth canal.

17. T F Fetal alcohol syndrome is most likely when pregnant women drink only an ounce of alcohol per day.

18. T F Radiation from video-display terminals is associated with retarded growth, leukemia, and mental retardation.

19. T F Higher levels of prenatal exposure to PCB is associated with lower verbal and memory skills.

20. T F Teratogens may be harmful to one species but not another.

21. T F The timing of exposure to a teratogen is not important.

22. T F Exposure to teratogens during the period of the embryo is most likely to result in major defects in bodily structure.

23. T F Teratogens usually affect a wide range of body systems.

24. T F Damage from teratogens is always apparent at birth.

25. T F Women whose mothers took DES while pregnant are more likely to develop cancer of the vagina and have difficulty becoming pregnant themselves.

26. T F Results from chorionic villus sampling can be obtained earlier than results from amniocentesis.

27. T F Miscarriages are slightly more likely after amniocentesis or chorionic villus sampling.

28. T F Fetal surgery involves removing a fetus from the uterus to perform surgery.

29. T F The use of gene therapy is common.

ANSWERS

Risk Factors and Teratogens

1. low levels of folic acid (84)
2. stress (84)
3. mother in her 40s (85)

12. marijuana (87)
13. alcohol (87)
14. cocaine/heroin (87)

4. thalidomide (86)
5. AIDS (86)
6. syphilis (86)
7. fetal alcohol syndrome (87)
8. lead (88)
9. inadequate nourishment (84)
10. stress (84)
11. genital herpes (86)
15. mercury (88)
16. cytomegalovirus (88)
17. aspirin (87)
18. PCB (88)
19. Rubella (86)
20. nicotine (87)
21. X-rays (88)
22. caffeine (87)

Prenatal Procedures

1. amniocentesis (93)
2. chorionic villus sampling (93)
3. ultrasound (92)
4. fetal medicine (93)
5. fetal surgery (93)
6. amniocentesis (93)
7. ultrasound (92)
8. chorionic villus sampling (93)
9. gene therapy (93)

Know the Details

1. false (84)
2. false (84)
3. false (84)
4. true (84)
5. true (84)
6. false (84)
7. true (84)
8. false (85)
9. true (85)
10. false (85)
11. false (85)
12. true (85)
13. false (85)
14. true (86)
15. true (86)
16. true (86)
17. false (87)
18. false (88)
19. true (89)
20. true (90)
21. false (90)
22. true (91)
23. false (91)
24. false (91)
25. true (91)
26. true (93)
27. true (93)
28. true (93)
29. false (93)

MODULE
4.3

Happy Birthday!

- *Labor and Delivery*
- *Approaches to Childbirth*
- *Birth Complications*
- *The Newborn*
- *Postpartum Depression*

HAPPY BIRTHDAY!

Textbook Learning Objectives

- **What are the stages in labor and delivery?**
- **What are "natural" ways of coping with the pain of childbirth? Is childbirth at home safe?**
- **How do we determine if a baby is healthy? What behavioral states are common in newborns?**
- **What are some of the complications that can occur during birth?**
- **What is postpartum depression and what are its effects?**

TO MASTER THESE LEARNING OBJECTIVES:

1. Know the terms associated with labor and delivery
2. Identify newborn assessment procedures and newborn behavioral states
3. Know the details of labor, delivery, newborn assessment, birth complications, and postpartum depression

Know the Terms Associated with Labor and Delivery: Match each definition with the correct term

Anoxia
Breech presentation
Cesarean section
Crowning
Infant mortality
Placental abruption
Premature
Small-for-date infants

1. The appearance of the top of the baby's head during labor.__________
2. Being born with feet or bottom emerging first.__________
3. Receiving an inadequate amount of oxygen.__________
4. When the placenta detaches from the wall of the uterus.__________
5. Removing the baby from an incision in the mother's abdomen and uterus.__________
6. Babies who are born less than 38 weeks after conception.__________
7. Infants who are much smaller than would be expected based on the length of time since conception.__________
8. The number of infants out of 1,000 births who die before their first birthday.__________

Identify Newborn Assessment Procedures and Behavioral States: Match the description with the correct term

Apgar score
Alert inactivity
Basic cry
Crying
Pain cry
Mad cry
Neonatal Behavioral Assessment Scale
Non-REM sleep
Rapid-eye movement (REM) sleep
Sleeping
Sudden Infant Death Syndrome (SIDS)
Waking activity

1. This score provides a quick assessment of the newborn's physical health.____________
2. A baby in this state has open but unfocused eyes and moves his arms or legs in bursts of uncoordinated motion.____________
3. This cry starts softly, then gradually becomes more intense and usually occurs when the baby is hungry or tired.____________
4. This cry is a more intense version of the basic cry.____________
5. Babies in this state cry vigorously and often use agitated, uncoordinated movements.____________
6. This scale evaluates a broad range of newborn abilities and behaviors such as reflexes, hearing, irritability, and consolability.____________

7. This cry begins with a sudden, long burst of crying that is followed by a long pause and gasping.____________
8. This state occurs when the baby's eyes are closed and the baby drifts between periods of regular and irregular breathing.____________
9. This state occurs when the baby is calm and attentive with open eyes.____________
10. This type of sleep is irregular and the body is quite active.____________
11. This is regular sleep when breathing, heart rate, and brain activity are steady.____________
12. This occurs when a healthy baby dies suddenly for no apparent reason.____________

Know the Details of Labor, Delivery, Birth Complications, Newborn Assessment, and Postpartum Depression

1. T F Labor begins with the contractions of the muscles of the uterus.
2. T F The transition phase of stage 1 of labor is the most painful part of labor.
3. T F The second stage of labor is the longest stage.
4. T F Most infants are born feet or bottom first.
5. T F The baby is born during the final stage of labor.
6. T F Babies whose mothers receive large doses of pain medication during labor often are withdrawn or irritable for days or weeks after birth.
7. T F The effects of pain medication during labor have a permanent effect on infants.
8. T F Childbirth classes emphasize visual imagery and deep-breathing as relaxation techniques.
9. T F Home birth is a safe option for any woman.
10. T F Birthing centers are best for deliveries that are expected to be trouble free.
11. T F Anoxia can lead to mental retardation or death.
12. T F For mothers, a C-section has no greater risks than a vaginal delivery.
13. T F Being a premature infant is more serious than being a small-for-date infant.
14. T F Premature infants continue to lag behind their full-term peers even into late childhood.
15. T F Small-for-date infants can thrive if they receive excellent medical care and their home environment is supportive and stimulating.
16. T F The United States has more babies with low birth weight than any other industrialized country.
17. T F A low birth weight baby is more likely if the mother receives inadequate or no prenatal care.
18. T F The Apgar scale assesses breathing, heart rate, muscle tone, reflexes, and skin tone.

19. T F The Neonatal Behavioral Assessment Scale measures behavioral characteristics such as irritability and consolability.

20. T F The cries that a newborn uses are not different in different circumstances.

21. T F Newborns sleep in a block of 16-18 hours daily.

22. T F During their waking hours, newborns move from alert inactivity, waking activity, and crying.

23. T F Most babies don't sleep through the night until they are 9 months old.

24. T F Approximately one-half of newborns' sleep is REM sleep.

25. T F REM sleep becomes more frequent as infants grow.

26. T F Some scientists believe that REM may stimulate the brain and foster growth of the nervous system.

27. T F Premature and low birth weight babies are more vulnerable to dying from SIDS.

28. T F SIDS is more likely when a baby sleeps on its back.

29. T F SIDS is more likely to occur in the summer.

30. T F Women are more likely to suffer from postpartum depression when they have particularly high hormone levels during the later phases of pregnancy.

31. T F Women are less likely to experience postpartum depression if they receive support from other adults around them.

32. T F Children of depressed mothers are no more likely to become depressed themselves than children of non-depressed mothers.

ANSWERS

Key Terms

1. crowning (96)
2. breech presentation (96)
3. anoxia (99)
4. placental abruption (99)
5. Cesarean section (99)
6. premature (99)
7. small-for-date infants (99)
8. infant mortality (100)

Newborn Assessment and Behavioral States

1. Apgar score (101)
2. waking activity (102)
3. basic cry (102)
4. mad cry (102)
5. crying (102)
6. Neonatal Behavioral Assessment Scale (102)
7. pain cry (102)
8. sleeping (102)
9. alert inactivity (102)
10. REM sleep (103)
11. regular or non-REM sleep (103)
12. sudden infant death syndrome (103)

Know the Details

1. true (95)
2. true (95)
3. false (96)
4. false (96)
5. false (96)
6. true (97)
7. false (97)
8. true (97)
9. false (98)
10. true (98)
11. true (99)
12. false (99)
13. false (99)
14. false (99)
15. true (100)
16. true (100)
17. true (101)
18. true (101)
19. true (102)
20. false (102)
21. false (103)
22. true (102)
23. false (103)
24. true (103)
25. false (103)
26. true (103)
27. true (103)
28. false (103)
29. false (103)
30. true (104)
31. true (104)
32. false (105)

SUMMARY

MODULE 4.1: FROM CONCEPTION TO BIRTH

two
implanted
differentiate

Period of the Zygote. The first period of prenatal development lasts __________ weeks. It begins when the egg is fertilized by the sperm in the fallopian tube and ends when the fertilized egg has __________ in the wall of the uterus. By the end of this period, cells have begun to __________.

eight
rapid
cephalocaudal; proximodistal

Period of the Embryo. The second period of prenatal development begins two weeks after conception and ends __________ weeks after. This is a period of __________ growth in which most major body structures are created. Growth in this period is __________ (the head develops first) and __________ (parts near the center of the body develop first).

size
seven
age of viability

Period of the Fetus. The third period of prenatal development begins 8 weeks after conception and lasts until birth. The highlights of this period are a remarkable increase in the __________ of the fetus and changes in body systems that are necessary for life. By __________ months, most body systems function well enough to support life. This is called the __________.

MODULE 4.2: INFLUENCES ON PRENATAL DEVELOPMENT

nutrition
stress
Teen-agers
health

General Risk Factors. Prenatal development can be influenced by several general factors. Prenatal development can be harmed if a pregnant mother does not provide adequate __________ for the developing organism and when women experience considerable __________ during pregnancy. A mother's age also is a factor in prenatal development. __________ often have problem pregnancies mainly because they rarely receive adequate prenatal care. Women in their 30s are likely to have problem-free pregnancies if they were in good __________ before becoming pregnant.

Teratogens: Diseases, Drugs, and Environmental Hazards. __________ are agents that can cause abnormal prenatal development. Several diseases are teratogens. Only by avoiding these diseases entirely can a pregnant woman escape their harmful consequences. Many __________ that adults take are teratogens. For most drugs, scientists have not established amounts that can be consumed safely. __________ teratogens are particularly dangerous because a pregnant woman may not know that these substances are present.

Teratogens
drugs
Environmental

How Teratogens Influence Prenatal Development. The impact of teratogens depends upon the __________ of the organism, the period of prenatal development when the organism is __________ to the teratogen, and the __________ of exposure. Sometimes the impact of a teratogen is not evident until __________ in life.

genotype
exposed; amount
later

Prenatal Diagnosis and Treatment. Many techniques are used to track the progress of prenatal development. A common component of prenatal care is __________, which uses sound waves to generate a picture of the fetus. This picture can be used to determine the position of the fetus, its sex, and if there are __________ deformities. When genetic disorders are suspected, __________ and __________ are used to determine the genotype of the fetus. Fetal medicine is a new field in which problems of prenatal development are corrected medically, with __________, or using genetic engineering.

ultrasound
gross physical
amniocentesis; chorionic villus sampling
surgery

MODULE 4.3: HAPPY BIRTHDAY!

Labor and Delivery. Labor consists of three stages. In Stage 1, the muscles of the uterus contract. The __________, which are weak at first and gradually become stronger cause the cervix to enlarge. In Stage 2, the baby moves through the birth canal. In Stage 3, the __________ is delivered.

contractions
placenta

Approaches to Childbirth. Natural or prepared childbirth is based on the assumption that parents should understand what takes place during pregnancy and birth. In natural childbirth, pain-relieving medications are __________ because this medication prevents women from pushing during labor and because it affects the fetus. Instead, women learn to cope with pain through __________, imagery, and with the help of a supportive coach. Most American babies are born in hospitals but many European babies are born at home. This procedure is safe when the mother is healthy, pregnancy and birth are __________, and a health-care professional is present to deliver the baby.

avoided
relaxation
trouble-free

Birth Complications. During labor and delivery, the flow of blood to the fetus can be disrupted, either because the umbilical cord is squeezed shut or because the placenta becomes detached from the wall of the uterus which is known as __________. This causes __________, a lack of oxygen to the fetus, and often results in a __________, an operation in which the baby is removed from the uterus surgically. Some babies are born prematurely and others are small for date. __________ babies develop more slowly at first but catch up by 2 or 3 years of age. Small-for-date babies often do not fare well, particularly if they weigh less than 1500 grams at birth and if their environment is __________. Infant mortality is relatively high in the United States, primarily due to __________ and inadequate prenatal care.

placental abruption; anoxia
Caesarean section
Premature
stressful
low birth weight

Answers	
Apgar behavioral alert inactivity through the night REM low birth weight stomach	*The Newborn.* The __________ score measures five vital signs to determine a newborn baby's physical well-being. The Neonatal Behavioral Assessment Scale provides a comprehensive evaluation of a baby's __________ and physical status. Newborns spend their day in one of four states: __________, waking activity, crying, and sleeping. Newborns spend approximately two-thirds of every day asleep and go through a complete sleep-wake cycle once every four hours. By three or four months, babies sleep __________. Newborns spend about half of their time asleep in __________ sleep. This type of sleep includes active brain waves and frequent movements of the eyes and limbs. Some healthy babies die from sudden infant death syndrome. Factors that contribute to SIDS are prematurity and __________. Also, babies are vulnerable to SIDS when they sleep on their __________, are overheated, and are exposed to cigarette smoke. A national campaign to encourage parents to have their babies sleep on their backs has reduced the number of SIDS cases.
crying disturbed	*Postpartum Depression.* After giving birth, many new mothers briefly experience irritation and __________ spells. A few experience postpartum depression--they are irritable, have poor appetite and __________ sleep, and are apathetic.

CHAPTER 4 PRENATAL DEVELOPMENT AND BIRTH

TEST YOURSELF

1. Which of the following events does NOT occur during the period of the zygote?
   a. Rapid division of the cells
   b. Differentiation of cells
   c. Development of body structures and internal organs
   d. Implantation
2. The __________ is where nutrients and wastes are exchanged between the mother and the developing organism.
   a. germ disc
   b. placenta
   c. ectoderm
   d. amnion
3. A fertilized egg is called a(n) __________.
   a. amnion
   b. umbilical cord
   c. mesoderm
   d. zygote
4. Once implantation is complete, the developing organism is called a(n) __________.
   a. fetus
   b. zygote

c. germ disc
d. embryo

5. The ectoderm will become
a. the arms and legs.
b. hair, the outer layer of skin, and the nervous system.
c. muscles, bones, and the circulatory system.
d. the digestive system and lungs.

6. The endoderm will become
a. the arms and legs.
b. hair, the outer layer of skin, and the nervous system.
c. muscles, bones, and the circulatory system.
d. the digestive system and lungs.

7. The mesoderm will become
a. the arms and legs.
b. hair, the outer layer of skin, and the nervous system.
c. muscles, bones, and the circulatory system.
d. the digestive system and lungs.

8. The __________ houses blood vessels that join the embryo to the placenta.
a. amnion
b. amniotic fluid
c. umbilical cord
d. placenta

9. The cephalocaudal principle means that growth proceeds from the
a. head to the base of the spine.
b. base of the spine to the head.
c. center of the body to the more distant parts of the body.
d. more distant parts of the body to the center of the body.

10. During the period of the fetus,
a. cells begin to differentiate.
b. most of the bodily structures and organs are formed.
c. an insulating layer of fat develops.
d. very little growth of the fetus occurs.

11. The age of viability occurs around the
a. third month of prenatal development.
b. fifth month of prenatal development.
c. seventh month of prenatal development.
d. ninth month of prenatal development.

12. Newborns whose mothers had read *The Cat in the Hat* aloud twice a day during the last 1 1/2 months of pregnancy
a. did not show any recognition of the story.
b. would activate tapes of their mother reading *The Cat in the Hat* but not other stories.
c. could not hear the story because their ears were not well-developed.
d. listened to *The Cat in the Hat* and other stories equally.

13. The weight of the baby, placenta, and amniotic fluid makes up about __________ of the weight that a pregnant woman gains.
a. one-quarter
b. one-third
c. one-half
d. all

14. When pregnant women to do not consume enough folic acid, they are likely to have babies born with
a. rubella.
b. low birth weight.
c. cytomegalovirus.
d. spina bifida.

15. Inadequate prenatal nourishment is associated with
a. damage to the nervous system.
b. blindness.
c. deafness.
d. encephalitis.

16. Which of the following is TRUE of the relation between maternal stress during pregnancy and outcomes for the baby?
a. Maternal stress increases the flow of blood to the fetus.
b. Women who report greater anxiety during pregnancy more often give birth early or have babies who weigh less than average.
c. Stress does not seem to affect a pregnant woman's immune system.
d. The effects of occasional, mild anxiety are the same as those associated with prolonged, extreme stress.

17. Teenage mothers
a. are more likely to have children who do less well in school and who have more behavioral problems.
b. are more likely to have babies with Down syndrome.
c. are less likely to have problems with pregnancy, labor, and delivery.
d. are more likely to seek out prenatal care.

18. Women who took thalidomide during pregnancy gave birth to offspring with a high incidence of
a. mental retardation.
b. deafness and blindness.
c. deformed arms, legs, hands, or fingers.
d. poor verbal and memory skills.

19. Cytomegalovirus (CMV)
a. is a genetic disorder.
b. can result in an abnormally small head.
c. is associated with deformed arms, legs, hands, or fingers.
d. is likely to result in encephalitis.

20. Children with fetal alcohol syndrome (FAS)
a. are usually born prematurely.
b. may have limited motor skills.
c. usually have normal levels of intelligence.
d. have deformed limbs.

21. Maternal exposure to PCB during pregnancy is associated with
a. hyperactivity.
b. deafness.
c. retarded growth.
d. below average verbal and memory abilities.

22. Prenatal exposure to X-rays is associated with
a. leukemia.
b. cerebral palsy.
c. deformed limbs.
d. blindness.

23. Which of the following statements is TRUE of the influence of teratogens on prenatal development?
a. If a teratogen is harmful to one species of mammals it will be harmful to all species of mammals.
b. Teratogens have wide-spread, not specific, effects on prenatal development.
c. The timing of exposure to a teratogen is important.
d. Damage from teratogens always is evident at birth.

24. If a doctor is trying to determine the presence of multiple fetuses, which procedure would she be **most** likely to use?
a. Amniocentesis
b. Ultrasound
c. Chorionic villus sampling
d. Fetal surgery

25. During labor,
a. the third stage lasts the longest amount of time.
b. the opening of the cervix gets larger.
c. the baby is born during the third stage of labor.
d. the second stage of labor is the most painful.

26. Being born feet first is known as
a. anoxia.
b. crowning.
c. dilation.
d. breech presentation.

27. Prepared childbirth classes emphasize
a. the use of visual imagery to increase relaxation.
b. the use of drugs for pain control.
c. that women should go through labor alone.
d. that home births are best.

28. Home births
a. usually involve the presence of a doctor.
b. are more expensive than hospital births.
c. make women feel as if they have less control over labor and delivery.
d. should only be attempted by healthy women who have had problem-free pregnancies.

29. Anoxia is likely to lead to
a. respiratory problems such as asthma.
b. blindness.

c. mental retardation.
d. hyperactivity.

30. Premature infants
a. continue to lag behind their peers into late childhood.
b. are born less than 38 weeks after conception.
c. are small-for-date infants.
d. do not have much of a chance of survival.

31. Low birth weight
a. is not related to infant mortality.
b. is more likely to occur in the United States than other industrialized nations.
c. cannot be prevented by good prenatal care.
d. has no long-term consequences for development.

32. The Neonatal Behavioral Assessment Scale measures
a. heart rate.
b. breathing.
c. skin tone.
d. irritability.

33. The Apgar Scale measures a newborn's
a. skin tone.
b. hearing.
c. vision.
d. alertness.

34. A newborn who is calm and attentive with open eyes is in the state of
a. crying.
b. waking activity.
c. alert inactivity.
d. sleeping.

35. A cry that begins suddenly with a long burst of crying that is followed by a long pause and gasping is known as the
a. basic cry.
b. mad cry.
c. pain cry.
d. hunger cry.

36. Rapid-eye movement (REM) sleep
a. becomes more frequent as infants grow older.
b. may stimulate the brain and foster growth of the nervous system.
c. makes up 90% of newborns' sleep.
d. involves steady heart rate, breathing, and brain activity.

37. Babies are more likely to die from Sudden Infant Death Syndrome
a. if their parents do not smoke.
b. if they were premature or low birth weight babies.
c. in the summer months.
d. while sleeping on their backs.

38. Postpartum depression is more likely in women who
a. were depressed before pregnancy.

b. planned to become pregnant.
c. have the support of other adults after the baby is born.
d. have particularly low levels of hormones in the later phases of pregnancy.

ESSAY QUESTIONS

1. Your friend Chloe is pregnant and she told you that she knows the three stages of prenatal development--the first trimester, the second trimester, and the third trimester--but she wasn't exactly sure about what happens during each of the stages. What can you tell Chloe about the 3 stages of prenatal development and the major events that occur during each of the stages?
2. Chloe also is concerned that her baby will be healthy when it is born. She is wondering if there is anything that she can do that will help ensure that her baby will be okay. What advice can you give Chloe about the steps that she can take toward a healthy baby?
3. Chloe also is concerned about the amount of weight that she will gain during pregnancy. She doesn't want to get "too fat." She has heard of women who gain only 10 pounds while pregnant and they wear their pre-maternity clothes home from the hospital. What can you tell Chloe about weight gain during pregnancy?
4. Chloe is in her 6th month of pregnancy and she isn't sure if she should take the prepared childbirth classes that are being offered at the local hospital. The class meets for 3 hours every Monday night for 6 weeks and that looks like a big time commitment to Chloe. What can you tell Chloe about the benefits of prepared childbirth classes?
5. Chloe wonders how long her labor will last. She has heard stories about women whose labors are so short that they had their babies in the back seat of a car or in an elevator. What can you tell Chloe about the typical length of labor for a first-born child?

ANSWERS

Multiple-Choice

1. c (76)
2. b (77)
3. d (76)
4. d (77)
5. b (77)
6. d (77)
7. c (77)
8. c (78)
9. a (79)
10. c (79)
11. c (80)
12. b (81)
13. b (84)
14. d (84)
15. a (84)
16. b (84)
17. a (85)
18. c (86)
19. b (86)
20. b (87)
21. d (88)
22. a (88)
23. c (90)
24. b (92)
25. b (95)
26. d (96)
27. a (97)
28. d (98)
29. c (99)
30. b (99)
31. b (99)
32. d (102)
33. a (101)
34. c (102)
35. c (102)
36. b (103)
37. b (103)
38. a (104)

Essays

1. Tell Chloe that even though people often refer to the 3 trimesters of pregnancy they do not correspond to the 3 stages of prenatal development. The first stage of prenatal development is called the period of the zygote and it lasts from conception until 2 weeks after conception. Rapid division of the cells and differentiation of the cells characterize this period. The period of the zygote ends when the zygote is completely implanted in the lining of the wall of the uterus. The second period is called the period of the embryo and it lasts from the third week to the eighth week after conception. During this period of prenatal development, most of the organs and systems of the body are formed. The third period is the period of the fetus. This period lasts from 9 weeks until 38 weeks after conception. During this final period, the fetus grows from 4 to 8 ounces to its birth weight of 7 to 8 pounds. Many of the bodily systems that were formed during the period of the embryo are refined during the period of the fetus to prepare the fetus for life outside the uterus. An insulating layer of fat also develops during this period. (76-81)
2. Chloe should visit her health care provider for regular prenatal checkups. Chloe also should eat a healthy diet that contains food from the 5 major food groups. Her diet also should include sufficient vitamins and minerals such as iron and folic acid. Cigarettes, drugs, alcohol, and caffeine should be avoided during pregnancy. Chloe should exercise during pregnancy to keep her body fit. Chloe should get enough rest and try to avoid stress so that she can avoid becoming ill. Chloe should also avoid chemicals such as cleaning products, paint strippers, etc. Finally, she should take prepared childbirth classes to help her prepare for labor and delivery. (82-90)
3. Chloe should not try to keep her weight gain to only 10 pounds. Pregnant women should increase their caloric intake by about 10-20%. Assuming that Chloe is an average-weight woman, she should plan to gain 25 to 35 pounds during pregnancy. Even a woman who is overweight before becoming pregnant should gain 15 pounds. Approximately one-third of the weight gained reflects the weight of the baby, placenta, and amniotic fluid; another third reflects an increase in the woman's fat stores; and the final third comes from increased blood volume, breast size, and uterus size. Remind Chloe that a healthy full-term baby weighs between 7 and 8 pounds. In other words, Chloe should plan to gain more than 10 pounds even if it means that she can't wear her pre-pregnancy clothes home from the hospital. (84)
4. The purpose of childbirth classes is to teach the mother-to-be strategies to manage the pain of labor without the use of drugs. During these classes, pregnant women are taught to relax using deep-breathing. Visual imagery, in which a pleasant event or reassuring scene is pictured, also is used to encourage relaxation. A supportive coach can contribute to relaxation by providing encouragement during labor. (97-98)
5. You can tell Chloe that very few women experience very short labor for first-born children. The average length of Stage 1 of labor for a first-born ranges from 12-24 hours. Stage 2 usually lasts about an hour for first-borns. While there is wide variability in length of labor, most babies do not arrive so quickly that they are born in cars or elevators. (95-96)

Chapter 5
Physical Development in Infants and Toddlers

Module 5.1 *Healthy Growth*

Module 5.2 *The Developing Nervous System*

Module 5.3 *Motor Development*

Module 5.4 *Sensory and Perceptual Processes*

This chapter covers basic information on physical growth, the development of the nervous system, motor development, and sensory and perceptual processes in infants.

HEALTHY GROWTH

MODULE
5.1

Healthy Growth

- *Features of Human Growth*
- *Variations on the Average Profile*
- *Mechanisms of Physical Growth*
- *Challenges to Healthy Growth*

Textbook Learning Objectives

- **What are the important features of physical growth in infants and toddlers? How do they vary from child to child?**
- **How do heredity, hormones, and nutrition contribute to physical growth?**
- **How do malnutrition, disease, and accidents affect infants' and toddlers' physical growth?**

TO MASTER THESE LEARNING OBJECTIVES:

1. Know the terms associated with physical growth.
2. Know the details of physical growth

Know the Terms Associated with Physical Growth: Match each definition with the correct term

Epiphyses

Secular growth trends

Hormones Thyroxine
Malnourished

1. The ends of the cartilage structures that turn to bone during prenatal development.__________
2. Changes in physical development from one generation to the next are known as __________
3. Chemicals that travel in the bloodstream to act on other body parts.__________
4. A hormone that is released by the thyroid gland that is essential for the proper development of nerve cells.__________
5. The condition of children who receive an inadequate diet and who are small for their age. __________

Know the Details of Physical Growth

1. T F Toddlers and young children have disproportionately small heads.
2. T F Most of the body's muscle fibers are not present at birth.
3. T F Fat accumulates rapidly the first year of life.
4. T F During prenatal development, cartilage turns to bone beginning with the ends of the cartilage structures.
5. T F Each generation is taller than the previous generation.
6. T F "Average" and "normal" mean the same thing.
7. T F Fraternal twins have more similar heights than identical twins.
8. T F Growth hormone is secreted by the pituitary gland.
9. T F Dwarfs do not have adequate amounts of growth hormone.
10. T F Thyroxine is necessary for the proper development of nerve cells.
11. T F Low levels of thyroxine lead to mental retardation.
12. T F Good nutrition is not important during infancy because infants have many years to catch up with well-nourished peers.
13. T F Infants need to consume fewer calories per pound than do adults.
14. T F Breast-fed babies are ill more often than bottle-fed babies.
15. T F Breast-fed babies are less prone to diarrhea and constipation.
16. T F Bottle-fed babies make the transition to solid food more easily than breast-fed babies.
17. T F Many new foods should be introduced at the same time to increase variety in the infant's diet.
18. T F Increased pickiness while eating occurs when growth slows in children who are around 2 years of age.
19. T F Malnutrition is not common in industrialized countries.
20. T F The effects of malnutrition are especially damaging during infancy.
21. T F Malnutrition affects a child's intelligence and ability to pay attention.
22. T F Malnourished children frequently are very active.

23. T F The effects of malnutrition can be cured simply by providing an adequate diet.

24. T F Most diseases that kill young children around the world do not have a cure.

25. T F Measles and diarrhea kill many young children each year.

26. T F In the United States, toddlers and preschoolers are more likely to die as a result of accidents than from any other single cause.

27. T F Drowning is the most common cause of accidental death in infants and toddlers.

ANSWERS

Know the Terms

1. epiphyses (113)
2. secular growth trends (113)
3. hormones (114)
4. thyroxine (114)
5. malnourished (116)

Know the Details

1. false (113)
2. false (113)
3. true (113)
4. true (113)
5. true (113)
6. false (114)
7. false (114)
8. true (114)
9. true (114)
10. true (114)
11. true (114)
12. false (117)
13. false (117)
14. false (115)
15. true (115)
16. false (115)
17. false (116)
18. true (116)
19. false (116)
20. true (117)
21. true (117)
22. false (117)
23. false (117)
24. false (117)
25. true (117)
26. true (119)
27. false (119)

MODULE 5.2

The Developing Nervous System
- *Organization of the Mature Brain*
- *The Developing Brain*

THE DEVELOPING NERVOUS SYSTEM

Textbook Learning Objectives

- **What are the parts of a nerve cell? How is the brain organized?**
- **When is the brain formed in prenatal development? When do different regions of the brain begin to function?**

TO MASTER THESE LEARNING OBJECTIVES:

1. Know the terms associated with the developing nervous system
2. Know the details of the developing nervous system

Know the Terms Associated with the Developing Nervous System: Match each definition with the correct term

Axon
Cell body
Neural plate
Neuron

Corpus callosum
Dendrite
Electroencephalogram (EEG)
Frontal cortex
Functional magnetic resonance imaging (F-MRI)
Hemispheres
Myelin
Neuroplasticity
Neurotransmitters
Positron emission tomography (PET)
Synapse
Synaptic pruning
Terminal buttons

1. A cell that specializes in receiving and transmitting information.__________
2. This structure at the center of the neuron contains the basic biological machinery that keeps the neuron alive (see #1 in figure below).__________
3. The receiving end of the neuron (see #2 in figure above).__________

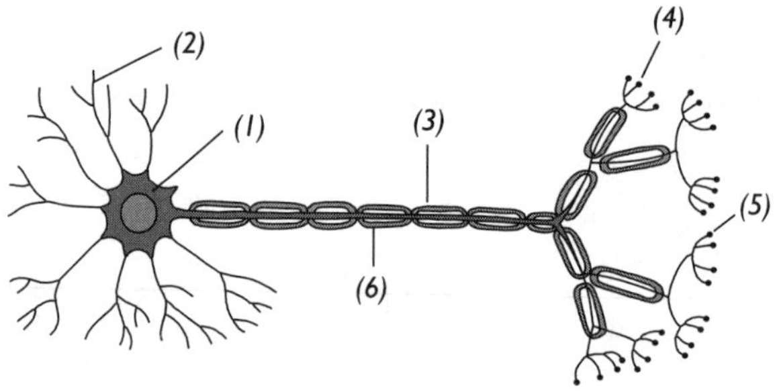

(2)
(1)
(3)
(4)
(5)
(6)

4. This tube-like structure sends information to other neurons (see #3 in figure above).__________
5. The small knobs at the end of the axons (see #4 in figure above). __________
6. Chemicals that carry information to nearby neurons. __________
7. The gap between one neuron and the next (see #5 in figure above). __________
8. The fatty sheath around neurons that will help them transmit information more rapidly (see #6 in figure above).__________
9. The right and left halves of the cortex.__________
10. The thick bundle of neurons that connects the hemispheres of the cortex.__________
11. The area of the cortex that controls personality and the ability to carry out plans.__________
12. A flat group of cells in the embryo that will become the nervous system.__________
13. The process by which synapses disappear gradually.__________
14. This measures the pattern of brain waves.__________
15. This uses magnetic fields to track the flow of blood in the brain.__________
16. This procedure traces the use of glucose in the brain. __________
17. The extent to which brain organization is flexible. __________

Know the Details of the Developing Nervous System

1. T F The nerve cell is called a neuron.

2. T F The cell body sends information to other neurons.

3. T F The part of the neuron called the axon sends information to other neurons.

4. T F The part of the neuron called the dendrite receives information from other neurons.

5. T F The gap between one neuron and another is the neurotransmitter.

6. T F The small knobs at the ends of the axons are called synapses.

7. T F The wrinkled surface of the brain is called the corpus callosum.

8. T F The right and left halves of the cortex are known as hemispheres.

9. T F The ability to produce and understand language is located in the left hemisphere of the brain.

10. T F The ability to perceive spatial relations is located in the left hemisphere of the brain.

11. T F The neural plate in the embryo will become the nervous system.

12. T F Almost all of the neurons that the brain will ever have are produced between 10 and 28 weeks after conception.

13. T F Around 7 months after conception, all 6 layers of the brain are in place.

14. T F Myelin slows down the transmission of information.

15. T F The gradual disappearance of synapses is known as synaptic pruning.

16. T F The left hemisphere cannot process language until the child is old enough to talk.

17. T F Electroencephalograms can tell scientists when different areas of the brain begin to function.

18. T F Music elicits greater electrical activity in the infant's right hemisphere than the left hemisphere.

19. T F Two functions of the right hemisphere, understanding spatial relations and recognizing faces, develop gradually but are under the control of the right hemisphere by the preschool years.

20. T F Active areas of the brain use more glucose than less active areas of the brain.

21. T F Positron emission tomography records electrical brain waves.

22. T F By 7 or 8 months of age, the activity in the frontal cortex reaches adult levels.

23. T F The frontal cortex controls deliberate, goal-directed behavior.

24. T F Throughout the preschool years, the frontal cortex achieves greater control over inappropriate responding.

25. T F Emotions such as curiosity stem from an organism's desire to avoid a stimulus.

26. T F The left frontal cortex regulates emotions stemming from the tendency to approach a stimulus.

27. T F According to Fox and his colleagues, infants who responded negatively to a novel stimulus at 4 months of age had greater left frontal activity at 9 months of age.

28. T F The human brain does not show plasticity when damaged.

ANSWERS

Know the Terms

1. neuron (120)
2. cell body (120)
3. dendrite (120)
4. axon (120)
5. terminal buttons (120)
6. neurotransmitters (120)
7. synapse (120)
8. myelin (120)
9. hemispheres (121)
10. corpus callosum (121)
11. frontal cortex (121)
12. neural plate (121)
13. synaptic pruning (122)
14. electroencephalogram (EEG) (122)
15. functional magnetic resonance imaging (123)
16. positron emission tomography (PET) (123)
17. neuroplasticity (125)

Know the Details

1. true (120)
2. false (120)
3. true (120)
4. true (120)
5. false (120)
6. false (120)
7. false (121)
8. true (121)
9. true (121)
10. false (121)
11. true (121)
12. true (121)
13. true (121)
14. false (122)
15. true (122)
16. false (123)
17. true (122)
18. true (123)
19. true (123)
20. true (123)
21. false (123)
22. true (123)
23. true (123)
24. true (123)
25. false (124)
26. true (124)
27. false (124)
28. false(125)

MODULE
5.3

Motor Development

- *The Infant's Reflexes*
- *Locomotion*
- *Fine-Motor Skills*
- *Maturation, Experience, and Motor Skill*

MODULE 5.3 MOTOR DEVELOPMENT

Textbook Learning Objectives

- **How do reflexes help infants interact with the world?**
- **What are the component skills involved in learning to walk, and at what age do infants typically master them?**
- **How do infants learn to coordinate the use of their hands? When and why do most children begin to prefer to use one hand?**
- **How do maturation and experience influence children's acquisition of motor skills?**

TO MASTER THESE LEARNING OBJECTIVES:

1. Know the terms associated with motor development
2. Know the details of motor development

Know the Terms Associated with Motor Development: Match the definition with the correct term

Babinski	Motor skills
Blink	Palmar
Differentiation	Reflexes
Dynamic systems	Rooting
Fine-motor skills	Stepping
Integration	Sucking
Locomotion	Withdrawal
Moro	

1. Coordinated movements of the muscles and limbs.____________
2. Moving about in the world.____________
3. Skills such as grasping, holding, and manipulating objects.____________
4. Unlearned responses that are triggered by a specific form of stimulation.____________
5. This reflex involves withdrawing one's foot when the sole is pricked with a pin.____________
6. This reflex occurs when a baby grasps an object that is placed in the palm of her hand.____________
7. This reflex occurs when a baby's toes fan out when the sole of the foot is stroked from heel to toe.____________
8. When a baby is held upright and moved forward, the baby will reflexively step rhythmically.____________
9. This reflex occurs when a baby closes her eyes in response to a bright light or loud noise.____________
10. This reflex occurs when a baby throws its arms and legs out and then inward in response to a loud noise or the falling of its head.____________
11. This reflex occurs when a baby's cheek is stroked, he will turn toward the stroking and open his mouth.____________
12. This reflex occurs when the baby sucks on an object that is placed in her mouth.____________
13. This involves breaking down complex motions into their component skills.____________
14. This involves combining the component skills of a complex motion in the proper sequence.____________
15. This theory states that motor development involves many distinct skills that are organized and reorganized over time to meet the demands of a specific task. __________

Know the Details of Motor Development

1. T F The rooting and sucking reflexes are not necessary for survival.
2. T F Some reflexes such as the stepping reflex serve as foundations for later motor activity.
3. T F Reflexes do not indicate the state of the newborn's nervous system.
4. T F By 4 months of age, most babies can sit upright with support.
5. T F By 9 months, most babies can stand using an object for support.
6. T F Most babies take their first steps at 24 months.
7. T F The ability to maintain an upright posture is one component skill of walking.
8. T F Cephalocaudal development means that it is easy for infants to stand upright during the first few months of life.
9. T F Maintaining one's balance is a component skill of walking.
10. T F The cues for balance come from the eyes, not the inner ears.
11. T F Moving the legs alternately while transferring body weight from one foot to the other is an essential element of walking.
12. T F Children typically step spontaneously around 10 months of age.
13. T F Some 3-month-olds show alternate stepping when they are held upright.
14. T F Infants use perceptual cues to decide whether a surface is safe for walking.
15. T F Most children take their first steps between 12 and 15 months of age.
16. T F Most infants cannot coordinate the motions of their hands until they are 12 months old.
17. T F Most 1-year-olds use spoons like adults do.
18. T F Almost 90% of the people in the world are left handed.
19. T F A preference for one hand over the other emerges around the first birthday.
20. T F By the time children enter kindergarten, handedness is well established.
21. T F Heredity is the only factor that determines handedness.
22. T F Motor development is influenced by both maturation and experience.
23. T F Experience can improve the rate of motor development.
24. T F The impact of practice on motor skills is widespread, not specific.

ANSWERS

Key Terms

1. motor skills (127)
2. locomotion (127)
3. fine-motor skills (128)
4. reflexes (128)
9. blink (128)
10. Moro (128)
11. rooting (128)
12. sucking (128)

5. withdrawal (128)
6. palmar (128)
7. Babinski (128)
8. stepping (128)
13. differentiation (131)
14. integration (131)
15. dynamic systems (129)

Know the Details

1. false (128)
2. true (128)
3. false (129)
4. true (129)
5. true (129)
6. false (129)
7. true (129)
8. false (130)
9. true (130)
10. false (130)
11. true (130)
12. true (130)
13. false (130)
14. true (130)
15. true (131)
16. false (131)
17. false (132)
18. false (132)
19. true (132)
20. true (132)
21. false (132)
22. true (133)
23. true (134)
24. false (134)

SENSORY AND PERCEPTUAL PROCESSES

MODULE
5.4

Sensory and Perceptual Processes

- *Smell, Taste, and Touch*
- *Hearing*
- *Seeing*
- *Integrating Sensory Information*

Textbook Learning Objectives

- **Are newborn babies able to smell, taste, and respond to touch?**
- **How well do infants hear? How do they use sounds to understand their world?**
- **How accurate is infants' vision? Do infants perceive color and depth?**
- **How do infants integrate information from different senses?**

TO MASTER THESE LEARNING OBJECTIVES:

1. Know the terms associated with sensation and perception.
2. Know the research results on perception of objects
3. Know the details of the development of the senses, perception of objects, and integration of the senses.

Know the Terms Associated with Sensation and Perception: Match each term with the correct definition

Auditory threshold
Cones
Edges
Interposition
Linear perspective
Relative size
Retinal disparity
Size constancy
Texture gradient
Visual acuity
Visual cliff

1. The smallest pattern that can be distinguished dependably.__________
2. Specialized neurons in the retina of the eye that detect color.__________
3. Paying less attention to a stimulus as it becomes more familiar.__________

4. The quietest sound that a person can hear.__________
5. A glass-covered platform that appears to have a steep drop-off, like a cliff. __________
6. The fact that the left and right eyes often see slightly different versions of the same scene. __________
7. The fact that parallel lines appear to come together at a single point in the distance. __________
8. The fact that the texture of objects changes from coarse but distinct for nearer objects to finer and less distinct for distant objects. __________
9. The fact that nearby objects look substantially larger than objects in the distance. __________
10. The fact that nearby objects partially obscure more distant objects. __________
11. Lines that mark the boundaries of objects. __________

Research Results: Circle the correct results for each study

1. Three-month-old infants were shown a simple square 6 different times. Then the infants were shown one of the four patterns shown below. Only pattern A creates the subjective experience of "seeing" a square.

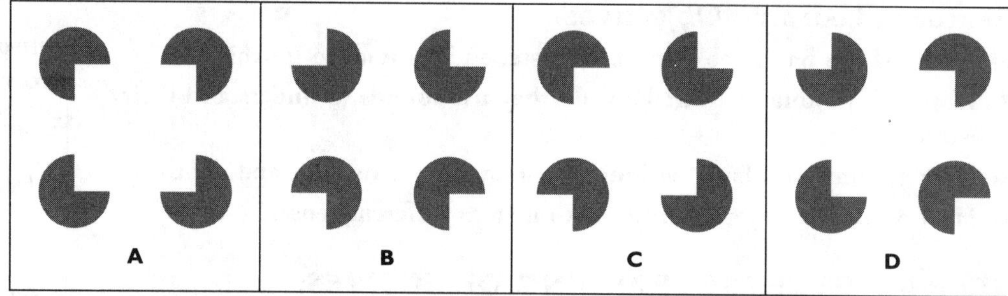

Result A-- Three-month-olds looked much longer at Patterns B-D than at Pattern A because they had habituated to seeing squares. In other words, infants could assemble a pattern from individual elements.

Result B--Three-month-olds look at all of the patterns equally because none of them resemble the squares that they saw earlier. In other words, infants cannot assemble a pattern from individual elements.

2. To see if infants understood the concept that elements of objects that move together are usually part of the same object, 2- to 4-month-olds were shown a pencil eraser and pencil point that moved together but were obscured by a colored square. Later, the colored square was removed to reveal either a single pencil or two pencil stubs that moved in unison. If infants had assumed that the pencil point and eraser were part of the same pencil they should have been surprised and should have looked longer at the two pencil stubs.

Result A--By 2 to 4 months of age, infants are surprised to see the two pencil stubs, indicating that they can use common motion to create objects from different parts.

Result B--Two- to four-month-olds looked an equal amount of time at the single pencil and the two pencil stubs, indicating that they cannot use common motion to create objects from different parts.

3. Four- and five-month-olds were shown an unfamiliar teddy bear. Then the bear was paired with a larger replica of the bear. If the babies have size constancy, they will recognize the first bear as familiar and the larger bear as novel, and be more likely to respond to the larger, novel bear. If they do not have size constancy, they will respond to both bears similarly because neither bear would be novel.

   Result A--Four- and five-month-olds respond equally to the two bears, indicating that they do not have size constancy.

   Result B--Four- and five-month-olds respond more to the larger, novel bear, indicating that they have size constancy.

4. To see if infants prefer to look at faces or just prefer stimuli that contain many of the elements that occur in faces, 1 1/2-month-old infants were shown faces or nonface stimuli that are matched for important variables (e.g., amount of black-white contrast and size and number of elements). If infants prefer faces, they should look at the faces more. If they merely prefer the elements that are found in faces, they should look at the face and matched nonface stimuli equally.

   Result A--Infants looked at the faces more, indicating that faces have an intrinsic attraction for infants.

   Result B--Infants looked at the face and matched nonface stimuli equally, indicating that they are not innately attracted to faces but are attracted to the elements found in faces.

5. In another study to test if babies are innately attracted to facelike stimuli, newborns were shown either faces or stimuli that had either facial elements or a facial configuration but not both. If babies have an innate preference for faces, they should follow a moving face more than they would follow the nonface stimuli. If infants do not have an innate preference for faces, they should follow the face and nonface stimuli equally.

   Result A--Newborns followed a moving face more than nonface stimuli, supporting the view that infants are innately attracted to faces.

   Result B--Newborns followed the moving face and nonface stimuli equally, indicating that faces are no more attractive to infants than similar nonface stimuli.

6. Lorraine Bahrick and her colleagues were interested in infants' ability to integrate sight and sound. They showed 4-month-olds and 7-month-olds videos of a man talking and a boy talking. The infants also heard a separate audio tape of either a man's voice or a boy's voice. If infants understand that the boyish voice should come from the boyish face (and the man-like voice should come from the man-like face), they should watch the video (either the man or boy) that corresponds to the audio tape that they hear.

   Result A--Infants were not able to link the video and audio tapes as indicated by the fact that they looked at matching and nonmatching videos equally.

Result B— Both 4- and 7-month-old infants looked longer at the matching videos than the nonmatching videos, indicating that they could integrate the typical appearance of faces and voices.

Know the Details of the Development and Integration of the Senses

1. T F Researchers often measure an infant's heart rate, facial expression, or head movements to see if the infant responds differently to 2 different stimuli.
2. T F Newborns cannot distinguish pleasant and unpleasant odors.
3. T F Young babies cannot identify their mother's scent.
4. T F Infants can differentiate sour, salty, bitter, and sweet tastes.
5. T F Infants prefer bitter and sour tastes.
6. T F An infant can detect changes in the taste of his mother's breast milk that reflect the mother's diet.
7. T F Infants have fewer pain receptors than do adults.
8. T F Infants hear as well as adults.
9. T F Infants best hear sounds with pitches that are in the range of human speech.
10. T F Infants can discriminate vowels from consonant sounds.
11. T F Infants cannot recognize their own names until they are 1 year old.
12. T F Infants cannot use sound to locate objects.
13. T F Tests of infants' visual acuity are based on the assumption that infants will prefer plain stimuli over patterned stimuli.
14. T F When testing an infant's visual acuity, looking at plain and patterned stimuli equally means that the infant cannot see the pattern.
15. T F Newborns can see as well as adults with normal vision.
16. T F Infants' color perception is similar to adults' by 3 or 4 months of age.
17. T F By 4 or 5 months, babies have mastered size constancy, brightness constancy, color constancy, and shape constancy.
18. T F Crawling infants are as likely to cross the deep as the shallow side of a visual cliff.
19. T F Babies who are 1 1/2 months old who cannot crawl yet are afraid when they are placed on the deep side of the visual cliff.
20. T F When objects are near, greater disparity in retinal images occurs.
21. T F By 4-6 months of age, infants use retinal disparity as a depth cue.
22. T F When texture gradient is used to infer depth, people judge blurred objects to be near.
23. T F When relative size is used to infer depth, people judge smaller objects as closer.
24. T F When interposition is used to infer depth, people judge partially obscured objects as more distant.

25. T F Edges play an important role in the perception of objects.
26. T F Young infants cannot assemble a pattern from individual elements.
27. T F Young infants (2- to 4-month-olds) cannot use motion to define objects.
28. T F When face and nonface stimuli are matched on a number of important variables, 1 1/2-month-olds typically look at the two types of stimuli equally.
29. T F By 3 or 4 months, babies can distinguish individual faces.
30. T F Infants cannot visually recognize an object that they had touched previously until they are 6 months old.
31. T F Infants as young as 4 months old can integrate the sound of child or adult voices with the appropriate child or adult face.

ANSWERS

Key Terms

1. visual acuity (138)
2. cones (143)
3. auditory threshold (140)
4. size constancy (139)
5. visual cliff (140)
6. retinal disparity (141)
7. linear perspective (141)
8. texture gradient (141)
9. relative size (141)
10. interposition (142)
11. edges (142)

Research Results

1. Result A (143)
2. Result A (143)
3. Result B (140)
4. Result B (144)
5. Result A (144)
6. Result B (145)

Know the Details

1. true (136)
2. false (136)
3. false (136)
4. true (136)
5. false (136)
6. true (136)
7. false (137)
8. false (137)
9. true (137)
10. true (137)
11. false (137)
12. false (137)
13. true (137)
14. true (138)
15. false (138)
16. true (139)
17. true (139)
18. false (140)
19. false (140)
20. true (141)
21. true (141)
22. false (141)
23. false (141)
24. true (142)
25. true (142)
26. false (143)
27. false (143)
28. true (144)
29. true (144)
30. false (144)
31. true (144)

SUMMARY

MODULE 5.1: PHYSICAL GROWTH

rapid *Features of Human Growth.* Physical growth is particularly __________ in infants
cephalocaudal and toddlers. Growth follows the __________ principle, in which the head and
trunk develop before the limbs. Physical growth refers to not only height and
weight, but also to the development of muscle, fat, and bones.

taller *Variations on the Average Profile.* Children are __________ today than in previous
generations. And children of the same age vary considerably in height and weight.

Mechanisms of Physical Growth. A person's height and weight as an adult are influenced by heredity. Also, hormones are important for physical development:
growth hormone; thyroxine __________ helps to develop bone and muscle, and __________, which helps to
develop nerve cells. Nutrition is particularly important during periods of rapid
adolescence growth such as infancy and __________. Breast milk provides babies with all of
antibodies the nutrients they need and it contains the mother's __________ which help protect the baby against illnesses.

Challenges to Healthy Growth. Many children face serious obstacles to healthy
development. Malnutrition is a problem worldwide--including the United States.
infancy That is particularly harmful during __________, when growth is so rapid. Malnutrition can cause brain damage, affecting children's intelligence and ability to
attention pay __________. Treating malnutrition requires improving children's diet and
stimulating environment training their parents to provide __________. Millions of children around the
world die annually from infectious diseases. Integrated Management of Childhood
Illness is a new integrated approach to promote children's health. In the United
accidents States, toddlers are more likely to die from __________ than any other single
cause.

MODULE 5.2: THE DEVELOPING NERVOUS SYSTEM

Organization of the Mature Brain. Nerve cells, called neurons, include a cell body,
dendrite a __________, and an axon. The mature brain consists of billions of neurons
organized into nearly identical left and right hemispheres connected by the
corpus callosum; frontal __________. The __________ cortex is associated with personality and goal-
language directed behavior; the cortex in the left hemisphere, with __________; and the
cortex in the right hemisphere, with nonverbal processes such as perceiving
music __________ and regulating emotions.

The Developing Brain. Brain structure begins in prenatal development, when neurons form at an incredible rate. After birth, the neurons in the central nervous
myelin system become wrapped in __________, allowing them to transmit information
more rapidly. Throughout childhood, unused synapses disappear gradually through
synaptic pruning a process called __________. Methods used to investigate brain functioning in
children include (a) studying children with brain damage, (b) recording electrical
EEG activity (__________), and (c) using imaging techniques. Research with these
methods reveals that an infant's brain begins to function early in life. The cortex
left in the __________ hemisphere specializes in language processing at (or soon after)
right birth. The cortex in the __________ hemisphere controls some nonverbal func-

tions, such as perception of music, very early in infancy; control of other right-hemisphere functions, such as understanding __________ relations, is achieved by the preschool years. The frontal cortex has begun to regulate goal-directed behavior and emotional responding by __________.

spatial
the first birthday

MODULE 5.3: MOTOR DEVELOPMENT

The Infant's Reflexes. Babies are born with many reflexes. Some help them to adjust to life outside the uterus, some __________ them, and some are the basis for later __________ behavior.

protect
motor

Locomotion. Infants progress through a sequence of motor milestones during the first year, culminating in __________ a few months after the first birthday. Like most motor skills, learning to walk involves __________ of individual skills, such as maintaining balance and stepping on alternate legs, and then __________ these skills into a coherent whole. This differentiation and integration of skills is central to the __________ theory of motor development.

walking
differentiation
integrating
dynamic systems

Fine-Motor Skill. Reaching and grasping become more precise in the first year as does __________ use of both hands. Most people are right handed, a preference that emerges after the __________ and that becomes well established during the preschool years. Handedness is determined by heredity but can also be influenced by __________.

coordinated
first birthday
cultural values

Maturation, Experience, and Motor Skill. Biology and experience both shape the mastery of motor skills. On the one hand, the basic developmental timetable for passing motor milestones is __________ worldwide, which indicates underlying biological causes. On the other hand, specific experience can accelerate motor development, particularly for __________ motor skills.

similar
complex

MODULE 5.4: SENSORY AND PERCEPTUAL PROCESSES

Smell, Taste, and Touch. Newborns are able to smell, and some can recognize their mother's odor; they also taste, preferring __________ substances and responding __________ to bitter and sour tastes. Infants respond to touch. They probably experience pain, because their responses to painful stimuli are __________ to those of older children.

sweet
negatively
similar

Hearing. Babies can hear, although they are __________ sensitive to higher- and lower-pitched sounds than adults. Babies can distinguish different sounds and use sound to __________ objects in space.

less
locate

Seeing. A newborn's visual acuity is relatively __________, but 1-year-olds can see as well as an adult with normal vision. Color vision develops as different sets of __________ begin to function; by 3 or 4 months of age, children can see color as well as adults. Infants, like adults, use __________ and motion to distinguish objects. By about 4 months, infants have begun to master size, shape, __________, and color constancy. Infants perceive depth by means of retinal disparity and other cues such as linear perspective, __________, relative size, and interposition. Infants perceive faces early in the first year. However, it is not clear

poor
cones
edges
brightness
texture gradient

whether perception of faces involves specific perceptual mechanisms or whether it is based on the same processes used to perceive other objects.

Integrating Sensory Information. Soon after birth, infants begin to coordinate information from different senses. They can recognize, by __________, an object that they've felt previously. And infants can integrate what they see with what they __________.

sight

hear

CHAPTER 5 PHYSICAL DEVELOPMENT IN INFANTS AND TODDLERS

TEST YOURSELF

1. Which of the following statements is true?
   a. The body's muscle fibers appear after birth.
   b. Very little fat accumulates after birth.
   c. Cartilage begins to turn to bone after birth.
   d. Toddlers and young children have disproportionately large heads.

2. "Average" physical growth
   a. varies from one generation to the next.
   b. does not vary from country to country.
   c. is the same as "normal" physical growth.
   d. is the same in Africa and Europe.

3. Which of the following statements is true of the role of hormones in growth?
   a. Growth hormone is secreted by the liver.
   b. Thyroxine triggers the release of somatomedin which causes muscles and bones to grow.
   c. Thyroxine is necessary for the proper development of nerve cells.
   d. Low levels of thyroxine cause dwarfism.

4. Which of the following is true of nutrition and physical growth?
   a. Nutrition is particularly important during infancy when growth is rapid.
   b. In a 2-month-old, almost 80% of the body's energy is devoted to growth.
   c. Young babies need fewer calories per pound of body weight than do adults.
   d. Nutrition is not related to physical growth.

5. Compared to bottle-fed babies, breast-fed babies
   a. are ill more often.
   b. are less prone to diarrhea and constipation.
   c. have a more difficult time making the transition to solid foods.
   d. do not receive the antibodies that are found in formula.

6. Malnutrition
   a. is common only in developing nations.
   b. does not affect children's size or intelligence.
   c. is especially damaging during middle childhood.
   d. needs to be treated by training parents to stimulate their children.

7. The most common cause of accidental death in children is
a. drowning.
b. motor vehicle accidents.
c. suffocation.
d. burns.

8. Each neuron consists of
a. a cell body.
b. an axon.
c. dendrites.
d. all of the above.

9. Chemicals that carry information from one neuron to the next are called
a. terminal buttons.
b. synapses.
c. myelin.
d. neurotransmitters.

10. The left hemisphere of the brain controls
a. artistic and musical abilities.
b. the perception of spatial relations.
c. the ability to produce and understand language.
d. the ability to recognize faces.

11. The entire nervous system arises from the embryonic structure known as the
a. medulla.
b. neural plate.
c. corpus callosum.
d. cerebral cortex.

12. The production of neurons
a. is not complete until the child is in school.
b. involves producing many more neurons than necessary.
c. does not begin until after birth.
d. is very slow and gradual.

13. Which of the following structures of the brain shows the most mature functioning at birth?
a. The left hemisphere
b. The right hemisphere
c. The frontal cortex
d. The corpus callosum

14. Damage to the frontal cortex of the brain is likely to affect which of the following functions?
a. Understanding and producing language
b. Musical ability
c. Spatial relations
d. Inhibiting behaviors that are no longer appropriate

15. The left frontal cortex regulates the emotions such as
a. disgust.
b. anger.
c. fear.
d. happiness.

16. Calkins, Fox, and Marshall (1996) measured brain frontal cortex activity to see if it was related to infants' responses to novel stimuli. They found that
a. there was no relation between frontal cortex activity and the infants' behavior.
b. infants who responded negatively to a novel stimulus at 4 months of age had more right frontal activity as 9-month-olds.
c. infants who responded negatively to a novel stimulus at 4 months of age had more left frontal activity as 9-month-olds.
d. the frontal cortex does not seem to regulate infant behavior in any predictable way.

17. When a newborn's foot is stroked from heel to toe, the infant will fan its toes. This is known as the
a. Moro reflex.
b. Babinski reflex.
c. palmar reflex.
d. rooting reflex.

18. Reflexes
a. are not important to the newborn's survival.
b. do not protect the infant from danger in the environment.
c. indicate whether or not the newborn's nervous system is working properly.
d. are not related to later motor behavior.

19. Most 4-month-olds
a. do not have the muscles necessary to help them stay upright.
b. use cues from the inner ears to maintain balance.
c. use only visual cues to maintain balance.
d. cannot maintain balance if they are blindfolded.

20. When infants are held upright over a treadmill,
a. most 3-month-olds demonstrated alternate stepping.
b. most 6- and 7-month-olds demonstrated alternate stepping.
c. only 10-months-olds demonstrated alternate stepping.
d. only infants who could walk already demonstrated alternate stepping.

21. Most children use a spoon like an adult by the time they are
a. 6 months old.
b. 12 months old.
c. 18 months old.
d. 24 months old.

22. A preference for one hand over the other
a. becomes apparent when children enter school.
b. is well established by the first birthday.
c. is influenced by one's culture.
d. is determined solely by heredity.

23. Dennis and Dennis (1940) found which of the following results from their study of Hopi children?
a. Cradle-board infants showed a large delay in the onset of walking.
b. Cradle-board infants were accelerated in the onset of walking.
c. Once cradle-board infants learned to walk they were less coordinated than other infants.
d. Cradle-board and noncradle-board infants both started to walk around 15 months of age.

24. Which of the following statements is true of the role of experience in motor development?
  a. Experience does not influence motor development.
  b. Experience can improve the rate of motor development.
  c. Experience has a widespread influence on many muscle groups.
  d. Experience is less important in mastering complex actions.

25. Newborns' sense of smell
  a. is so poor that they cannot identify their mothers using the sense of smell.
  b. is very different from that of adults. Newborns will turn away from odors that adults find pleasant (e.g., honey or chocolate).
  c. is well-developed at birth.
  d. is poorly developed because they do not turn away from unpleasant smells (e.g., rotten eggs).

26. Newborns are able to detect which of the following tastes?
  a. Salty and sour tastes
  b. Sweet and salty tastes
  c. Bitter and sour tastes
  d. Salty, sour, bitter, and sweet tastes

27. Most newborns prefer which of the following tastes?
  a. Salty tastes
  b. Bitter tastes
  c. Sweet tastes
  d. Sour tastes

28. The pain cry in infants
  a. often is accompanied by agitated movements of hands and arms.
  b. has a low pitch.
  c. is easily soothed.
  d. begins gradually.

29. Which of the following is true of infants' auditory perception?
  a. Infants have higher auditory thresholds than adults.
  b. Infants can hear high-pitched sounds the best.
  c. Infants cannot use sound to locate an object.
  d. Infants cannot discriminate vowel and consonant sounds.

30. Three-month-old infants
  a. cannot see color.
  b. can see the full range of color.
  c. cannot differentiate red from green.
  d. cannot differentiate yellow from red.

31. To test size constancy, infants were shown an unfamiliar teddy bear. Then the bear was paired with a larger replica of the bear. How did infants react to the bears?
  a. At 5 months, infants treated both bears similarly, indicating that they do not have size constancy.
  b. At 5 months, infants treated both bears similarly, indicating that they do have size constancy.
  c. At 5 months, infants responded more to the larger, novel bear, indicating that they do have size constancy.
  d. At 5 months, infants responded more to the smaller bear that they have seen previously, indicating that they do not have size constancy.

32. The majority of the crawling infants in the Gibson and Walk study of depth perception using a visual cliff
a. demonstrated no fear of crawling over the deep side.
b. displayed depth perception.
c. would crawl over the deep side when called by their mothers.
d. could not discriminate the shallow side from the deep side.

33. Retinal disparity cues are used to infer depth
a. in the newborn.
b. beginning at 3 months of age.
c. by 4 to 6 months of age.
d. after the first birthday.

34. To see if infants can assemble a pattern from individual elements, 3-month-olds were shown a square. After 6 presentations of the square, the infants were shown diagrams of circles arranged in various patterns. In Pattern A the circles were arranged in the shape of a square, but in Patterns B-D the arrangements did not resemble a square. What did the researcher find?
a. Infants looked longer at Patterns B-D, indicating that they recognized the square in Pattern A.
b. Infants looked longer at Pattern A, indicating that they did not recognize the square in Pattern A.
c. Infants looked at all of the patterns equally, indicating that they did not recognize the square in Pattern A.
d. Infants did not look at any of the patterns, indicating that they do not like to look at patterns.

35. Which of the following is true of perception of faces in infants?
a. There is clear-cut evidence that infants have an innate preference for faces.
b. One-month-old infants focus on the interior features of the face such as the eyes and lips.
c. Three-month-olds focus on the outer edges of the face.
d. By 4 months of age, babies can distinguish individual faces.

36. To see if infants can match child faces with child voices and adult faces with adult voices, Lorraine Bahrick and her colleagues simultaneously showed infants a picture of an adult and a picture of a child while playing an audio tape of either an adult voice or a child voice. If infants can match the child voice to the child picture, they should look at the picture of the child while the audio tape of the child voice is played. How did the infants react?
a. Infants always looked at the picture of the adult regardless of which audio tape they heard.
b. Infants were more likely to look at the picture that matched the audio tape.
c. Infants were more likely to look at the picture that did not match the audio tape.
d. Infants looked at both pictures equally regardless of which audio tape they heard.

ESSAY QUESTIONS

1. Your friend Lafon has a newborn son named Lamar. Lamar was a healthy full-term infant who weighed 7 pounds 6 ounces at birth. While you and Lafon are shopping for clothes for Lamar in a very expensive children's store, you notice that Lafon is loading her cart with lots of 0-3 month size clothes. You ask Lafon if she thinks it's a good idea to spend so much money on clothes that Lamar will outgrow very quickly. What can you tell Lafon about physical growth during the first year of life that may change her mind about these clothes?
2. Your friends Alex and Katya are concerned that their 9-month-old daughter Mariana often uses her left hand to pick up objects. Alex and Katya are both right-handed and they do not want Mariana to be left-handed because it is a right-handed world. What can you tell your friends about the roles of heredity and environment in the development of hand preference?
3. Based on what you know about the infant's visual system, how would you decorate a child's nursery so that it is consistent with the young infant's visual ability? Include information on acuity and pattern perception.
4. Your friend Shane has noticed that his 3-week-old daughter Fran seems to drink more from her bottle when it contains sugar water than when it contains formula. Shane thinks that he saw Fran lick her lips when she was given a bottle of sugar water. Shane thinks that he is crazy because he doesn't think that the senses are functioning in babies who are so young. What can you tell Shane about the sense of taste that might make him feel better?
5. Your friends have an 18-month-old who often becomes fussy when he is in his car seat for long periods of time so they will take him out of the car seat. What can you tell your friends that might make them change their minds about this unsafe practice?

ANSWERS

Multiple Choice

1. d (113)
2. a (114)
3. c (114)
4. a (115)
5. b (115)
6. d (116)
7. b (119)
8. d (120)
9. d (120)
10. c (121)
11. b (121)
12. b (121)
13. a (123)
14. d (123)
15. d (124)
16. b (124)
17. b (128)
18. c (128)
19. b (129)
20. b (130)
21. d (132)
22. c (132)
23. d (133)
24. b (134)
25. c (136)
26. d (136)
27. c (136)
28. a (137)
29. a (137)
30. b (139)
31. c (140)
32. b (140)
33. c (141)
34. a (143)
35. d (144)
36. b (145)

Essay

1. The first year of life is a time of very rapid physical growth. The average baby will grow 13 inches and will gain 15 pounds before his second birthday. If Lafon buys clothes that fit Lamar perfectly now, he probably won't be able to fit in them in a few short weeks. After telling these facts to Lafon, you might want to ask her if she will get her money's worth out of these expensive, little outfits. Fortunately, this rapid growth does taper off and Lafon might want to buy more expensive clothes when Lamar is older and is not growing so quickly. (112-113)
2. Most 6-9-month-olds use their left and right hands equally so it is unlikely that Mariana's use of her left hand now will predict her later hand preference. By 13 months, most children start to show a preference for one hand over the other. Throughout the preschool years, preference for one hand becomes stronger and more consistent so that by the time the child enters kindergarten hand preference is well established. Heredity does influence handedness. Most left-handed people have a parent or grandparent that was left-handed. Given that both Alex and Katya are right-handed, it is less likely that they have genes for left-handedness to pass along. Experience also plays a role in the development of hand preference. For example, in China where writing with the left hand is a cultural taboo, virtually no one is left-handed. However, when Chinese children are raised in other cultures where left-handedness is accepted the rate of left-handedness has become common. Given that Mariana has two right-handed parents who are likely to encourage right-handed behavior, she will probably become right-handed but it is too early to tell. (132-133)
3. The visual acuity in newborns is very poor so any visual stimuli (such as a mobile in a crib) would need to be placed close to the infant. Infants prefer patterned objects to plain objects so objects with patterns would be better than plain objects in the nursery. Infants like to look at patterns that resemble faces. In fact, some manufacturers make mobiles and other infant toys that contain drawings of faces. (138; 144)
4. Even infants who are Fran's age have a highly developed sense of taste. They can tell the difference between sweet, salty, bitter, and sour tastes. In fact, infants seem to react to those tastes in ways that are similar to adults' reactions. For example, most infants will smile and lick their lips while drinking a sweet substance. Infants also grimace after tasting sour and bitter substances. So, Shane is not going crazy--Fran probably does have a sweet tooth and is reacting positively to the sugar water. (136)
5. You can tell your friends that accidental deaths are the most common cause of death in toddlers and preschoolers in the United States. Furthermore, the most common cause of accidental death is motor vehicle accidents. Many of these motor vehicle deaths could have been prevented if the children had been restrained in an approved car seat. When children aren't restrained, they often are thrown through the windshield or onto the road, which causes fatal injuries. If your friends' son becomes fussy in his car seat on long trips, a better solution to his fussiness is to stop and take a break rather than removing him from his car seat while the car is in motion. (119)

Chapter 6
Cognition in Infants and Toddlers

Module 6.1 *Piaget's Theory*

Module 6.2 *Information Processing*

Module 6.3 *Language*

This chapter examines Piaget's first stage of cognitive development, information processing in infants and toddlers, and language development during the first 2 years.

PIAGET'S THEORY

MODULE
6.1

Piaget's Theory

- *Basic Principles of Piaget's Theory*
- *Piaget's Sensorimotor Stage*
- *Evaluating Piaget's Account of Sensorimotor Thought*
- *The Child as Theorist*

Textbook Learning Objectives

- **How do assimilation, accommodation, and equilibration explain how children's thinking changes with age?**
- **How does thinking become more advanced as infants progress through the six substages of the sensorimotor stage?**
- **What are some criticisms of Piaget's account of cognitive processes in infants and toddlers?**
- **What are young children's naive theories of physics and biology?**

TO MASTER THESE LEARNING OBJECTIVES:

1. Know the terms associated with Piaget's theory of cognitive development
2. Know the details of Piaget's theory of cognitive development

Know the Terms Associated with Piaget's Theory: Match each definition with the correct term

Accommodation	Schemes
Assimilation	Secondary circular reactions

Equilibration
Object permanence
Primary circular reactions
Sensorimotor
Tertiary circular reactions

1. Psychological structures that organize experiences.__________
2. This type of adaptation occurs when new experiences are incorporated readily into existing schemes.__________
3. This type of adaptation occurs when schemes are modified based on experience.__________
4. The process of reorganizing one's schemes to return to a state of equilibrium.__________
5. During this stage, the infant progresses from simple reflex actions to symbolic processing. __________
6. This is an action that an infant tries to repeat over and over again. This action is focused on the world outside the infant.__________
7. This is a chance, pleasurable event that infants try to reproduce. This is centered on the infant's body.__________
8. This involves repeating old schemes with new objects.__________
9. The understanding that objects exist independently of oneself and one's actions. __________

Know the Details of Piaget's Theory of Cognitive Development

1. T F According to Piaget, children do not want to make sense of their experiences.
2. T F Schemes help children understand the world.
3. T F During infancy, most schemes are based on conceptual representations.
4. T F Older children and adolescents use schemes that are based on abstract properties.
5. T F Extending an existing grasping scheme to a new object is an example of accommodation.
6. T F Changing an existing scheme so that it works for new objects or ideas is known as assimilation.
7. T F When children spend much more time accommodating than assimilating new information and experiences, they discover that their current schemes are not adequate.
8. T F When disequilibrium occurs, children replace their current, outmoded schemes with qualitatively different, more advanced schemes.
9. T F Children move to a new stage of cognitive development when their current "theories" seem to be wrong most of the time.
10. T F Each stage of cognitive development is a distinctive way of thinking about and understanding the world.
11. T F Smart children can skip one or more of Piaget's stages.
12. T F Primary circular reactions are actions or events that are oriented toward objects and activities that are beyond the infant's body.

13. T F Primary circular reactions represent an infant's first efforts to learn about objects in the environment.

14. T F Tertiary circular reactions involve active experimenting.

15. T F The end of the sensorimotor stage is marked by the infant's ability to use mental symbols.

16. T F The ability to use symbols allows children to anticipate the consequences of actions mentally.

17. T F Baillargeon's studies of object permanence using impossible and possible events indicates that infants as young as 4 1/2 months old have some understanding of object permanence.

18. T F Children base their early naive theories on their experiences.

19. T F By 3 or 4 months of age, infants understand that objects cannot move through other objects.

20. T F Toddlers who are 18 months old are just beginning to understand that one object striking another should make the second object move.

21. T F Children who are 1 year old do not understand the importance of gravity.

22. T F Toddlers do not understand the different properties of animate and inanimate objects.

23. T F Toddlers understand that animate objects drink, but inanimate objects do not.

24. T F Toddlers try to use keys to open both toy houses and toy animals.

ANSWERS

Key Terms

1. schemes (152)
2. assimilation (152)
3. accommodation (153)
4. equilibration (154)
5. sensorimotor (155)
6. secondary circular reactions (155)
7. primary circular reactions (155)
8. tertiary circular reactions (156)
9. object permanence (157)

Know the Details

1. false (152)
2. true (152)
3. false (152)
4. true (153)
5. false (153)
6. false (153)
7. true (154)
8. true (154)
9. true (154)
10. true (155)
11. false (155)
12. false (155)
13. false (155)
14. true (156)
15. true (156)
16. true (156)
17. true (157)
18. true (158)
19. true (159)
20. false (159)
21. false (160)
22. false (160)
23. false (160)
24. true (160)
25. false (160)

MODULE
6.2

Information Processing
- *Basic Features of the Information-Processing Approach*
- *Learning*
- *Memory*
- *Understanding the World*
- *Individual Differences in Ability*

INFORMATION PROCESSING

Textbook Learning Objectives

- **What are the basic characteristics of the information-processing approach?**
- **How do infants learn and remember?**
- **What do infants and toddlers understand about number and about their environments?**
- **How is intelligence measured in infants and toddlers?**

TO MASTER THESE LEARNING OBJECTIVES:

1. Know the characteristics of the information-processing components
2. Know the terms associated with information processing
3. Know the details of information processing

Know the Characteristics of the Information-Processing Components: Match each statement with the correct component

Long-term memory
Mental hardware
Mental software
Sensory memory
Working memory

1. Built-in mental and neural structures that allow the mind to operate.__________
2. This has 3 components: sensory memory, working memory, and long-term memory.__________
3. This holds information in a raw, unanalyzed form for a few seconds.__________
4. This includes ongoing cognitive processes and the information that they require.__________
5. This is a limitless, permanent storehouse of knowledge.__________
6. This resembles random-access memory (RAM) in a computer.__________
7. This is like a computer's hard drive.__________
8. This refers to mental programs that are used to perform specific tasks.__________

Know the Terms Associated with Information Processing: Match each definition with the correct term

Autobiographical memory
Infantile amnesia
Memory strategies
Script

1. When presented with a strong or unfamiliar stimulus, people start, fix their eyes on the stimulus, and show changes in heart rate and brain wave activity. __________
2. The diminished response to a stimulus as it become familiar. __________
3. A neutral stimulus elicits a response that was originally produced by another stimulus. __________
4. The relation between the consequences of a behavior and the likelihood that the behavior will reoccur. __________

5. The inability to remember events from one's early life. __________
6. Thinking of the positions of objects in space exclusively in terms of the objects' position relative to one's own body. __________
7. Thinking of the positions of objects in space as relative to the positions of other objects in space. __________

Know the Details

1. T F Mental hardware refers to the mental programs that are used to perform particular tasks.
2. T F Mental hardware has 3 components: sensory memory, working memory, and long-term memory.
3. T F Sensory memory is a limitless, permanent storehouse for information.
4. T F Ongoing cognitive processes are included in working memory.
5. T F Information rarely is forgotten from long-term memory.
6. T F An orienting response involves changes in heart rate and brain wave activity.
7. T F Responding less and less as a stimulus becomes more familiar is known as an orienting response.
8. T F Operant conditioning occurs when a previously neutral stimulus elicits a response that was originally produced by another stimulus.
9. T F Classical conditioning gives infants a sense of order in their worlds.
10. T F When a child's behavior leads to pleasant consequences, the child is more likely to repeat the behavior in the future.
11. T F Young babies can remember events for days or weeks at a time.
12. T F Even after they were given a reminder, babies did not remember that kicking would make a crib mobile move.
13. T F Most adults can recall events that occurred when they were 3 or 4 years old.
14. T F Changing language ability from infancy to adulthood is not related to infantile amnesia.
15. T F The child's changing sense of self may be related to infantile amnesia.
16. T F When shown pictures like the ones below, most 5-month-olds can distinguish two objects from three. (see figure below)
17. T F Most 18-month-olds have an egocentric frame of reference.
18. T F The Bayley Scales of Infant Development consist of mental and motor scales.
19. T F Scores from infant intelligence tests are highly related to later IQ scores.

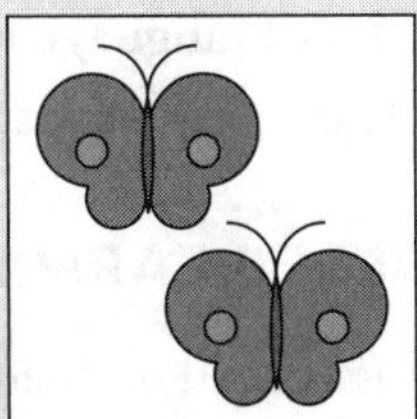
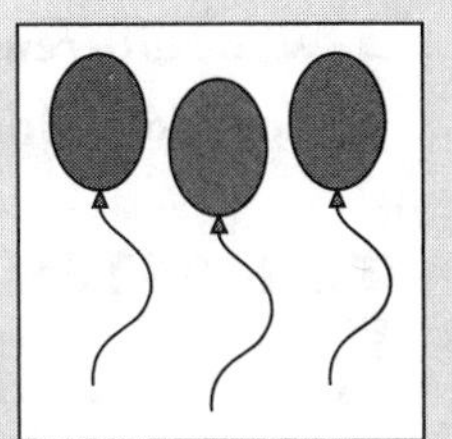

20. T F Infant tests place more emphasis on sensorimotor skills and less emphasis on tasks involving cognitive processes such as language, thinking, and problem solving.

21. T F Young infants who habituate to visual stimuli more rapidly tend to have higher IQ scores as children.

22. T F The Bayley Scale can be used to detect the impact of prenatal teratogens.

ANSWERS

Characteristics of Components

1. mental hardware (162)
2. mental hardware (163)
3. sensory memory (163)
4. working memory (163)
5. long-term memory (163)
6. working memory (163)
7. long-term memory (163)
8. mental software (164)

Key Terms

1. orienting response (164)
2. habituation (164)
3. classical conditioning (165)
4. operant conditioning (165)
5. infantile amnesia (166)
6. egocentric frame of reference (168)
7. objective frame of reference (168)

Know the Details

1. false (162)
2. true (163)
3. false (163)
4. true (163)
5. true (163)
6. true (164)
7. false (164)
8. false (165)
9. true (165)
10. true (165)
11. true (166)
12. false (166)
13. true (166)
14. false (167)
15. true (167)
16. true (168)
17. false (168)
18. true (169)
19. false (169)
20. true (169)
21. true (169)
22. true (170)

MODULE 6.3 LANGUAGE

Textbook Learning Objectives

- **When can infants hear and produce basic speech sounds?**
- **What is babbling and how do children make the transition from babbling to talking?**
- **What different styles of language learning do young children use?**
- **How do children learn new words?**

TO MASTER THESE LEARNING OBJECTIVES:

1. Know the terms associated with language development
2. Know the details of language development

Know the Terms Associated with Language Development: Match each definition with the correct term

Babbling
Cooing
Expressive
Fast mapping
Infant-directed speech
Intonation
Naming explosion
Overextension
Phoneme
Referential
Underextension

1. The sounds of a language that are its basic building blocks. __________
2. The type of speech in which adults speak slowly with exaggerated changes in pitch and loudness.__________
3. Vowel-like sounds that are produced by young babies.__________
4. Speech-like sounds that have no meaning but consist of a consonant and vowel combined.__________
5. A pattern of rising or falling pitch.__________
6. A period of time when children learn new words at a very rapid pace. __________
7. Children's ability to make connections between new words and referents so rapidly that they cannot be considering all possible meanings for the new word.__________
8. A common mistake in early word learning in which children define a word too broadly.__________
9. A common mistake in early word learning in which a word is defined too narrowly.__________
10. A language learning style in which children's vocabularies are dominated by the names of objects, persons, or actions.__________
11. A language learning style in which children's vocabularies include some names but many social phrases that are used like a single word.__________

Know the Details of Language Development

1. T F Phonemes include both consonant and vowel sounds.
2. T F Infants as young as 1 month can discriminate different speech sounds.
3. T F Young infants cannot discriminate sounds that they have never heard before.
4. T F By 11-13 months of age, children of English-speaking parents cannot discriminate speech sounds that are not found in English.
5. T F Infants who are 7 to 8 months old cannot recognize sound patterns that they hear repeatedly.
6. T F Infant-directed speech is more rapid and has fewer changes in pitch and intonation than adult-directed speech.
7. T F Cooing involves combining vowel and consonant sounds.
8. T F Intonation is not present in early babbling.
9. T F Spoken babbling occurs at approximately the same age in deaf and hearing children.

10. T F Common early words denote animals, food, and toys.

11. T F The use of symbols is not related to language development.

12. T F Gestures are symbols that children use to communicate.

13. T F At about 18 months of age, many children experience a naming explosion.

14. T F Children systematically consider all possible meanings of a word before connecting new words and referents.

15. T F Children are more likely to learn a word name when adults are not looking at an object when they name it.

16. T F When an unfamiliar word is heard, children will assume that the word refers to an object that is present that doesn't have a name.

17. T F Children assume that a name refers to a whole object and not the parts of an object.

18. T F If an object already has a name and another name is presented, children will assume that the new name denotes a subcategory of the original name.

19. T F If a child knows the name *dinosaur* and sees that one dinosaur is consistently called *Dino*, the child will conclude that *Dino* is the name of the dinosaur.

20. T F Children ignore sentence cues when learning the meanings of words.

21. T F Calling all four-legged animals *doggie* is an example of an underextension.

22. T F Overextension is more common in word production than in word comprehension.

23. T F Expressive children's vocabularies include a large percentage of words that are names of objects, people, or actions.

24. T F Children with a referential style use language as a social tool.

ANSWERS

Key Terms

1. phoneme (171)
2. infant-directed speech (173)
3. cooing (174)
4. babbling (174)
5. intonation (174)
6. naming explosion (176)
7. fast mapping (176)
8. overextension (178)
9. underextension (178)
10. referential (178)
11. expressive (178)

Know the Details

1. true (171)
2. true (171)
3. false (172)
4. true (172)
9. false (174)
10. true (175)
11. false (175)
12. true (175)
17. true (177)
18. true (177)
19. true (177)
20. false (178)

5. false (172)
6. false (173)
7. false (174)
8. true (174)
13. true (176)
14. false (176)
15. false (176)
16. true (177)
21. false (178)
22. true (178)
23. false (178)
24. false (178)

SUMMARY

MODULE 6.1: PIAGET'S THEORY

Basic Principles of Piaget's Theory. In Piaget's view, children construct their own understanding of the world by creating __________; mental categories of related events, objects, and knowledge. Infants' schemes are based on __________ but older children's and adolescents' schemes are based on functional, __________, and abstract properties. Schemes change constantly. In __________, experiences are readily incorporated into existing schemes. In __________, experiences cause schemes to be modified. When accommodation becomes much more frequent than assimilation, this is a sign that children's schemes are __________, so children reorganize them. This reorganization produces four different phases of mental development from infancy through adulthood. All individuals go through all four phases, but not necessarily at the same __________.

schemes
actions
conceptual
assimilation
accommodation
inadequate
rate

Piaget's Sensorimotor Stage. The first two years of life constitute Piaget's sensorimotor phase, which is divided into six stages. As infants progress through the stages, schemes become more __________. By 8-12 months, one scheme is used in the service of another; by 12-18 months, infants experiment with schemes; and, by 18-24 months, infants engage in __________.

sophisticated
symbolic processing

Evaluating Piaget's Account of Sensorimotor Thought. Piaget's theory has been faulted because children's performance on tasks, such as __________, is sometimes better explained by ideas that are not part of his theory.

object permanence

The Child As Theorist. In contrast to Piaget's idea that children create a comprehensive theory that __________ all their knowledge, the modern view is that children are __________, generating naive theories in particular domains, including physics, psychology, and biology.

integrates
specialists

MODULE 6.2: INFORMATION PROCESSING

Basic Features of the Information-Processing Approach. According to the information processing approach, cognitive development involves changes in mental hardware and mental software. Mental hardware refers to mental processes that are built-in and allow the mind to function, including sensory, working, and __________ memories. Mental software refers to mental programs that allow people to perform __________ tasks.

long-term
specific

Learning. Infants habituate, that is, they respond __________ as stimuli become more familiar. They also are capable of classical conditioning, particularly when the

less

pleasant
consequences

stimuli are associated with feeding or other __________ events; operant conditioning, in which the __________ of behavior determine whether the behavior is likely to repeated in the future; and imitation, in which they learn from watching others.

remember
language

Memory. Studies of kicking show that infants can __________, forget, and be reminded of events that occurred in the past. Infantile amnesia, children's and adults' inability to remember events from early in life, may reflect the acquisition of __________ or a sense of self.

egocentric
objective

Understanding the World. Infants can distinguish quantities, probably by means of basic perceptual processes. Before 12 months of age, infants know the positions of objects in relation to their own bodies, which is known as __________ frame of reference. Beyond 12 months, they are more likely to know positions of objects relative to other objects, which is known as __________ frame of reference.

not highly
Habituation

Individual Differences in Ability. Infant tests like the Bayley Scales include mental and motor scales. Typically, scores on these tests are __________ correlated with adult IQ but they are useful for determining if development is progressing normally. __________ predicts later IQ more accurately.

MODULE 6.3: LANGUAGE

Phonemes
not used
slower

Perceiving Speech. __________ are the basic units of sound that make up words. Infants can hear phonemes soon after birth. They can even hear phonemes that are __________ in their native language, but this ability is lost by the first birthday. Before they speak, infants can recognize words, apparently by noticing stress and syllables that go together. Infants prefer infant-directed speech — adults' speech to infants that is __________ and that has greater variation in pitch and loudness — because it provides them additional language clues.

cooing
longer
signs

First Steps to Speaking. Newborns are limited to crying, but at about 3 months of age, babies produce vowel-like sounds known as __________. Babbling soon follows, consisting of a single syllable; over several months, infants' babbling includes __________ syllables and intonation. Deaf children babble later than children with normal hearing but they make partial __________ that are thought to be analogous to babbling.

symbols
gestures

First Words. Children's first words represent a cognitive accomplishment that is not specific to language. Instead, the onset of language is due to a child's ability to interpret and use __________. Consistent with this view, there are parallel developments in the use of __________ and words.

all plausible
narrower
overextension

Fast Mapping Meanings to Words. Most children learn the meanings of words too rapidly for them to consider __________ meanings systematically. Instead, children use a number of fast-mapping rules to determine probable meanings of new words. Joint attention, constraints, and sentence cues all help children learn words. The rules do not always lead to the correct meaning. An underextension denotes a child's meaning that is __________ than an adult's meaning; an __________ denotes a child's meaning that is broader.

Styles of Learning Language. Some youngsters use a referential style in learning words that emphasizes words as names and that views language as an __________ tool. Other children use an expressive style that emphasizes __________ and that views language as a social tool.

intellectual
social phrases

CHAPTER 6 COGNITION IN INFANTS AND TODDLERS

TEST YOURSELF

1. According to Piaget, which of the following would be a scheme?
  a. A functional category like "tools my mom uses in the garden"
  b. A conceptual category like "butterflies"
  c. Sucking on objects
  d. All of the above

2. Which of the following is the correct order of Piaget's stages?
  a. Sensorimotor, concrete operational, preoperational, and formal operational
  b. Sensorimotor, preoperational, concrete operational, and formal operational
  c. Sensorimotor, preoperational, formal operational, and concrete operational
  d. The order varies from individual to individual

3. The type of adaptation that involves changing one's existing schemes to fit the new experience is called
  a. accommodation.
  b. assimilation.
  c. equilibration.
  d. disequilibrium.

4. The type of adaptation that involves readily incorporating new information into existing schemes is called
  a. accommodation.
  b. assimilation.
  c. equilibration.
  d. disequilibrium.

5. The process of using assimilation and accommodation to reach a new state of equilibrium is called
  a. accommodation.
  b. assimilation.
  c. equilibration.
  d. disequilibrium.

6. In substage 1 of the sensorimotor period, the infant's behavior
  a. is largely reflexive.
  b. is purposeful.
  c. involves primary and tertiary circular reactions.
  d. includes mental representations.

7. The critical difference between primary circular reactions and secondary circular reactions is that
   a. secondary circular reactions focus on the infant's own body and primary circular reactions focus on interesting events in the outside world.
   b. primary circular reactions are deliberate whereas secondary circular reactions are not.
   c. primary circular reactions are attempts to produce something new whereas secondary circular reactions are attempts to reproduce a previous action.
   d. primary circular reactions are focused on the infant's body and secondary circular reactions are focused on interesting events that occur outside of the infant's body.

8. Which of the following actions is a primary circular reaction?
   a. Repeatedly throwing one's spoon from a high chair
   b. Repeatedly shaking a rattle
   c. Repeatedly kicking a crib to shake a mobile
   d. Repeatedly sucking one's thumb

9. Which of the following is *true* of tertiary circular reactions?
   a. They are unintentional
   b. They are systematically varied as they are repeated
   c. They are centered on the infant's body
   d. They are concerned with exactly reproducing previous events

10. The infant is capable of mental representation in which of the substages of the sensorimotor period?
   a. The third substage
   b. The fourth substage
   c. The fifth substage
   d. The sixth substage

11. Which of the following abilities marks the end of the sensorimotor period?
   a. The ability to use mental symbols
   b. Walking
   c. Talking
   d. The decline of egocentrism

12. By the first birthday, infants' naive theory of physics leads them to believe that
   a. gravity is not important so floating objects are not unusual.
   b. one object striking a second object does not affect the second object.
   c. objects cannot move through other objects.
   d. objects move along disconnected, discontinuous paths.

13. According to the information-processing approach, the mental hardware consists of
   a. one's cognitive skills.
   b. the cognitive tasks that one completes.
   c. built-in mental and neural structures.
   d. mental programs that are used to perform specific tasks.

14. Sensory memory
   a. holds raw, unanalyzed information.
   b. is limitless and permanent.
   c. passes information to long-term memory.
   d. holds information for many days.

15. Working memory
   a. holds visual images for a few seconds.
   b. is a limitless, permanent storehouse of knowledge.
   c. is like a computer's hard drive.
   d. is the site of ongoing cognitive activity.

16. Long-term memory
   a. is a permanent storehouse of information.
   b. is like a computer's random-access memory (RAM).
   c. holds raw, unanalyzed information.
   d. is the site of ongoing cognitive activity.

17. Carol begged her father for some candy when they were in the grocery store. Eventually, Carol's father gave in and bought Carol some candy. According to theories of operant conditioning, what is likely to happen the next time Carol and her father go to the grocery store?
   a. Carol will not beg for candy because her father punished her begging the last time that they were in the store.
   b. Carol will not beg for candy because her father reinforced her begging the last time that they were in the store.
   c. Carol will beg for candy because her father reinforced her begging the last time they were in the store.
   d. Carol will beg for candy because her father punished her begging the last time they were in the store.

18. Carolyn Rovee-Collier's work on infant memory in which she taught infants to kick to make a crib mobile move indicated that
   a. infants could not remember an event for more than a day or two.
   b. after several weeks infants forgot how to move the mobile and they could not be reminded.
   c. after several weeks infants had forgotten how to move the mobile, but a single reminder helped them to remember.
   d. infants never forgot how to move the mobile.

19. Infantile amnesia
   a. means that adults can remember many events that occurred in their lives before the age of 3 years.
   b. means that infants are not able to form memories.
   c. may be related to the young child's well-developed sense of self.
   d. may be related to an individual's changing language ability.

20. Five-month-old infants
   a. cannot distinguish one object from two objects.
   b. use the one-to-one principle.
   c. can distinguish two objects from three objects.
   d. do not seem to be sensitive to quantity as a characteristic of stimuli.

21. In experiments designed to investigate frames of reference, infants learn that a buzzer will sound and a face will appear in a window to their left. After infants have learned this, they are turned 180 degrees so that they are facing the opposite direction and the window with the face is to their right. Now, when the buzzer sounds, infants
   a. with an egocentric frame of reference will look to their left.
   b. with an objective frame of reference will look to their left.
   c. who are 6 months old will usually look to their right.
   d. with an objective frame of reference will look straight ahead.

22. Which of the following statements *best* describes the relation between infant intelligence tests, such as the Bayley Scales, and later IQ?
   a. The infant tests predict later IQ very well.
   b. The infant tests do not predict later IQ.
   c. The predictive power of infant tests improves if the test is administered after a child is 18 to 24 months old.
   d. The infant tests emphasize cognitive processes and later tests emphasize sensorimotor skills.

23. Infant tests, such as the Bayley Scales, have been useful in predicting
   a. developmental progress early in life.
   b. academic success.
   c. superior perceptual skills.
   d. superior athletic ability.

24. Tests of infant intelligence do not generally predict later behavior because
   a. individual differences in ability are too large in infants.
   b. infant tests are not reliable.
   c. infant tests tap different abilities than do later tests.
   d. infant tests have not been standardized like later tests have been.

25. The basic building blocks of language that are used to form words are called
   a. morphemes.
   b. grammars.
   c. lexicals.
   d. phonemes.

26. Infants who are younger than 6 months of age
   a. do not need to experience speech sounds in their environments to be able to discriminate them.
   b. must experience speech sounds in their environments to be able to discriminate them.
   c. only can discriminate the sounds found in their native language.
   d. cannot discriminate any speech sounds which explains why they can't talk.

27. When 7- to 8-month-olds hear a word repeatedly in different sentences, later they
   a. pay less attention to that word than to words they haven't heard previously.
   b. pay more attention to that word than to words they haven't heard previously.
   c. pay the same amount of attention to the previously heard word and new words.
   d. cannot recognize sound patterns that they hear repeatedly.

28. Young infants seem to identify words by
  a. paying attention to unusual combinations of syllables.
  b. paying more attention to stressed syllables rather than unstressed syllables.
  c. paying more attention to words they have never heard before.
  d. paying attention to the meaning of words.

29. Which of the following is *true* of infant-directed speech?
  a. Infants prefer adult-directed speech to infant-directed speech.
  b. Only mothers use infant-directed speech.
  c. Infant-directed speech seems to attract the infant's attention.
  d. The use of infant-directed speech makes it more difficult for infants to identify speech sounds.

30. The production of syllables that contain vowels and consonants is called
  a. cooing.
  b. babbling.
  c. fast mapping.
  d. intonation.

31. Which of the following statements is *true* of the development of babbling?
  a. Infants produce complex speech sounds before simpler sounds.
  b. Intonation is added to later babbling.
  c. Early babbling contains combinations of many different sounds.
  d. Babbling is the production of vowel-like sounds.

32. When young children are learning new words, they
  a. require many presentations of the new word to learn the correct referent.
  b. systematically consider all possible hypotheses about the connection between the word and the correct referent.
  c. are more likely to learn an object's name when adults look at the object while saying its name.
  d. do not use sentence cues.

33. According to the rules that young children use to learn the meanings of new words, when Ravisha points to a picture of a boy in a blue shirt and says "boy," her 13-month-old son will assume that the word "boy" refers to
  a. the boy.
  b. the boy's shirt.
  c. the color blue.
  d. the book that Ravisha is reading.

34. When Utsav is riding in the car with his mother, he will point at buses, vans, bikes, and trucks and say "car." This is an example of
  a. an overextension.
  b. an underextension.
  c. fast mapping.
  d. overregularization.

35. Defining a word too narrowly is known as
  a. an overextension.
  b. an underextension.
  c. fast mapping.
  d. overregularization.

36. Children with expressive language-learning styles
   a. have vocabularies that primarily consist of the names of objects, people, and actions.
   b. have vocabularies that consist of many social phrases.
   c. use language as an intellectual tool.
   d. have vocabularies that contain many question words such as "what."

ESSAY QUESTIONS

1. Your friend Andre is the father of a 6-month-old daughter, Brooke, who has just begun to eat sitting in a high chair. Meal time has become a very frustrating time for Andre because Brooke repeatedly pushes her tippy cup off the high chair and onto the floor. The first time that the cup fell on the floor it appeared to Andre that it was an accident but now he is convinced that his daughter is deliberately pushing her cup onto the floor to annoy him. Based on what you know about circular reactions, what can you tell Andre that might make him feel better?
2. Your friends Elmo and Dawn have a 3-year-old daughter, Courtney. Dawn stays at home with Courtney during the day while Elmo is at work. Often in the evening, Courtney will say "Mom, Mom, Mom" repeatedly before Dawn responds to her. Elmo cannot understand why Dawn keeps ignoring Courtney. When Courtney says "Dad" he always responds right away. How would you explain what's happening, using what you know about the selective nature of attention, orienting responses, and habituation?
3. Your friends have a 3-month-old son, Zack. Two weeks ago, when Zack was at your house he had been interested in kicking at a ball that makes noise when it rolls. Yesterday when Zack was at your house, he kicked at the ball again as if he remembered moving the ball and hearing its noise. When you pointed out this "memory" to Zack's parents, they said that "everyone knows that babies don't have any memories." What can you tell your friends about memory in infants that might change their minds?
4. Your friends Bernie and Miriam have a 6-month-old daughter, Rachel. Rachel was tested using the Bayley Scales of Infant Development and she received a very high score. Bernie and Miriam are convinced that this means that Rachel will be gifted when she is older. What can you tell your friends about the relation between infant intelligence test scores and later IQ that might contradict their beliefs?
5. Your sister and brother-in-law have a newborn baby and they are wondering when she will begin talking. They hope that it will occur soon, so they have begun saying *mama* and *dada* to their daughter. What can you tell them about the course of language development during the first year of life?

ANSWERS

Multiple Choice

1. d (152)
2. b (154)
3. a (153)
4. b (153)
5. c (154)
6. a (155)
7. d (155)
8. d (156)
9. b (156)
10. d (156)
11. a (156)
12. c (159)
13. c (162)
14. a (163)
15. d (163)
16. a (163)
17. c (165)
18. c (166)
19. d (166)
20. c (167)
21. a (168)
22. c (169)
23. a (169)
24. c (169)
25. d (171)
26. a (172)
27. b (172)
28. b (173)
29. c (173)
30. b (174)
31. b (174)
32. c (176)
33. a (177)
34. a (178)
35. b (178)
36. b (178)

Essay

1. You should tell Andre that Brooke is in the sensorimotor period of cognitive development and, more specifically, she is at an age when secondary circular reactions are typical. These secondary circular reactions are interesting events that infants try to repeat. The first case of Brooke's cup falling on the floor was an accident that she found pleasurable. She may have liked the way the cup sounded as it hit the floor or she may have liked the stream of milk that flowed from the cup on the floor. In any case, her repeated throwing of her cup is only meant to recreate the original interesting event. Her behavior is NOT meant to annoy Andre. Knowing that this behavior is a normal part of cognitive development may help Andre's anger and frustration as he mops the floor. (155-156)

2. When people are first presented with a stimulus (such as someone calling "Mom") they show an orienting response. They may startle, look toward the stimulus (in this case, Courtney), and respond. When a stimulus is repeated over and over people will eventually habituate. In other words, they will pay less attention to the stimulus with repeated exposure. In the case of Dawn and Courtney, Dawn hears Courtney say "Mom" hundreds of times during the day before Elmo gets home from work. Dawn has habituated to the stimulus of Courtney saying "Mom" so by evening she often does not pay attention to this stimulus. Elmo, however, has not been around Courtney as much and has not habituated to her saying "Dad." Dawn isn't being a bad mother, but has habituated to hearing "Mom" all day long. (164)

3. Tell your friends that young babies remember events for days or weeks at a time. Carolyn Rovee-Collier connected 2- or 3-month-olds' legs to a crib mobile using a ribbon. The infants quickly learned to kick their legs to make the mobile move. Even after a few weeks had passed, infants remembered that kicking moves the mobile. Based on the results of this research, it is

quite likely that Zack does remember kicking at the ball at your house and your friends are wrong about his memory ability. (166)

4. You can tell Bernie and Miriam that, in general, scores from infant intelligence tests such as the Bayley Scales are not related to later IQ scores. Children must be at least 18 to 24 months old before the scores from infant tests can predict later IQ scores. The reason for this is that infant tests place more emphasis on sensorimotor skills and later tests emphasize cognitive processes such as language, thinking, and problem solving. A high score on the Bayley should reassure Bernie and Miriam that Rachel is developing normally but it should not lead them to believe that Rachel will be gifted later in life. (168-170)

5. Your sister and brother-in-law will have a few months to wait until their daughter is talking because most babies say their first words around their first birthdays. Even though it will be months before their daughter says her first words, she will begin to make language-like sounds within the next few months. Around 2 or 3 months of age, babies start producing vowel-like sounds that are called cooing. Around 5 or 6 months of age, babies start combining vowels with consonants to produce babbling. Early babbling consists of single syllables but later babbling consists of combinations of syllables. Around 7 months of age, intonation (rising and falling pitch) is added to babbling. This intonation will mimic the intonation found in the language that the child hears. Around the first birthday, advanced babbling will become early words. (174-175)

Chapter 7 Social Behavior and Personality in Infants and Toddlers

Module 7.1 *Emotions*

Module 7.2 *Relationships with Others*

Module 7.3 *Self-Concept*

Module 7.4 *Temperament*

This chapter covers the emergence of emotions, the relationships with parents and peers, the understanding of self, and the different behavioral styles that are seen in children.

EMOTIONS

MODULE 7.1

Emotions

- *Basic Emotions*
- *Complex Emotions*
- *Recognizing and Using Others' Emotions*
- *Regulating Emotions*

Textbook Learning Objectives

- **When do infants begin to express basic emotions?**
- **What are complex emotions and when do they develop?**
- **When do infants begin to understand other people's emotions? How do they use this information to guide their own behavior?**
- **When do infants and toddlers begin to regulate their own emotions?**

TO MASTER THESE LEARNING OBJECTIVES:

1. Know the terms associated with emerging emotions
2. Know the details of emerging emotions

Know the Terms Associated with Emerging Emotions: Match each definition with the correct term

Social referencing
Social smiles
Stranger wariness

1. These first appear around 2 months of age when infants see another human face.__________
2. This occurs around 6 months of age when infants become wary of unfamiliar adults.__________
3. This occurs when infants look at their parents as if searching for cues to interpret unfamiliar or ambiguous situations.__________

Know the Details of Emerging Emotions

1. T F Basic emotions consist of a subjective feeling, a physiological change, and an overt behavior.
2. T F Basic emotions are not experienced the same way in all cultures but complex emotions are experienced similarly around the world.
3. T F Anger is a complex emotion.
4. T F Facial expressions are not reliable predictors of an infant's emotional state.
5. T F Babies who are a few weeks old use social smiles.
6. T F Around the first birthday, infants will laugh in response to both physical and psychological stimulation.
7. T F Distinct displays of anger emerge between 4 and 6 months of age.
8. T F The first distinct signs of fear emerge around 6 months when babies show stranger wariness.
9. T F Infants are more fearful of strangers in a familiar environment.
10. T F Wariness of strangers declines as infants learn to interpret facial expressions.
11. T F Complex emotions depend on the child having some understanding of the self.
12. T F Complex emotions emerge between 18 and 24 months of age.
13. T F Six-month-olds cannot discriminate different facial expressions.
14. T F By 6 months of age, infants often match their own emotions to other people's emotions.
15. T F Social referencing shows that infants rely on their parents' emotions to regulate their own behavior.
16. T F The regulation of emotions doesn't begin until the preschool years.

ANSWERS

Key Terms

1. social smiles (185)
2. stranger wariness (186)
3. social referencing (187)

Know the Details

1. true (184)
2. false (184)
7. true (186)
8. true (186)
13. false (187)
14. true (187)

3. false (184)
4. false (185)
5. false (185)
6. true (186)
9. false (186)
10. true (186)
11. true (187)
12. true (187)
15. true (187)
16. false (188)

MODULE
7.2

Relationships with Others

- *The Growth of Attachment*
- *Quality of Attachment*
- *Onset of Peer Interactions*

RELATIONSHIPS WITH OTHERS

Textbook Learning Objectives

- **How does an attachment relationship develop between an infant and primary caregiver?**
- **What different types of attachment relationships are there? What are the consequences of different types of relationships? How does child care affect attachment relationships?**
- **How do infants and toddlers interact with peers?**

TO MASTER THESE LEARNING OBJECTIVES:

1. Know the characteristics of each of the types of attachment and the attachment representations of adults
2. Know the different types of play
3. Know the details of attachment and peer interaction

Know the Characteristics of the Types of Attachment and Attachment Representations: Match each statement with the correct type of attachment or attachment representation

Autonomous
Avoidant
Dismissive
Disorganized (disoriented)
Preoccupied
Resistant
Secure

1. This baby seems confused when the mother leaves and when she returns.__________
2. This baby is upset when the mother leaves and remains upset or angry when she returns, and is difficult to console.__________.
3. This baby may or may not cry when the mother leaves, but when she returns, the baby wants to be with her.__________
4. This baby is not upset when the mother leaves and when she returns the baby may ignore her or turn away.__________
5. The largest group of American babies have this type of attachment.__________
6. The smallest group of American babies have this type of attachment.__________
7. These adults describe childhood experiences in very general terms and often idealize their parents. __________

8. These adults describe childhood experiences objectively and mention both positive and negative aspects of their parents. __________
9. These adults describe childhood experiences emotionally and often express anger or confusion regarding relationships with their parents. __________
10. Adults with this attachment representation are more likely to provide sensitive caregiving to their own children. __________

Know the Different Types of Play

Cooperative play
Parallel play
Nonsocial play
Simple social play

1. The type of play that involves playing alone or watching others play. __________
2. The type of play in which youngsters play alone but maintain interest in what other children are doing.__________
3. The type of play in which youngsters engage in similar activities, talk or smile at one another, and offer each other toys.__________
4. The type of play in which children organize their play around a distinct theme and take on special roles based on the theme. __________

Know the Details of Attachment and Peer Interaction

1. T F Attachment is an enduring social-emotional relationship.
2. T F According to John Bowlby, children are more likely to survive if they form an attachment to an adult.
3. T F The first step in the development of attachment is for the infant to learn the difference between people and other objects.
4. T F Mothers and infants try to avoid being "on" at the same time.
5. T F Around 7 months of age, the attachment figure becomes a stable social-emotional base.
6. T F Most American infants become attached to their mothers but not their fathers.
7. T F Fathers are more likely than mothers to read to and play games like peek-a-boo with their babies.
8. T F When infants are distressed they prefer to be comforted by their fathers.
9. T F As you can see in the graph below, secure attachments are the most common type of attachment throughout the world.

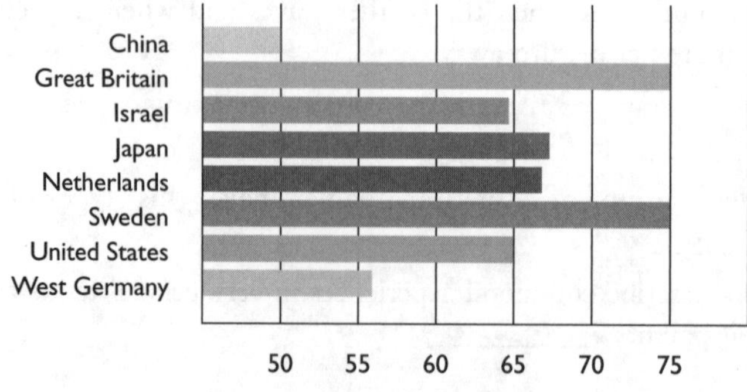

10. T F Children with secure attachment relationships have higher-quality friendships and fewer conflicts with peers than children with insecure attachment relationships.

11. T F Children with insecure attachment relationships are more likely to have behavior problems than children with secure attachment relationships.

12. T F A secure attachment is most likely when parents respond to infants predictably and appropriately.

13. T F An internal working model is a set of expectations about parents' availability and responsivity.

14. T F Adults with a dismissive attachment representation are the most likely to provide the sensitive caregiving that promotes secure attachment relationships in their own children.

15. T F Babies with difficult temperaments are more likely to form secure attachments.

16. T F Mothers cannot be taught how to interact more sensitively, affectionately, and responsively to their babies.

17. T F Children in poor quality child care with less sensitive and less responsive mothers are more likely to have insecure attachments.

18. T F Sensitive, responsive caregiving is the key to high-quality child care.

19. T F The first signs of peer interaction appear around 6 months of age.

20. T F The first signs of peer interaction include pointing to or smiling at another infant.

21. T F During parallel play children engage in similar activities, talk or smile at one another, and offer each other toys.

22. T F Cooperative play usually appears around the first birthday.

ANSWERS

Types of Attachment and Attachment Representations

1. disorganized (disoriented) (192)
2. resistant (192)
3. secure (192)
4. avoidant (192)
5. secure (192)
6. disorganized (disoriented) (192)
7. dismissive (194)
8. autonomous (194)
9. preoccupied (194)
10. autonomous (194)

Types of Play

1. nonsocial play (196)
2. parallel play (196)
3. simple social play (197)
4. cooperative play (197)

Know the Details

1. true (189)
2. true (190)
3. true (190)
9. true (192)
10. true (193)
11. true (193)
17. true (195)
18. true (195)
19. true (196)

4. false (190)
5. true (190)
6. false (190)
7. false (191)
8. false (191)
12. true (193)
13. true (193)
14. false (194)
15. false (194)
16. false (194)
20. true (196)
21. false (196)
22. false (197)

MODULE
7.3

Self Concept
- *Origins of Self-Recognition*
- *Moving Beyond Self-Recognition*

SELF CONCEPT

Textbook Learning Objectives

- **When do infants first recognize themselves?**
- **Following self-recognition, how do infants acquire a self-concept?**

TO MASTER THESE LEARNING OBJECTIVES:

1. Know the details of self-recognition and self-concept

Know the Details of Self-Recognition and Self-Concept

1. T F The first step in the development of self-concept is the child's awareness that he or she exists independently of others.
2. T F A typical 1-year-old who has a red mark on her nose will touch her own nose when she sees the red mark in the mirror.
3. T F Self-awareness emerges between 18 and 24 months.
4. T F When 3-year-olds are shown a videotape of themselves with a sticker on their heads, almost all of them reached up and tried to remove the sticker.
5. T F Three-year-olds have a very strong sense of self that is linked across time.
6. T F When children with Down syndrome achieve a mental age of approximately 18 months, they typically recognize themselves in the mirror.
7. T F Self-aware toddlers were more likely to say, "Mine!" while playing with toys than were children who were not yet self-aware.

ANSWERS

Know the Details

1. true (198)
2. false (199)
3. true (199)
4. false (199)
5. false (199)
6. true (199)
7. true (200)

TEMPERAMENT

MODULE
7.4

Temperment
- *What is Temperment?*
- *Hereditary and Environmental Contributions to Temperment*
- *Stability of Temperment*
- *Temperment and Other Aspects of Development*

Textbook Learning Objectives

- **What are different features of temperament?**
- **How do heredity and environment influence temperament?**
- **How stable is a child's temperament across childhood?**
- **What are the consequences of different temperaments?**

TO MASTER THESE LEARNING OBJECTIVES:

1. Know the terms associated with temperament
2. Know the details of temperament

Know the Terms Associated with Temperament: Match each definition with the correct term

Activity	Sociability
Emotionality	Temperament

1. Consistent mood and style of behavior.__________
2. The strength of the infant's emotional response to a situation, the ease with which the response is triggered, and the ease with which the infant can be returned to a nonemotional state.__________
3. The tempo and vigor of a child's movements. __________
4. Preference for being with other people.__________

Know the Details of Temperament

1. T F In the New York Longitudinal Study, the largest group of babies was classified as "slow-to-warm-up."
2. T F An infant who is always busy, who likes to explore the environment, and who enjoys vigorous play would be high on the emotionality dimension of temperament.
3. T F Rhythmicity is one of the nine dimensions of temperament suggested by Thomas and Chess.
4. T F The results of twin studies provide evidence that heredity does not influence temperament.
5. T F Infants of mothers who interact easily and confidently with them are more likely to develop intense, difficult temperaments.
6. T F Japanese and Chinese babies are more likely to become upset in stressful situations than European American babies.
7. T F Temperament during infancy is not related to temperament later in life.
8. T F Prenatal activity level is not related to activity level during infancy.
9. T F Persistent, active, and distractible children are all as likely to succeed in school.
10. T F Shy children often have difficulties interacting with peers and often do not cope effectively with problems.

11. T F Anxious, fearful children are less likely to comply with a parent's rules and requests.

12. T F A resistant temperament in a child leads to behavior problems even when the mother exerts control over the child.

13. T F The influence of temperament often depends on the environment in which children develop.

ANSWERS

Key Terms

1. temperament (201)
2. emotionality (202)
3. activity (202)
4. sociability (202)

Know the Details

1. false (201)
2. false (202)
3. true (202)
4. false (203)
5. false (203)
6. false (203)
7. false (204)
8. false (204)
9. false (205)
10. true (205)
11. false (205)
12. true (205)
13. true (206)

SUMMARY

MODULE 7.1: EMERGING EMOTIONS

facial expressions / social smile / stranger wariness

Basic Emotions. Scientists often use infants' __________ to judge when different emotional states emerge in development. The earliest indicator of happiness is the __________, which emerges at about two months. Laughter appears at 4 months. Anger and fear are both evident by about 6 months of age. Fear first appears in infancy as __________; fears of specific objects develop later in childhood.

embarrassment

Complex Emotions. Complex emotions have an evaluative component and include guilt, __________, and pride. They appear between 18 and 24 months and require more sophisticated cognitive skills than basic emotions like happiness and fear.

unfamiliar

Recognizing and Using Others' Emotions. By 6 months, infants have begun to recognize the emotions associated with different facial expressions. They use this information to help them to evaluate __________ situations.

looking away

Regulating Emotions. Infants use simple strategies (e.g., __________) to regulate emotions such as fear.

MODULE 7.2 RELATIONSHIPS WITH OTHERS

The Growth of Attachment. Attachment is an enduring __________ relationship between infant and parent. Many of the behaviors that contribute to the formation of attachment are biologically programmed. Attachment develops gradually over the first year of life; by about __________ months, infants have identified an attachment figure, typically the mother. In the ensuing months, infants often become attached to other family members, including fathers, whose usual role is __________.

social-emotional
6 or 7
playmate

Quality of Attachment. Research with the Strange Situation, in which infant and mother are separated briefly, reveals four primary forms of attachment. Most common is a __________ attachment, in which infants have complete trust in the mother. Less common are three types of attachment relationships that lack this trust. In __________ relationships, infants deal with the lack of trust by ignoring the mother; in __________ relationships, infants remain angry and difficult to console when mother returns; in __________ relationship, infants seem to not understand the mother's absence.

secure
avoidant
resistant
disorganized (disoriented)

Children who have had secure attachment relationships during infancy often interact with their peers more readily and more skillfully. Secure attachment is most likely to occur when mothers __________ sensitively and consistently to their infant's needs. Adults who have __________ representations of attachment to their own parents are most likely to use the __________ caregiving that promotes secure attachments with their own infants.

respond
autonomous
sensitive

Many U.S. children are cared for at home by a father or other relative, in a day care provider's home, or in a day-care center. Attachment relationships in infants and toddlers are not harmed by such arrangements as long as the care is __________ and parents remain __________ to their children.

high quality, responsive

Onset of Peer Interactions. Children's first real social interactions, at about 12 to 15 months, take the form of __________ play, in which infants play alone while watching each other. A few months later, __________ play emerges, in which infants engage in similar activities and interact with one another. At about 2 years of age, __________ play organized around a theme becomes common.

parallel
simple social
cooperative

MODULE 7.3: SELF-CONCEPT

Origins of Self-Recognition. Beginning at about 15 months, infants begin to recognize themselves in the mirror, which is one of the first signs of __________. They also begin to prefer to look at pictures of themselves, begin to refer to themselves by name (or use personal pronouns), and sometimes know their __________ and gender. Evidently, by two years, most children have the rudiments of self awareness, but this early understanding is __________.

self-recognition
age
fragile

Moving Beyond Self-Recognition. After toddlers become self aware, they begin to acquire a self-concept. __________ are one of the first elements in young children's self-concepts.

Possessions

MODULE 7.4: TEMPERAMENT

patterns of behavior / difficult / sociability

What is Temperament? Temperament refers to stable __________ that are evident soon after birth. The New York Longitudinal Study suggests three temperamental patterns: easy, __________, and slow-to-warm-up; other research suggests that the dimensions of temperament are emotionality, activity, and __________. The major theories of temperament include many of the same elements, organized differently.

alike / abrupt

Hereditary and Environmental Contributions to Temperament. The major theories agree that both heredity and environment contribute to temperament. For many dimensions of temperament, identical twins are more __________ than fraternal twins. Positive emotionality reflects environmental influences, and difficult temperament is linked to __________ parenting.

moderately / does

Stability of Temperament. Temperament is somewhat stable during infancy and the toddler years and __________ stable into childhood and adolescence. The correlations are not very strong, which means that, for many children, temperament __________ change as they develop.

behavioral problems / Persistent / compliant / environment

Temperament and Other Aspects of Development. Many investigators have shown that temperament is related to other aspects of development. Difficult babies are more likely to have __________ by the time they are old enough to attend school. __________ children are more successful in school, shy children sometimes have problems with peers, anxious children are more __________ with parents, and inhibited children are less likely to help a stranger in distress. However, the impact of temperament always depends on the __________ in which children develop.

CHAPTER 7 SOCIAL BEHAVIOR AND PERSONALITY IN INFANTS AND TODDLERS

TEST YOURSELF

1. Basic emotions
   a. do not involve a physiological change.
   b. are not expressed in an overt behavior.
   c. vary from culture to culture.
   d. involve a subjective feeling.

2. Research on the link between facial expressions and emotions has shown that
   a. changes in facial expressions are not linked to physiological changes that are associated with emotions.
   b. infants and adults worldwide express basic emotions with similar facial expressions.
   c. in the first few weeks of life, infants produce social smiles.
   d. infants' facial expressions do not change in a predictable, meaningful fashion until around the first birthday.

3. Complex emotions
   a. emerge before basic emotions.
   b. are universal.
   c. involve an understanding of the self.
   d. include feelings of happiness, anger, and disgust.

4. Which of the following emerges first?
   a. Guilt
   b. Embarrassment
   c. Pride
   d. Fear

5. Which of the following emerges first?
   a. Laughter in response to physical stimulation
   b. Laughter in response to psychological stimulation
   c. Social smiles
   d. Smiles that are related to internal physiological states

6. Stranger wariness
   a. emerges a few weeks after birth.
   b. provides a natural restraint against the tendency for mobile infants to wander away from familiar caregivers.
   c. is greater when infants are in a familiar environment.
   d. is not related to the stranger's behavior.

7. The ability to recognize others' emotions
   a. can be used in social referencing.
   b. emerges after the first birthday.
   c. is not related to the ability to discriminate different facial expressions.
   d. decreases with age.

8. The regulation of emotions
   a. doesn't begin until children are about 2 years old.
   b. is not related to the quality of interactions and relationships with one's peers.
   c. involves the use of cognitive strategies (e.g., reminding oneself to ignore something) in school-age children and adolescents.
   d. involves the use of physical strategies (e.g., moving closer to a parent) in school-age children and adolescents.

9. The ethological view of attachment is
   a. that it is learned through reinforcement and punishment.
   b. it is the result of the resolution of conflicts that are centered on various parts of the body.
   c. it increases the infant's likelihood of survival.
   d. that it was important to human evolution but has no value in modern society.

10. Which is the first step in the development of attachment?
   a. Discriminating familiar and unfamiliar people
   b. Singling out the attachment figure
   c. Synchronizing behavior with the caregiver's behavior
   d. Learning the difference between people and objects

11. Fathers
  a. interact with their babies in the same ways that mothers do.
  b. are more likely to engage in physical play with their babies than mothers.
  c. are more likely than mothers to be a source of comfort when babies are distressed.
  d. spend more time taking care of their children than playing with them.

12. The infant singles out the attachment figure at approximately what age?
  a. Four weeks
  b. Two months
  c. Six months
  d. One year

13. When Kylie's mother left her at the babysitter's house, Kylie was upset and cried. When Kylie's mother returned, Kylie was still angry and would not be consoled by her mother. Which type of attachment does Kylie seem to have?
  a. Disorganized (disoriented)
  b. Resistant
  c. Avoidant
  d. Secure

14. Children who had a secure attachment as infants
  a. tend to have less satisfying later social relationships.
  b. have more fights with friends when they are older.
  c. show high levels of hostility as preschoolers.
  d. interact more skillfully with peers as 11-year-olds at summer camp.

15. A secure attachment is most likely to occur when
  a. parents spend a lot of time with their child.
  b. parents respond to their child in an inconsistent manner.
  c. babies have difficult temperaments.
  d. parents are sensitive and responsive to their baby.

16. Jude is an adult who describes her own childhood in very general terms and seems to idealize her parents. Which type of attachment representation does Jude seem to have?
  a. Autonomous
  b. Dismissive
  c. Preoccupied
  d. Resistant

17. Which of the following statement *best* reflects the relation between day care and infant attachment?
  a. An insecure attachment is more likely when a child is in poor quality day care and has less responsive, sensitive parents.
  b. An insecure attachment is more likely when a child is cared for in a day care center than when she is cared for in a home setting.
  c. A secure attachment relationship is less likely when child-care arrangements are changed frequently.
  d. An insecure attachment is more likely when children are in full-time, rather than part-time, day care.

18. Soon after the first birthday, children commonly engage in
  a. cooperative play.
  b. pretend play.

c. parallel play.
d. role-playing.

19. Parallel play involves
a. pretending.
b. assigning different roles for each child to play.
c. playing alone but maintaining interest in what other children are doing.
d. complex social and cognitive skills so it is not found in toddlers.

20. Ricky and Kyle are building a castle of blocks together in their kindergarten class. Ricky is building the turrets and Kyle is building the moat. This interaction illustrates
a. imitation.
b. parallel play.
c. pretend play.
d. cooperative play.

21. Laura and Kyle are sitting next to each other and are drawing pictures. Periodically, they will trade crayons and comment on the other's picture. This is an example of
a. parallel play.
b. simple social play.
c. cooperative play.
d. pretend play.

22. Evidence for growing self-awareness between the ages of 18 and 24 months includes the fact that children of this age
a. cannot recognize themselves in a mirror.
b. they look less at photographs of themselves than at photos of other children.
c. they do not refer to themselves by name.
d. they sometimes know their own age and gender.

23. When a 3-year-old is shown a videotape of himself in which an experimenter surreptitiously places a sticker on his head, the typical 3-year-old
a. does not recognize himself in the video tape.
b. will reach up and remove the sticker that is still on his head.
c. shows that his sense of self is limited to the present.
d. reacts just like the typical 4-year-old.

24. Twenty- to twenty-eight-month-olds who were self aware were
a. more likely to say "Mine!" when playing with toys than children who were not self aware.
b. less likely to say positive things to their playmates than children who were not self aware.
c. more confrontational and aggressive than children who were not self aware.
d. less likely to consider the toy to be part of a definition of himself than children who were not self aware.

25. An infant's consistent mood and style of behavior is called
a. emotionality.
b. rhythmicity.
c. temperament.
d. intensity of reaction.

26. Results of the New York Longitudinal Study indicated that the largest group of babies was categorized as
a. easy babies.
b. difficult babies.
c. slow-to-warm-up babies.
d. average babies.

27. Which of the following is *not* one of the dimensions of temperament that was proposed by Buss and Plomin?
a. Emotionality
b. Rhythmicity
c. Sociability
d. Activity

28. Jevan is an infant who seems to cry easily and who is difficult to console once he starts crying. Jevan would be high on which of Buss and Plomin's dimensions of temperament?
a. Distractibility
b. Sociability
c. Activity
d. Emotionality

29. Studies of temperament in twins have found that
a. fraternal twins are more alike in temperament than are identical twins.
b. identical twins are more alike in temperament than are fraternal twins.
c. there are no differences in the degree of similarity in temperament in fraternal and identical twins.
d. heredity does not seem to influence temperament.

30. Cross-cultural studies of temperament have shown
a. that Japanese and Chinese babies are more emotional in stressful situations than European American babies.
b. that European American babies are more emotional in stressful situations than Asian babies.
c. that any cultural differences in emotionality cannot be explained by the behavior of the mothers.
d. no differences in emotionality between Asian and American babies.

31. Which of the following statements *best* describes the stability of temperament?
a. Temperament during the first few weeks of life is not related to temperament later in infancy.
b. Temperament during the preschool years is strongly related to temperament during childhood and adolescence.
c. Irritability is the least stable dimension of temperament between the ages of 3 and 9 years.
d. An active fetus is more likely to be an active infant.

32. Studies of links between temperament and developmental outcomes have found
a. distractible children are more likely to succeed in school.
b. anxious children are less likely to comply with parents' rules.
c. shy children often have problems interacting with peers.
d. persistent children are less likely to succeed in school.

ESSAY QUESTIONS

1. Recently, your friend went out for the evening and got a babysitter. They have gotten babysitters in the 7 months since their baby was born, but this time the baby cried when the babysitter came in the door and rushed to pick him up. A few weeks ago when the same sitter came to the house, the baby was willing to go to her. Your friends can't figure out what happened to the baby or the babysitter to change the situation. What can you tell your friends about stranger wariness that might explain the baby's behavior?
2. Your friend Jamal has a 12-month-old daughter, Kia. Recently, they ran into one of Jamal's coworkers who Kia did not know. When this "stranger" approached, Jamal thought that Kia looked at him to gauge his reaction to the "stranger" and then smiled after she saw Jamal greet the "stranger" in a friendly manner. When Jamal told this story to his wife, Yolanda, she laughed and told him that he was giving Kia more credit than a 1-year-old should get. Is Jamal or Yolanda correct? Explain your answer.
3. Your friends have a 6-month-old son, Ethan. Ethan often seems unhappy, is irritable, and does not adjust well to new situations. Your friends are hoping that Ethan is just "in a bad stage" and that he will outgrow his behavior. Which category of temperament would you put Ethan in and what can you tell your friends about the stability of temperament?
4. Your friend Beth has a 9-month-old baby and she is considering returning to work full-time. She has heard that infants who are in daycare full-time have a slightly higher risk of forming an insecure attachment. She told you that she is willing to take that risk because attachment only lasts a few years and doesn't affect other behaviors. What can you tell Beth about the relation between attachment and later social behavior?
5. Your friend Brad is concerned about his 12-month-old son Phillip's social development. Brad has noticed that Phillip will sit next to another child his own age and each of them will do his own puzzle rather than cooperating on one puzzle together. Occasionally, they will look at each other, smile, and say a word or two. Brad feels that Phillip should be interacting more with his peers. What can you tell Brad about the development of play in toddlers that will alleviate his concerns?

ANSWERS

Multiple Choice

1. d (184)
2. b (185)
3. c (187)
4. d (186)
5. d (186)
6. b (186)
7. a (187)
8. c (188)
9. c (190)
10. d (190)
11. b (191)
12. c (190)
13. b (192)
14. d (193)
15. d (193)
16. b (194)
17. a (195)
18. c (196)
19. c (196)
20. d (197)
21. b (197)
22. d (199)
23. c (199)
24. a (200)
25. c (201)
26. a (201)
27. b (202)
28. d (202)
29. b (203)
30. b (203)
31. d (204)
32. c (205)

Essay

1. You can tell your friends that around 6 months of age, stranger wariness emerges in infants. So, infants who had gone to strangers readily just a few weeks before will not fuss or cry when approached by a stranger. In general, infants show less stranger wariness in familiar environments than unfamiliar environments. Infants also show more wariness when someone rushes at them (like the babysitter did) and less wariness when they are given time to "warm up" to the stranger. This wariness will decline as your friends' baby learns to interpret facial expressions and recognizes when strangers are friendly or hostile. (186-187)
2. You can tell Jamal and Yolanda that Kia was engaging in social referencing. Social referencing occurs when infants encounter unfamiliar or ambiguous situations in the environment and involves looking at a parent to find cues to help interpret the situation. The approach of the coworker who was a stranger to Kia would be an unfamiliar or ambiguous situation. Kia is old enough to use social referencing so she looked at Jamal to see how he reacted to this "stranger." When Jamal was friendly to the "stranger," Kia smiled at the "stranger." In other words, Jamal's ideas about Kia's behavior were correct. (187-188)
3. You can tell your friends that Ethan's behavior is typical of "difficult" infants. Will this difficult stage pass? Studies of the stability of temperament indicate that temperament is somewhat stable. There is a moderate correlation between infant temperament during the first few months of life and later temperament. A difficult temperament during the preschool years is related to behavior problems by the time children enter school. Based on the studies of the stability of temperament, no one can say with certainty that Ethan will continue to be difficult but he is more likely to be a difficult child than someone else who is an easy infant. The environment also plays a role in the stability of temperament so that your friends' skillful parenting may help Ethan to become less difficult. (201; 204-206)
4. Attachment does last longer than a few years and a secure attachment is related to better social relationships later in life. There is much evidence that children who form secure attachments as infants have better social relationships with peers later in life. For example, children with secure attachment relationships have higher quality friendships and fewer conflicts with friends than children with insecure attachments as infants. Also, school-age children are less likely to have behavior problems if they have a secure attachment relationship. Finally, 11-year-olds at summer camp who had secure attachments as infants interacted more skillfully with peers and had more friends than those children who had been insecurely attached as infants. (192-193)
5. First, Brad should know that Phillip is engaging in parallel play. This type of play is quite common in 12- to 15-month-old children. In parallel play, social interactions are as basic as one child smiling and talking with the other child responding. Around 15 to 18 months, children's social interactions become truly interactive when simple social play appears. It isn't until around the second birthday that cooperative play, such as building a tower together with blocks, begins to appear. So, Brad shouldn't expect to see cooperative play in Phillip for at least another year. (196-197)

Chapter 8
Physical Growth in Preschool Children

This chapter covers the physical growth, motor development, the factors that promote healthy development, and the maltreatment of children.

PHYSICAL GROWTH

MODULE
8.1

Physical Growth
- *Body Growth*
- *Brain Development*
- *Sleep*

Textbook Learning Objectives

- **What changes take place in preschool children's growing bodies?**
- **How does the brain become more powerful during the preschool years?**
- **How much do preschool children sleep? What problems disrupt their sleep?**

TO MASTER THESE LEARNING OBJECTIVES:

1. Know the details of physical growth

Know the Details of Physical Growth

1. T F Growth during the preschool years is not as rapid as during the infant and toddler years.
2. T F The range of normal growth is very small during the preschool years.
3. T F Gender differences in physical development during the preschool years are large.

4. T F Preschool children still have the "top-heavy" look that is characteristic of infants.
5. T F Preschoolers have a more slender look than do infants.
6. T F Most children have all of their primary teeth by age 3 years.
7. T F Parents don't need to worry about brushing their children's teeth until all of the primary teeth have appeared.
8. T F By age 3, the brain has achieved 80% of its mature weight.
9. T F Much of the myelinization of the neurons in the corpus callosum occurs between the ages of 1 and 5 years.
10. T F The more specialized brain is more likely to recover from injury.
11. T F Around age 4, most preschoolers give up their afternoon nap.
12. T F Bedtime struggles are a regular occurrence in most preschool children.
13. T F Parents should seek professional help even when their child has occasional nightmares.
14. T F Children usually remember night terrors when they wake up the next morning.
15. T F Occasional bed wetting is normal in preschool children.
16. T F Most children grow out of bed wetting by age 5 or 6.

ANSWERS

Know the Details

1. true (214)
2. false (214)
3. false (214)
4. false (215)
5. true (215)
6. true (215)
7. false (215)
8. true (216)
9. true (216)
10. false (216)
11. true (216)
12. false (216)
13. false (217)
14. false (217)
15. true (218)
16. true (218)

MODULE

8.2

Motor Development

- *Gross-Motor Skills*
- *Fine-Motor Skills*
- *Handedness*
- *Gender Differences in Motor Skills*

MOTOR DEVELOPMENT

Textbook Learning Objectives

- **How do children's gross-and-fine-motor skills improve during the preschool years? How do preschool children draw?**
- **How similar are left- and right-handed children?**
- **Do preschool boys and girls differ in their motor skills?**

TO MASTER THESE LEARNING OBJECTIVES:

1. Know the stages of drawing ability
2. Know the details of motor development

Know the Stages of Drawing Ability: Match each statement with the correct stage

Design Pictorial
Shape

1. Most children in this stage draw 6 basic shapes. __________
2. Children in this stage depict recognizable objects such as people, animals, and plants. __________
3. Children in this stage combine the 6 basic shapes to create more complex patterns. __________

Know the Details of Motor Development

1. T F Most 2-year-olds have a "true run" rather than a hurried walk.
2. T F The average 3-year-old can hop for long distances or can alternate hopping from one foot to the other.
3. T F Most 2-year-olds are not very skilled at catching and throwing a ball.
4. T F Most 2-year-olds can use zippers, but not buttons.
5. T F Most 5-year-olds can dress and undress themselves.
6. T F Most children cannot tie their own shoes until they are 6 years old.
7. T F Most 3-year-olds use an adult, 1-finger grip. (see figure below)
8. T F Most 3-year-olds seem to be experimenting with different ways to hold a pen.
9. T F Most 2-year-olds produce drawings that consist mainly of scribbles.

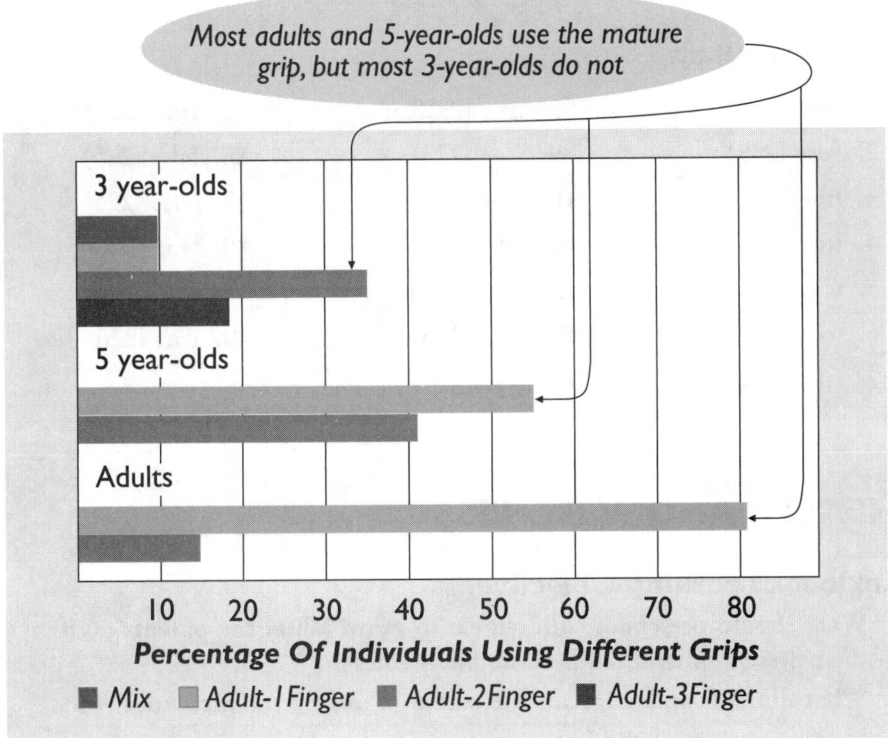

10. T F Most 3-year-olds are in the pictorial stage of drawing.

11. T F Children in the design stage of drawing produce pictures that contain 6 basic shapes.

12. T F The right hemisphere of the brain is usually the dominant hemisphere in right-handed people.

13. T F Language functions are localized in the right hemispheres of some left-handed people.

14. T F Left-handed people are more likely to have migraine headaches and allergies than right-handed people.

15. T F Left-handed individuals are more likely to be talented artistically and spatially.

16. T F Preschool girls and boys do not differ in the amount of muscle that they have.

17. T F Boys and girls do not differ in their activity levels.

18. T F Girls tend to be better at fine-motor skills than boys.

19. T F Boys tend to be more skilled at activities that require coordination of limbs such as hopping or skipping.

20. T F Gender differences in motor skill in preschool children may be due to social encouragement to participate in gender stereotyped activities.

ANSWERS

Stages of Drawing

1. shape (223)
2. pictorial (224)
3. design (224)

Know the Details

1. false (219)
2. false (219)
3. true (219)
4. true (221)
5. true (221)
6. true (221)
7. false (222)
8. true (222)
9. true (223)
10. false (224)
11. false (224)
12. false (225)
13. true (225)
14. true (225)
15. true (225)
16. false (225)
17. false (225)
18. true (226)
19. false (226)
20. true (226)

MODULE
8.3

Health and Wellness
- *Nutrition*
- *Threats to Children's Development*

HEALTH AND WELLNESS

Textbook Learning Objectives

What should preschool children eat to grow? What can parents do if their preschool children become picky eaters?

What illnesses and accidents are common during the preschool years?

How do preschool children react to being hospitalized?

TO MASTER THESE LEARNING OBJECTIVES:

1. Know the details of health and wellness

Know the Details of Health and Wellness

1. T F Preschoolers need to eat more per pound than do infants and toddlers.
2. T F According to the American Academy of Pediatrics, parents should not let children eat their food in any order that they want.
3. T F Parents should force their children to try new foods.
4. T F Food should never be used to reward or punish a child.
5. T F The average preschool child has 7 or 8 colds per year.
6. T F Minor illnesses help prepare children for later, more serious illnesses.
7. T F Diabetes is the most common chronic disease of childhood.
8. T F Accidents are the leading cause of death in preschool children.
9. T F Children who are under stress are no more likely to be ill or have an accident than other children.
10. T F Children who live in poverty are more prone to illness than children who do not live in poverty.
11. T F Like most European nations, the United States guarantees basic health care for young children.
12. T F When health-care professionals give hospitalized children choices about food and schedules, children don't feel so powerless in the hospital environment.

ANSWERS

Know the Details

1. false (227)
2. false (228)
3. false (228)
4. true (228)
5. true (229)
6. true (229)
7. false (229)
8. true (230)
9. false (231)
10. true (231)
11. false (231)
12. true (231)

CHILD NEGLECT AND MALTREATMENT

MODULE
8.4

Child Neglect and Maltreatment

- *Consequences of Maltreatment*
- *Causes of Maltreatment*
- *Preventing Maltreatment*

Textbook Learning Objectives

- **What are the consequences of child maltreatment?**
- **What factors cause parents to mistreat their children?**
- **How can maltreatment be prevented?**

TO MASTER THESE LEARNING OBJECTIVES:

1. Know the details of child neglect and maltreatment

Know the Details of Child Abuse

1. T F Physical abuse occurs when children do not receive adequate food, clothing, or medical care.
2. T F Social, emotional, and intellectual development often is harmed in children who are abused.
3. T F Adults who were abused as children are no more likely to have emotional problems such as depression.
4. T F Countries that accept physical punishment have lower rates of child abuse.
5. T F Child abuse is more common in families that live in poverty.
6. T F Child abuse is more likely to occur when parents have a lot of contact with neighbors and other relatives.
7. T F Parents who maltreat their children often have high expectations for their children but do little to help the children achieve these goals.
8. T F Older children are more likely to be abused than infants and preschoolers.
9. T F Children who are frequently ill are abused more often than healthy children.
10. T F Stepchildren are more prone to abuse and neglect than biological children.
11. T F Parents can be taught more effective ways of dealing with their children so that abuse is less likely.
12. T F Social support for parents is not likely to reduce child abuse.

ANSWERS

Know the Details

1. false (233)
2. true (233)
3. false (234)
4. false (234)
5. true (235)
6. false (235)
7. true (235)
8. false (236)
9. true (236)
10. true (236)
11. true (237)
12. false (237)

SUMMARY

MODULE 8.1: PHYSICAL GROWTH

Body Growth. Preschool children grow steadily, adding about 2-3 inches and 4 pounds each year. However, the range of normal heights and weights is very
wide __________ in this period. Preschool children begin to look more mature because
fat their bodies have more adult-like proportions and less __________. During these years, much cartilage turns to bone and children acquire, typically by age 3, all 20
primary (baby) __________ teeth.

Brain Development. Between 2 and 5 years, unnecessary neurons are __________ and many additional neurons — particularly those in the __________ and the sensory and motor regions of the brain — are wrapped in myelin. In addition, the brain becomes more specialized with specific functions (e.g., comprehending speech) becoming localized in particular brain regions.

pruned
corpus callosum

Sleep. Preschool children typically sleep about 12 hours each night. Many children occasionally have problems falling asleep. The best approach is to follow a __________ routine that allows children to make a __________ shift from daytime activities to a relaxed state that's conducive to sleep. Many children experience occasional __________; less common are __________ and sleep walking. Normally none of these sleep disturbances poses a special problem for children. Many preschool children wet their beds during the night; this, too, is not a problem unless it persists in the __________ years.

consistent, gradual
nightmares, night terrors
elementary-school

MODULE 8.2: MOTOR DEVELOPMENT

Gross-Motor Skills. Children's gross motor skills improve steadily throughout the preschool years. They become more skilled at __________ and hopping as well as throwing and catching a ball. Most 2- or 3-year-olds, for example, throw a ball using only their __________ but 6-year-olds use their arm, upper body, and legs.

running
forearms

Fine-Motor Skills. Preschool children become much more dextrous, which makes it possible for them to feed and __________ themselves. Their greater fine-motor coordination also means that their drawings become more __________. Children's first drawings — at about age 2 — consist of __________; youngsters rapidly progress to shapes and combining shapes. At about 4 or 5, children begin to draw __________ objects such as people and animals.

clothe
complex
scribbles
recognizable

Handedness. Most preschool children use their __________ hand most of the time. For most children, language functioning is typically localized in the __________ hemisphere. However, language is localized in the __________ hemisphere for some left-handed children and in both hemispheres for other left-handed children. Left-handed children and adults are more prone to some health problems and __________ disorders, but are more talented artistically, __________, and mathematically.

right
left, right
language
spatially

Gender Differences in Motor Skills. Young boys tend to be more __________ than girls and have an advantage on tasks that rely on strength. However, girls perform better than boys on tasks that require coordinated movements of the limbs or __________ motor coordination.

active
fine

MODULE 8.3: HEALTH AND WELLNESS

Nutrition. Most preschool children need a diet of roughly 1500-1700 calories, from each of the five food groups, and that is low in fat and sugar. Preschool children are often picky eaters but parents can do a number of things to prevent this from happening. They can allow children to __________ their food and eat it in any order they want. Parents should not __________ children to eat everything on their plate and should not spend mealtimes talking about the child's eating.

choose
force

immunities, illness
asthma

Threats to Children's Development. Preschool children frequently have minor illnesses, such as colds. Having a minor illness benefits children by helping them develop __________ and teaching them about the nature of __________ and recovery. Most chronic illnesses are rare, but several million U.S. children are afflicted with __________, in which they have difficulty breathing because air passages in their lungs are inflamed. Children with asthma can lead normal lives as long as they follow several guidelines, such as taking proper medications.

accidents
stress, poverty
fear of unknown

Preschool children die from __________ more than any other cause. Parents can avoid most accidents entirely (e.g., by ensuring that children cannot get to poisons) or they can reduce the risk of injury from an accident (e.g., by having children always ride in a car seat). Children are more prone to illness when they are living in __________ and when they live in __________. Hospitalization disturbs children because of the separation from parents, the __________, and the loss of control. By addressing these concerns, parents and health-care professionals can make hospitalization less traumatic for children.

MODULE 8.4: CHILD NEGLECT AND MALTREATMENT

peer
academic

Consequences of Maltreatment. Children who are maltreated sometimes suffer permanent physical damage. Their __________ relationships are often poor and they tend to lag behind in cognitive development and __________ performance.

poverty
unhealthy

Causes of Maltreatment. A culture's views on violence, __________, and social isolation can foster child maltreatment. Parents who abuse their children are often unhappy, socially unskilled individuals. Younger, __________ children are more likely to be targets of maltreatment, as are stepchildren.

coping
resources

Preventing Maltreatment. Prevention should target each of the factors that contribute to child maltreatment. In reality, prevention programs often focus on providing families with new ways of __________ with problems and providing parents with __________ to help them cope with stress.

CHAPTER 8 PHYSICAL DEVELOPMENT IN PRESCHOOL CHILDREN

TEST YOURSELF

1. Which of the following is *true* of physical growth during the preschool years?
   a. Growth at this time is as rapid as growth during the infant and toddler years.
   b. Gender differences in physical development are large during the preschool years.
   c. Adult height cannot be predicted from preschool height since growth during the preschool years is so erratic.
   d. Preschoolers lose baby fat which makes them appear more slender than infants.

2. In most children,
  a. the first tooth appears at about 18 months.
  b. all primary teeth have erupted by age 3 years.
  c. the first primary tooth is lost around 8 years.
  d. the first tooth is usually an upper, front tooth.

3. According to the American Academy of Pediatric Dentistry, proper dental care
  a. doesn't need to begin until all the primary teeth are in place.
  b. includes flossing for preschool children.
  c. should involve visiting the dentist twice a year.
  d. is not necessary for primary teeth since they will be replaced by secondary teeth later.

4. The brain of the preschooler
  a. has achieved 90% of its mature weight by 3 years.
  b. has completed synaptic pruning during the toddler years.
  c. has completed hemispheric specialization.
  d. is making progress on the myelinization of neurons, particularly those neurons in the corpus callosum.

5. During the preschool years,
  a. sleep is important because most growth hormone is secreted while children are sleeping.
  b. a regular bedtime routine is not important.
  c. sleep patterns include an afternoon nap until most children are 6 years old.
  d. bedtime struggles occur on a nightly basis in most children.

6. In nightmares, children
  a. usually appear to wake in a panic and are often breathing rapidly and perspiring heavily.
  b. usually don't remember the episode in the morning.
  c. have vivid, frightening dreams.
  d. often don't respond to parents.

7. Bedwetting
  a. is common in most 4-year-olds.
  b. is usually outgrown by the time children are 5 or 6.
  c. is more common in girls than boys.
  d. in preschool children is a sign of underlying physical or psychological problems.

8. Typical motor development means that most 2-year-olds
  a. use a "hurried walk" rather than a "true" run.
  b. can use their legs to move to a ball that is thrown at them.
  c. step into their throw when throwing a ball.
  d. can hop for long distances and can alternate feet while hopping.

9. Which child would you expect to dress himself?
  a. 2-year-old Jacob
  b. 3-year-old Lance
  c. 4-year-old Muhammed
  d. 5-year-old Claude

10. Tammy Greer and Jeffrey Lockman (1998) tested 3-year-olds, 5-year-olds, and college students to see if 3-year-olds were experimenting with different ways to hold a pen and to see if their grip would vary depending on the diameter of the pen and the type of writing task. They found that
a. only the 3-year-olds varied their grip to adjust to the size of the pen.
b. both 3-year-olds and 5-year-olds varied their grip to adjust to the size of the pen.
c. neither 3-year-olds nor 5-year-olds used the adult, 1-finger grip in an effective manner.
d. very few 3-year-olds used the adult, 1-finger grip and they were more likely to be experimenting with different grips.

11. Four-year-old Matt loves to draw. Matt's pictures usually contain combinations of circles, squares, and triangles to form somewhat complex patterns. Which stage of drawing does Matt seem to be in?
a. Design stage
b. Imagery stage
c. Pictorial stage
d. Shape stage

12. Which of the following statements is *true* of handedness?
a. Right-handed individuals are more likely to have migraine headaches and allergies.
b. The right hemisphere is usually the dominant hemisphere in right-handed people.
c. In some left-handed people, language functions occur in the right hemisphere of the brain.
d. Left-handed people are not more likely to have more artistic talent.

13. During the preschool years, typical gender differences in motor skills are reflected in the fact that
a. girls are stronger than boys.
b. boys are more active than girls.
c. girls are less coordinated than boys in activities such as skipping and hopping.
d. boys are more skilled at tasks that require fine motor coordination.

14. Parents of preschool children who are picky eaters should
a. allow children to choose from among a number of healthy food choices.
b. not allow children to eat foods in any order that they want because they will fill up on dessert.
c. force children to clean their plates.
d. reward children with dessert if they finish their main course.

15. During the preschool years, minor illnesses such as colds
a. occur about 2 or 3 times per year.
b. usually require a visit to a health-care professional.
c. do not help children's bodies develop immunity to more serious illnesses.
d. help prepare children for more serious future illnesses.

16. The most common chronic illness during childhood is
a. asthma.
b. cancer.
c. diabetes.
d. leukemia.

17. Children with asthma
   a. cannot participate in most of the activities that their friends do.
   b. should avoid things that may trigger an asthma attack.
   c. should visit a physician once a month.
   d. can usually be cured.

18. Which of the following should be done to make a hospital stay less traumatic for a child?
   a. The parents shouldn't spend too much time with the child because they will get in the way of the medical professionals.
   b. Medical professionals shouldn't explain procedures to children because the explanations will scare the children.
   c. Parents should be allowed to room in.
   d. Health-care professionals shouldn't give children choices because they aren't mature enough to make the choices.

19. Which type of maltreatment occurs when parents do not provide adequate food, clothing, or medical care?
   a. Physical abuse
   b. Psychological abuse
   c. Neglect
   d. Sexual abuse

20. Abused children
   a. have normal relationships with peers.
   b. get lower grades in school.
   c. do not have behavior problems in school.
   d. are likely to be promoted a grade in school.

21. Child abuse is more likely to occur when
   a. children are infants or preschoolers than when they are older.
   b. children are healthy.
   c. parents have frequent contact with and receive help from friends and relatives.
   d. parents have low expectations for their children.

ESSAY QUESTIONS

1. Your friend Shereka has a 4-year-old son named Jerome. Jerome occasionally wets the bed at night and Shereka is afraid that this will be a problem for Jerome when he is older. What can you tell Shereka about bedwetting in preschool children that might put her mind at ease?

2. Reggie is quite athletic and he would like his 3-year-old daughter Cheryl to be athletic also, but he is concerned that she is a klutz. When she runs she doesn't have the fluid motion that most good runners have, when he plays catch with her she doesn't move to the ball, and when she throws the ball she only uses her forearms rather than her whole body. What can you tell Reggie about motor development that might relieve some of his worries?

3. Your friend Regina is quite worried that her 3-year-old son Randall cannot dress himself and tie his shoes. Whenever Randall goes to the bathroom, Regina needs to help him get his clothes back on properly. What can you tell Regina about the development of fine motor skill that will help her understand Randall's ability to dress himself?

4. Your daughter has been diagnosed with asthma and your spouse is worried that she won't be able to participate in sports and other activities. What can you tell your spouse about asthma and children's activities that might change your spouse's opinion?

ANSWERS

Multiple Choice

1. d (214)
2. b (215)
3. c (215)
4. d (216)
5. a (216)
6. c (217)
7. b (218)
8. a (219)
9. d (221)
10. d (222)
11. a (224)
12. c (225)
13. b (225)
14. a (228)
15. d (229)
16. a (229)
17. b (230)
18. c (231)
19. c (233)
20. b (233)
21. a (235)

ESSAY

1. Most children in the United States are toilet trained as 2- or 3-year-olds. Once toilet trained, most children stay dry during the day, but may wet the bed at night. In fact, about 25% of 4-year-olds wet their bed occasionally. Also, boys tend to wet the bed at night more than girls do. Occasional bedwetting in preschoolers is quite normal and most children will outgrow their bedwetting by the time they are 5 or 6. So, given Jerome's age and gender it isn't unusual that he occasionally wets the bed. If the problem gets worse or continues past age 6, then Shereka should look into methods that help prevent bedwetting such as alarms that wake children and exercises that strengthen sphincter muscles. (218)

2. You can tell Reggie that Cheryl's motor behavior is quite typical for a child her age. Much development in coordination and fluidity of motion occurs between the ages of 2 and 6 years. For example, most 2-year-olds don't run in a fluid motion, but use a hurried walk instead, but by age 5 or 6 years, children run easily. Also, a 2-year-old can only catch a ball that lands on her extended arms, but by age 6 the same child will move toward a thrown ball. Similarly, 2-year-olds only use their forearms to throw a ball, but 6-year-olds step into a throw and use their bodies to propel a thrown ball. In other words, Cheryl's behavior is quite typical of a 3-year-old and much refinement in her motor skill will occur in the next 3 years. So, Reggie should relax because it may be too early to tell if Cheryl will be a gifted athlete. (219-220)

3. You can tell Regina that Randall's fine-motor skill is fairly typical of children his age. Most 2- or 3-year-olds can put on simple clothing such as elastic-waist pants and sweatshirts and can use zippers, but not buttons. Most 3- or 4-year-olds can fasten buttons and take off their clothes when they go to the bathroom. However, most kids can't dress and undress themselves unassisted until they are 5 and they usually can't tie their shoes until they are 6. Also, Regina should keep in mind that boys tend to be less skilled at fine-motor tasks. So, Regina needs to change her expectations and/or find Randall more simple clothes that do not have buttons, zippers, or shoe laces. (220-221)

4. Asthma is the most common chronic illness affecting children in the United States. Asthma attacks account for nearly half a million trips to the hospital and a few hundred deaths each year so it is an illness that should be taken seriously. However, asthma can be managed effectively and children with asthma participate in sports and other physical activities. By visiting a physician regularly, taking medication appropriately, monitoring changes in symptoms, and avoiding things such as pet hair and dust mites that might trigger an asthma attack, children and their parents can control the disease. Also, you might want to tell your spouse that children whose parents view asthma as a problem that can be solved, tend to have children who handle their asthma better than children whose parents view the illness as an insurmountable barrier to activities. (229-230)

Chapter 9 Cognitive Development in Preschool Children

This chapter examines cognitive development, language development, and the education of preschool children.

COGNITIVE PROCESSES

MODULE 9.1

Cognitive Processes

- *Piaget's Account*
- *Information-Processing Perspectives on Preschool Thinking*
- *Vygotsky's Theory of Cognitive Development*

Textbook Learning Objectives

- **What are the distinguishing features of thinking during the preoperational stage?**
- **How does children's information processing improve during the preschool years?**
- **Why did Vygotsky view development as an apprenticeship?**

TO MASTER THESE LEARNING OBJECTIVES:

1. Know the terms associated with cognitive development
2. Know the details of cognitive development

Know the Terms Associated with Cognitive Development: Match each definition with the correct term

Animism
Attention
Autobiographical memory
Centration
Cardinality
Egocentrism
Inner speech
One-to-one
Preoperational
Private speech
Scaffolding
Stable-order
Theory of mind
Zone of proximal development

1. This is marked by the child's use of symbols to represent objects and events. __________
2. This refers to the young child's difficulty in seeing the world from another's perspective.__________
3. This refers to the preoperational child's tendency to attribute life or life-like properties to inanimate objects.__________
4. Piaget's terms for narrowly focused thought that is characteristic of preoperational children.__________
5. A naive understanding of the relations between mind and behavior. __________
6. The process by which we select information that will be processed further. __________
7. People's memory of significant events and experiences of their own lives. __________
8. The counting principle that states that there must be one and only one name for each object that is counted. __________
9. The counting principle that states that number names must be counted in the same order. __________
10. The counting principle that states that the last number name denotes the number of objects in a set. __________
11. The difference between what a child can do with assistance and what he can do alone. __________
12. A teaching style that matches the amount of assistance to the learner's needs. __________
13. Comments not directed toward others but that are intended to help children regulate their own behavior. __________
14. Vygotsky's term for thought. __________

Know the Details of the Stages of Cognitive Development

1. T F Most two year-olds cannot think of scale models of rooms as symbols of life-size rooms.
2. T F Thought during the preoperational period is egocentric.
3. T F On the problems like the one shown at right, preoperational children do not demonstrate egocentrism.
4. T F Thinking that the sun is happy because it is shining is an example of animism.

5. T F One reason that preoperational children fail conservation tasks is that their thought is centered on one aspect of the task.

6. T F Preoperational children who look at a glass of milk through red glasses will say that the milk looks red and the milk really is red.

7. T F The preoperational child's confusion about appearance and reality is easily changed with a little training.

8. T F Most 4-year-olds understand that inanimate objects cannot move themselves.

9. T F Most 4-year-olds do not understand that growth does not occur in inanimate objects.

10. T F By 4 years of age, children understand that the insides of animate and inanimate objects differ.

11. T F By 4 years of age, children understand that broken objects do not heal themselves.

12. T F According to theory of mind, 2-year-olds are not aware of their wants and likes.

13. T F Most 3-year-olds can distinguish the mental world from the physical world.

14. T F By age 4, children understand that behavior is based on beliefs, even when those beliefs are wrong.

15. T F Attention is the process by which we select information that will be processed further.

16. T F After a stimulus is presented repeatedly, infants pay more attention to it. This increase in attention is called habituation.

17. T F Habituation indicates that attention is selective.

18. T F Older preschoolers show more focused attention than do younger preschoolers.

19. T F Older children and adults have better attentional skills because they remind themselves to pay attention more often.

20. T F Older children and adults do not know any more attentional strategies than do young children.

21. T F Autobiographical memory begins in late childhood.

22. T F Most child-protection workers and law-enforcement officials are very accurate at distinguishing truthful children from lying children.

23. T F When questioning children, interviewers should pursue only 1 explanation of what happened.

24. T F Interviewers should question children repeatedly on a single issue.

25. T F Children should be warned that interviewers may try to trick them or suggest things that didn't happen.

26. T F The one-to-one principle states that the last number name denotes the number of objects being counted.

27. T F The stable-order principle states that number names must be counted in the same order.

28. T F The cardinality principle states that there must be one and only one number name for each object that is counted.

29. T F By 4 years of age, most American youngsters can count to 20.

30. T F English-speaking children often stop counting at a number ending in 9 (e.g., 29) because they don't know the next decade name.

31. T F Preschoolers in the United States count more accurately than preschoolers in Asian countries.

32. T F According to Vygotsky, the difference between what a child can do independently and what she can do with assistance defines the zone of proximal development.

33. T F Scaffolding matches the amount of assistance to the learner's needs.

34. T F Comments that are not intended for others but are used by children to regulate their own behavior are known as private speech.

35. T F Children use private speech more on easy tasks than on difficult tasks.

ANSWERS

Key Terms

1. preoperational (242)
2. egocentrism (242)
3. animism (243)
4. centration (243)
5. theory of mind (248)
6. attention (249)
7. autobiographical memory (251)
8. one-to-one (252)
9. stable-order (252)
10. cardinality (252)
11. zone of proximal development (254)
12. scaffolding (254)
13. private speech (254)
14. inner speech (255)

Know the Details

1. true (245)
2. true (242)
3. false (242)
4. true (243)
5. true (243)
6. true (245)
7. false (247)
8. true (248)
9. false (248)
10. true (248)
11. true (248)
12. false (248)
13. true (248)
14. true (249)
15. true (249)
16. false (250)
17. true (250)
18. true (250)
19. true (250)
20. false (250)
21. false (251)
22. false (252)
23. false (252)
24. false (252)
25. true (252)
26. false (252)
27. true (252)
28. true (252)
29. true (253)
30. false (253)
31. true (254)
32. true (254)
33. true (254)
34. false (255)

MODULE
9.2

Language

- *Encouraging Word Learning*
- *From Two-Word Speech to Complex Sentences*
- *How Children Acquire Grammar*

LANGUAGE

Textbook Learning Objectives

- **What conditions help preschoolers to expand their vocabulary?**
- **How do children progress from speaking single words to complicated sentences?**
- **How do children acquire the grammar of their native language?**

TO MASTER THESE LEARNING OBJECTIVES

1. Know the terms associated with the development of language
2. Know the details associated with the development of language

Know the Terms Associated with the Development of Language: Match each definition with the correct term

Grammatical morphemes
Overregularization
Semantic bootstrapping hypothesis
Telegraphic speech

1. Speech that consists only of words that are directly relevant to meaning. __________
2. Word or endings of words that make a sentence grammatical. __________
3. Applying grammatical rules to words that are exceptions to the rule.__________
4. Relying upon one's knowledge of the meanings of words to discover grammatical rules.__________

Know the Details of the Development of Language

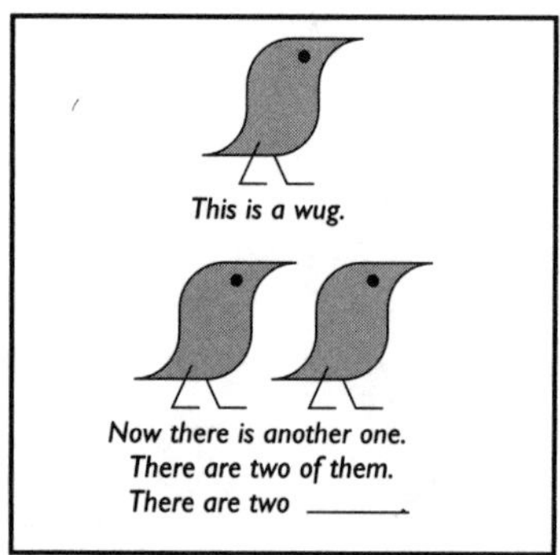

This is a wug.
Now there is another one.
There are two of them.
There are two ______.

1. T F Naming objects that are the focus of a child's attention can help the child learn new words.
2. T F Children whose parents asked them questions while reading a story to them were more likely to comprehend and produce target words than children whose parents only read to them. (see figure at left)
3. T F Preschoolers who watch television shows such as cartoons tend to have larger vocabularies than other children.
4. T F Bilingualism is very confusing for children and, consequently, bilingual children show more cognitive deficits than monolingual children.
5. T F The production of two-word speech only occurs in English-speaking children.
6. T F The production of two-word speech does not follow any rules.
7. T F Children learn general rules about grammatical morphemes.
8. T F Two *mans* is an example of overregularization.
9. T F Adding -s and -ing are simple grammatical morphemes that are mastered at an early age.
10. T F During the stage of two-word speech, children use *wh* words when asking questions.

11. T F Preschoolers completely understand sentences in the passive voice.

12. T F Learning theorists claimed that all aspects of language could be learned through imitation and reinforcement.

13. T F A specific area of the brain, usually the left hemisphere, plays a critical role in processing language.

14. T F Chimpanzees learn grammar as easily as young children.

15. T F People can easily acquire language at any point in life.

16. T F Individuals master the grammar of a foreign language at the level of a native speaker only if they are exposed to the language prior to adolescence.

17. T F Language experience is important to the semantic bootstrapping hypothesis because it provides the information from which grammatical rules are inferred.

18. T F Parents do not adjust their speech to include examples of speech that their child is trying to master.

19. T F The majority of the time parents do not correct their child's grammar.

20. T F Parents respond to correct grammar by simply continuing the conversation.

21. T F Parents correct ungrammatical speech by rephrasing or elaborating the child's speech.

ANSWERS

Key Terms

1. telegraphic speech (259)

2. grammatical morphemes(259)

3. overregularization (260)

4. semantic bootstrapping hypothesis (263)

Know the Details

1. true (257)

2. true (257)

3. false (257)

4. false (258)

5. false (259)

6. false (259)

7. true (260)

8. true (260)

9. true (260)

10. false (260)

11. false (261)

12. true (261)

13. true (262)

14. false (262)

15. false (262)

16. true (262)

17. true (263)

18. false (263)

19. true (263)

20. true (263)

21. true (263)

MODULE
9.3

Communicating with Others

- *Taking Turns*
- *Speaking Effectively*
- *Listening Well*

COMMUNICATING WITH OTHERS

Textbook Learning Objectives

- **When and how do children learn to take turns in conversations?**
- **What are the skills required to be an effective speaker?**
- **What is involved in becoming a good listener?**

TO MASTER THESE LEARNING OBJECTIVES

1. Know the details of effective communication

Know the Details of Effective Communication

1. T F Western parents wait until after their children say their first words before they encourage turn-taking.
2. T F By 3 years of age, children understand that a comment should be followed by a response.
3. T F The first deliberate attempts to communicate typically emerge at 10 months.
4. T F Infants' early attempts to communicate include pointing, touching, or making noises.
5. T F Four-year-olds are more likely to use attention-getting phrases and shorter sentences when describing a toy to an adult than when describing the same toy to a 2-year-old.
6. T F Most toddlers understand that one's reply to comments should be related to the comment.
7. T F Young children usually ask for clarification when they are given somewhat ambiguous instructions.

ANSWERS

Know the Details

1. false (266)
2. true (266)
3. true (266)
4. true (266)
5. false (267)
6. false (268)
7. false (268)

MODULE
9.4

Early Childhood Education

- *Varieties of Early Childhood Education*
- *Preschool Programs for Economically Disadvantaged Children*
- *Using Television to Educate Preschool Children*

EARLY CHILDHOOD EDUCATION

Textbook Learning Objectives

- **What are the aims of preschool programs? How are they best achieved?**
- **How effective is Head Start?**
- **Can television be used to educate preschool children?**

TO MASTER THESE LEARNING OBJECTIVES:

1. Know the details of early childhood education

Know the Details of Early Childhood Education

1. T F The distinction between preschools and day-care centers is clear-cut.
2. T F Child-centered preschools follow an explicit curriculum to achieve explicit goals for cognitive, social, and emotional growth.
3. T F Chinese parents are more likely to desire a preschool that emphasizes academic preparation.
4. T F American parents are more likely to desire a preschool that focuses on being a good group member.
5. T F According to Piaget, teachers should tell children information rather than letting them discover it on their own.
6. T F The best teaching experiences are slightly ahead of children's current skills.
7. T F Teachers should encourage children to look at the consistency in their own thinking.
8. T F Children who are graduates of Head Start are just as likely to repeat a grade in school as children who were not in Head Start.
9. T F Head Start graduates are more likely to graduate from high school than children who did not attend Head Start.
10. T F Children who watch *Sesame Street* regularly have larger vocabularies than those who watch infrequently.
11. T F Children are more likely to behave prosocially when they watch TV shows that emphasize prosocial behavior.
12. T F Girls are more likely than boys to benefit from viewing prosocial TV shows.
13. T F Children who watch a lot of TV have reduced levels of attention.
14. T F Studies consistently find that children who watch a lot of TV show lower levels of creativity.

ANSWERS

Know the Details

1. false (270)
2. false (270)
3. true (270)
4. false (270)
5. false (270)
6. true (271)
7. true (271)
8. false (273)
9. true (273)
10. true (273)
11. true (274)
12. false (274)
13. false (274)
14. false (274)

SUMMARY

MODULE 9.1: COGNITIVE PROCESSES

egocentrism
centered
appearance
animate and inanimate
beliefs

Piaget's Account. From 2 to 7 years of age, children are in Piaget's preoperational stage. Although now capable of using symbols, their thinking is limited by __________, the inability to see the world from another's point of view. Preoperational children also are __________ in their thinking and sometimes confuse __________ with reality. During these years, children's theories of biology clearly distinguish properties of __________ objects and their theories of psychology gradually include the idea that behavior is based on people's __________ about events and situations.

pay attention

Information-Processing Perspectives on Preschool Thinking. Compared to older children, preschool children are less able to __________, primarily because they lack well-developed strategies for paying attention.

past events
suggest
cardinality

Autobiographical memory emerges early in the preschool years, often prompted by parents questioning children about __________. Young children's memory of the past is inaccurate when they're questioned repeatedly because they cannot distinguish what actually happened from what adults __________ may have happened. Preschoolers begin to count at 2 and by 3 most have mastered the one-to-one, stable-order, and __________ principles, at least when counting small sets of objects.

social setting
zone of proximal development
scaffolding
difficult

Vygotsky's Theory of Cognitive Development. Vygotsky believed that cognition first develops in a __________ and only gradually comes under the child's independent control. The difference between what children can do with assistance and what they can do alone defines the __________. Control of cognitive skills is most readily transferred from others to the child through __________, a teaching style that allows children to take on more and more of a task as they master its different components. Children often talk to themselves, particularly when the task is __________ or after they have made a mistake.

MODULE 9.2: LANGUAGE

Encouraging Word Learning. Children's word learning is fostered by experience, including reading to children, watching television, and, for school-age children, reading to themselves. The key ingredient is making children __________ about the meanings of new words. think

From Two-Word Speech to Complex Sentences. Not long after the first birthday, children produce two-word sentences that are based on simple __________ for expressing ideas or needs. These sentences are sometimes called __________ because they focus solely on meaning. Moving from two-word to more complex sentences involves adding __________ . Children first master grammatical morphemes that express simple relations, then those that denote complex relations. As children acquire grammatical morphemes they also extend their speech to other sentence forms, such as questions, and, later, to more complex constructions, such as passive sentences. rules telegraphic speech grammatical morphemes

How Children Acquire Grammar. Some researchers claim that grammar is too complex for children to learn solely from their __________; instead, the brain must be pre-wired to simplify the task. Findings consistent with this argument are specialized regions in the brain for __________, the inability of chimpanzees to master grammar, and __________ in language acquisition. Other researchers believe that children use general cognitive skills to __________ grammatical rules from regularities in the speech that they hear. Language experience is important for learning grammar. Parents provide examples of the rules of speech that their children are trying to master and they provide children with __________ concerning grammatical rules. experience processing language critical periods infer feedback

MODULE 9.3: COMMUNICATING WITH OTHERS

Taking Turns. Parents encourage turn-taking __________ infants talk and, later, demonstrate both the speaker and listener roles for their children. By age 3 years, children spontaneously take turns and will expect a __________ to a comment. before response

Speaking Effectively. Before they can speak, infants use __________ and noises to communicate. During the preschool years, children gradually become more skilled at constructing clear messages, in part by adjusting their speech to fit their listeners' needs. They also begin to monitor their listeners' __________, repeating messages if necessary. gestures comprehension

Listening Well. Toddlers are not good conversationalists because their remarks __________ to the topic. Preschoolers are unlikely to identify __________ in another's speech. don't relate, ambiguities

MODULE 9.4: EARLY CHILDHOOD EDUCATION

Varieties of Early Childhood Education. Most early childhood education programs emphasize play but academically-oriented programs embed play in explicit __________. According to Piaget's theory, early childhood education is most effective when it emphasizes children's __________, provides experiences that are just instructional goals discovery

current skills ahead of the child's __________, and allows children to discover inconsistencies in their thinking. Guidelines by the NAEYC for developmentally appropriate
caring teaching practice call for creating a __________ community of learners, teaching that enhances development, assessing children's learning, and establishing rela-
families tionships with __________.

Preschool Programs for Economically-Disadvantaged Children. Head Start was created in the 1960s as part of President Johnson's War on Poverty. Children from low-income families who participate in high-quality Head Start programs are
healthier __________ and do better in school.

Using Television to Educate Preschool Children. Children who watch *Sesame Street*
school regularly improve their academic skills and adjust to __________ more readily. When children watch programs that emphasize prosocial skills such as *Mister*
prosocially *Rogers' Neighborhood,* they are more likely to behave __________. Although critics have suggested that frequent TV-viewing leads to reduced attention and
has not reduced creativity, research __________ consistently found evidence that supports these criticisms.

CHAPTER 9 COGNITIVE DEVELOPMENT IN PRESCHOOL CHILDREN

TEST YOURSELF

1. Which of the following statements describes preoperational children's thought?
   a. They do not confuse appearance and reality.
   b. They may credit inanimate objects with life-like properties.
   c. They do not narrowly focus on one characteristic of a task.
   d. Their thinking is not egocentric.
2. Judy DeLoache (1995) had 2 1/2-year-olds and 3-year-olds watch an adult hide a toy in a full-size room, then asked them to try to find the toy in a scale model of the room. She found that
   a. neither the 2 1/2-year-olds nor the 3-year-olds could find the toy in the scale model.
   b. only the 2 1/2-year-olds could find the toy in the scale model.
   c. only the 3-year-olds could find the toy in the scale model.
   d. both the 2 1/2-year-olds and the 3-year-olds could find the toy in the scale model.
3. DeLoache and her colleagues (1997) hid a toy in a full-size room and then asked 2 1/2-year-olds to find the hidden toy in either a scale model of the room or in a scale model of the room that they had pretended to shrink. They found that 2 1/2-year-olds
   a. could not find the toy in either the "shrinking" room condition or the regular scale model condition.

b. could find the toy in the "shrinking" room condition but not the regular scale model condition.
c. could find the toy in the regular scale model condition but not the "shrinking" room condition.
d. could find the toy in both the regular model and "shrinking" room conditions.

4. When preoperational children are asked to identify different perspectives of model mountains on a table, which of the following characteristics of preoperational thought do they demonstrate?
a. Egocentrism
b. Animism
c. Centration
d. Intellectual realism

5. The preoperational child's confusion of appearance and reality
a. is changed easily with a little training.
b. does not occur when the instructions used in the study are reworded.
c. is present when some materials are used and not present when others are used.
d. is a deep-seated characteristic of thinking at this stage.

6. Many 4-year-olds believe that
a. inanimate objects move by themselves.
b. adopted children will physically resemble their adoptive parents.
c. inanimate objects can grow.
d. the internal parts of animate and inanimate objects are the same.

7. According to theory of mind, at 3 years of age children
a. do not understand that they and other people have desires.
b. do not understand that desires can cause behavior.
c. do not emphasize desires when trying to explain other people's behavior.
d. do not understand that other people's behavior is based on beliefs.

8. Research on attention in preschoolers in which children's focused attention was evaluated while they watched a puppet show or while they engaged in free play, indicated that
a. younger and older preschoolers did not differ in their focused attention in either the puppet show or free play settings.
b. older preschoolers showed more focused attention in the puppet show setting, but did not show more focused attention in the free play setting.
c. older preschoolers showed more focused attention in the free play setting, but did not show more focused attention in the puppet show setting.
d. older preschoolers showed more focused attention in both the free play and puppet show settings.

9. To obtain reliable testimony from preschoolers
a. interviewers should pursue only one explanation for what happened.
b. children should be warned that sometimes interviewers may try to trick them.
c. children should be questioned repeatedly on a single issue.
d. adults should suggest possible events to cue the child's memory.

10. The __________ principle is illustrated by a child who counts a set of Star Wars figures "1, 2, 5, 8...Eight! There are eight Star Wars figures."
a. cardinality
b. stable-order
c. one-to-one
d. addition

11. According to Vygotsky, development is optimal when
a. the child learns independently.
b. a child is guided by someone with more skill.
c. someone with more skill does NOT interfere by trying to structure a task for the child.
d. the amount of assistance given exceeds the amount that the child needs.

12. Private speech
a. eventually becomes inner speech.
b. involves talking aloud to others.
c. is more likely to occur while performing easy tasks than difficult tasks.
d. occurs before children's behavior is regulated by speech from other people.

13. Which of the following statements is *true* regarding the influence of the environment on language development?
a. The frequency of parental speech is not related to the size of a child's vocabulary.
b. Naming objects that are the focus of a child's attention is not related to word learning.
c. Children who are passively exposed to television shows such as cartoons have larger vocabularies than other children.
d. Questioning children while reading to them forces them to identify the meanings of new words.

14. Bilingual children
a. have lower IQ scores than monolingual children.
b. do not understand the fine points of grammar as well as monolingual children.
c. are at a linguistic disadvantage when they begin elementary school.
d. are more likely than monolingual children to understand that words are simply arbitrary symbols.

15. The production of two-word speech
a. often is called telegraphic speech.
b. is haphazard and is not based on any rules.
c. follows rules that are very different from language to language.
d. usually occurs around the first birthday.

16. Children's use of grammatical morphemes is based primarily on
a. learning individual words.
b. the use of rules.
c. inflection.
d. telegraphic speech.

17. Which of the following is an example of overregularization?
a. Mans
b. Women

c. Children's
d. Mice

18. The order in which children acquire grammatical morphemes depends on
a. the complexity of the morpheme with the acquisition of simpler morphemes occurring before that of more complex morphemes.
b. the frequency of occurrence of the morpheme in the language.
c. the frequency with which children's parents use the morpheme.
d. the age at which children begin speaking.

19. Which would occur first in language development?
a. Comprehension of passive sentences
b. Use of negation
c. Use of intonation to indicate a question
d. Use of embedded sentences

20. Which of the following statements reflects how children acquire grammar?
a. Children learn grammar by means of reinforcement and imitation.
b. The human brain is not specialized to process language.
c. Humans seem to be innately prepared to process language and learn grammar.
d. Language can be acquired easily at any time during one's life.

21. Which of the following statements reflects parents' responses to children's speech?
a. The majority of children's grammatical errors go uncorrected by parents.
b. When parents rephrase children's statements they do not correct the grammatical errors.
c. When parents repeat children's statements they do not expand the statements.
d. Parents usually do not continue the conversation following grammatically correct statements by children.

22. Turn taking
a. is not encouraged by parents until after children say their first words.
b. is apparent in preschoolers who expect that a comment will be followed by a response.
c. does not occur spontaneously in conversations between children and adults until after children have entered school.
d. is discouraged when parents take both the speaker and listener roles.

23. When 4-year-olds describe a toy to a 2-year-old, they
a. use fewer attention-getting phrases than they do with an adult listener.
b. use longer sentences than they do with an adult listener.
c. use simpler grammar than they do with an adult listener.
d. do not adjust their speech when talking to a younger child.

24. Which of the following is an implication of Piaget's theory for teaching practices?
a. Teachers should tell children facts that they can absorb passively.
b. Children should be encouraged to look at the consistency of their own thinking and to sort out any inconsistencies.
c. The best teaching experiences are slightly behind a child's current level of thinking.
d. Teachers should construct a child's understanding of the world.

25. Which of the following parents would be most likely to want a preschool that educates the "whole child"?
   a. Parents from China
   b. Parents from Japan
   c. Parents from Brazil
   d. Parents from the United States

26. Compared to economically-disadvantaged children who did not attend Head Start, children who attend a high quality Head Start program are
   a. more likely to be ill.
   b. more likely to graduate from high school.
   c. more likely to repeat a grade in school.
   d. less likely to do well in school.

27. Viewing prosocial television shows
   a. has a much greater impact on children than viewing televised violence.
   b. has a much greater impact on girls than on boys.
   c. is easy to do because there are many television shows that emphasize prosocial behavior.
   d. has no influence on children's prosocial behavior.

28. Compared to infrequent viewers, preschoolers who watch *Sesame Street* regularly
   a. have smaller vocabularies as 5-year-olds.
   b. are less proficient at the targeted academic skills.
   c. adjust to school more readily.
   d. are more likely to be bored in school because they are used to a lot of visual stimulation while learning.

ESSAY QUESTIONS

1. You are the parent of two young children, ages 4 and 6 years. They have been playing outside and they come running inside asking for a drink. All of the drinking glasses in the house, except two, are dirty. One of these glasses is tall and narrow and the other is short and squat. You know that your children will argue with each other if one thinks that the other child is getting more to drink. Based on your knowledge of conservation of liquid in preoperational children, what should you do to avoid an argument? Explain your answer.

2. Your brother, Pretesh, is concerned that his two-year-old daughter's counting ability is well below average. When she counts, his daughter will say, "one, two, c, door...door balls" when counting the four balls in a picture book. What can you tell Pretesh about the mastery of the principles of counting that will reassure him that his daughter's counting ability is fine?

3. You have been watching your friend Deb trying to teach her son Sean how to do a puzzle. Sean has done this puzzle many times and he usually just needs help with the pieces that are in a difficult area that is all black. Deb is trying to help Sean but her instructions would be appropriate for a child who has never done the puzzle before. What can you tell Deb about Vygotsky's theory, in general, and scaffolding, in particular, that might help her teach Sean in more effective ways?

4. Your friend Angelina wants to know what she can do to stimulate her son Mario's language development. What should Angelina do in her interactions with Mario and how should she structure his home environment to maximize his language development?
5. Your friends Kumi and Hugh have a 6-month-old son, Joe. Kumi is a native speaker of Japanese and Hugh is a native speaker of English. They are thinking about raising Joe to be bilingual but they are wondering if there are any benefits or drawbacks to this. What can you tell Kumi and Hugh about the impact of bilingualism on language development?
6. Your friend Chuck does not have a TV in his house because he feels that TV will only have negative effects on his children--they will become more impulsive, they will have shorter attention spans, and they will be less creative. Chuck feels that nothing good can come from TV viewing. What can you tell Chuck about the research on the effects of television on children?

ANSWERS

Multiple Choice

1. b (242)
2. c (245)
3. b (246)
4. a (242)
5. d (245)
6. b (248)
7. d (249)
8. d (250)
9. b (252)
10. a (252)
11. b (253)
12. a (254)
13. d (256)
14. d (258)
15. a (259)
16. b (259)
17. a (260)
18. a (260)
19. c (261)
20. c (261)
21. a (263)
22. b (266)
23. c (267)
24. b (270)
25. d (270)
26. b (273)
27. a (273)
28. c (273)

ESSAY

1. Both of your children are in the preoperational period of cognitive development. You know from your knowledge of Piaget's theory that children who are in the period of preoperational thinking cannot do conservation of liquid tasks. These children will focus narrowly on the height of the liquid without considering the circumference of the container. If you give your children equal amounts of juice but use the tall, thin glass and the short, squat glass, they will center on the height of the juice and will conclude that the child with the tall, narrow glass received more juice than the other child. To avoid an argument, fill the glasses so that the height of the liquid is the same in both glasses. (243)
2. You can reassure your brother that your niece is doing well in the area of counting. Most children begin counting around their second birthday and have mastered the counting principles around age 5 years. Your niece has mastered the one-to-one principle in which she assigns one and only one number name to each object to be counted. She also has mastered the stable-

order principle in which the same names for numbers are used in a consistent order. Your niece also seems to understand that the last number name denotes the number of items in the set (the cardinality principle). In other words, your niece's mastery of counting principles is more advanced than most two-year olds. Tell your brother to relax. Your niece has plenty of time to learn the "real" number names. (252-253)

3. According to Vygotsky's principle of zone of proximal development, Sean will do better on the puzzle if he is assisted by someone who has more puzzle-building expertise than he does. Deb does have more puzzle-building experience so she could be a good teacher. However, according to the concept of scaffolding, a skilled teacher will gauge her instruction to the learner's needs. In other words, a beginner should get more instruction than someone who is close to mastering a task. Sean is close to mastering this puzzle and Deb should stop providing so much instruction and should only provide help on the section where Sean needs help. (253-255)

4. Angelina should speak frequently to Mario. Parents who speak frequently with their children provide their children with more opportunities to learn words. Language development also is fostered when parents name objects or activities that are the focus of a child's attention. Reading books to a child increases the child's encounters with unfamiliar words which leads to an increase in vocabulary. Also, asking Mario questions while reading to him will force him to identify the meanings of new words.

   The type of television shows that Mario watches may influence his language development. Watching television shows like *Sesame Street* in which Mario can actively participate and is challenged to use his emerging language skills probably will lead to improved language development. (256-257)

5. Initially, language development in bilingual children may be slower than that of monolingual children but there are many benefits in the long run. When 1- and 2-year-olds are reared in a bilingual home, their language development often progresses slowly at first because they mix words from both languages. By 3 or 4 years of age, however, children can separate the two languages. By the time they enter school, most bilingual children are as proficient as monolinguals in both languages. During the elementary-school years, most bilingual children have a better understanding of many aspects of language such as understanding fine points of grammar and understanding that words are arbitrary symbols. So, in the long run Joe will not be harmed and should benefit from his bilingual upbringing. (258)

6. Chuck is mostly, but not entirely, correct. Some negative effects are associated with large amounts of television viewing, but some of Chuck's worries are not supported by research. In fact, increased TV viewing per se does not lead to reduced attention, greater impulsivity, reduced task persistence, or increased activity levels. However, the content of TV shows may have negative influences. For example, children who watch impulsive models behave impulsively themselves. As for TV viewing stifling creativity, some studies find no effects on creativity and other studies show more viewing is related to less creativity. On the positive side, children are more likely to engage in prosocial behavior if they see it modeled on TV and children who watch educational programs like *Sesame Street* have larger vocabularies, are more profi-

cient at the targeted academic skills, and adjust more readily to school. Unfortunately, there are many more poor quality television programs than there are prosocial, educational programs. If Chuck monitors what his children watch and he limits their viewing, they could learn some good things from television. (273-274)

Chapter 10
Social Behavior and Personality in Preschool Children

This chapter covers preschool children's understanding of self, their relationships with parents, siblings, and peers, and their efforts to regulate their own behavior.

MODULE
10.1

Self

- *Gender Roles*
- *Gender Identity*
- *Self-Esteem*

SELF

Textbook Learning Objectives

- **What are gender stereotypes? How do they differ for males and females? What do preschoolers know about gender stereotypes?**
- **How do people, children themselves, and biology contribute to children's learning of gender roles?**
- **Do preschool children have high self-esteem?**

TO MASTER THESE LEARNING OBJECTIVES:

1. Know the terms associated with gender stereotypes, gender identity, and self-esteem
2. Know the details of gender stereotypes, gender identity, and self-esteem

Know the Terms Associated with Gender and Self: Match each definition with the correct term

Constricting
Enabling
Expressive
Gender consistency
Gender constancy
Gender identity
Gender labeling
Gender-schema
Gender stability
Gender roles
Gender stereotypes
Instrumental
Purpose
Self-esteem
Social role

1. A set of cultural guidelines for how a person should behave.__________
2. The culturally prescribed behaviors that are considered appropriate for males and females.__________
3. The perception of oneself as either male or female. __________
4. Beliefs about how males and females differ in personality traits, interests, and behaviors.__________
5. Traits that are associated with males that describe individuals who act on the world and influence it.__________
6. Traits that are associated with females that describe emotional functioning and individuals who value personal relationships.__________
7. A person's judgments and feelings about his or her own worth. __________
8. Interactions that are characterized by actions and remarks that tend to support others and sustain social interactions.__________
9. Interactions that are characterized by threatening, contradicting, exaggerating, etc.__________
10. Children's ability to understand that they are either boys or girls and to label themselves correctly.__________
11. Children's understanding that gender is stable throughout development.__________
12. Children's understanding that gender does not change over situations or according to personal wishes.__________
13. This occurs when children understand gender labeling, gender constancy, and gender stability.__________
14. According to this theory, children first decide if an object, activity, or behavior is male or female, then use this information to decide whether they should learn more about the object, activity, or behavior.__________
15. According to Erikson, this occurs when there is a balance between individual initiative and willingness to cooperate with others. __________

Know the Details of Gender Stereotypes

1. T F Instrumental traits are associated with women.
2. T F Expressive traits are associated with men.
3. T F Gender stereotypes are more extreme in America than in many other countries.

4. T F Preschool children think that gender stereotypes are flexible and are not related to behavior.
5. T F According to social learning theorists, children learn gender roles through reinforcement and observational learning.
6. T F Mothers are more likely than fathers to treat sons and daughters differently.
7. T F Children are very accepting of peers who engage in cross-gender play.
8. T F Children select same-sex playmates solely because they are pressured to do so by adults.
9. T F Reluctance to play with members of the opposite sex is restricted to gender-typed games and does not extend to gender-neutral activities.
10. T F The choice of same-sex playmates may occur, in part, because boys' competitive and rough play is aversive to girls.
11. T F Girls' interactions with each other are typically constricting.
12. T F Boys' interactions with each other are typically enabling.
13. T F In general, television portrays women and men in a very stereotyped manner.
14. T F Children who watch a lot of television have more stereotyped views of males and females.
15. T F A preschool boy who believes that he will grow up to be a woman is demonstrating gender stability.
16. T F Interest in gender-typical behavior emerges after children understand gender constancy.
17. T F According to gender-schema theories, children pay more attention to experiences and events that are gender-appropriate.
18. T F How expressive or instrumental a child is depends, in part, on heredity.
19. T F Females who are exposed to large amounts of male hormones during prenatal development do not differ from other females.
20. T F Preschool children have very high levels of self-esteem.

ANSWERS

Key Terms

1. social role (280)
2. gender roles (280)
3. gender identity (282)
4. gender stereotype (280)
5. instrumental (281)
6. expressive (281)
7. self-esteem (280)
8. enabling (284)
9. constricting (284)
10. gender labeling (285)
11. gender stability (285)
12. gender consistency (285)
13. gender constancy (285)
14. gender-schema (286)
15. purpose (288)

Know the Details

1. false (281)
2. false (281)
3. true (281)
4. false (281)
5. true (283)
6. false (283)
7. false (283)
8. false (284)
9. false (284)
10. true (284)
11. false (284)
12. false (284)
13. true (284)
14. true (284)
15. false (285)
16. true (285)
17. true (286)
18. true (287)
19. false (287)
20. true (288

MODULE
10.2

Relationships with Parents

- *The Family as a System*
- *Dimensions and Styles*
- *Parental Behavior*
- *Children's Contributions*
- *Family Configuration*

RELATIONSHIPS WITH PARENTS

Textbook Learning Objectives

- **What is the systems view of family dynamics?**
- **What are the primary dimensions of parenting?**
- **What parental behaviors affect children's development?**
- **How do children help determine how parents rear them?**
- **What role does family configuration play in children's development?**

TO MASTER THESE LEARNING OBJECTIVES:

1. Know the terms associated with parenting
2. Know the details of parenting

Know the Terms Associated with Parenting: Match each definition with the correct term

Authoritarian
Authoritative
Counterimitation
Direct instruction
Disinhibition
Dispensing-family-wisdom
Distant
Formal
Fun-seeking
Indifferent-uninvolved
Indulgent-permissive
Inhibition
Negative reinforcement trap
Punishment
Reinforcement
Surrogate parent
Time-out

1. This type of parenting combines high levels of control with little warmth.__________
2. This type of parenting combines a fair degree of parental control with being warm and responsive to children.__________
3. These parents are warm and caring but exert little control over their children.__________
4. These parents are neither warm nor controlling.__________
5. Telling a child what to do, when to do it, and why. __________
6. Learning what should not be done through observational learning.__________

7. An increase in all behaviors like those observed in others. __________
8. A decrease in the likelihood that an entire class of behaviors will occur. __________
9. Any action that increases the likelihood of the response that it follows.__________
10. Any action that discourages the reoccurrence of the response that it follows.__________
11. Unwittingly reinforcing the behaviors that one wants to discourage.__________
12. A form of punishment in which a misbehaving child must briefly sit alone in a quiet, unstimulating location.__________
13. Grandparents who express strong interest in a grandchild but maintain a hands-off attitude toward rearing the child.__________
14. Grandparents who see themselves as a primary source of fun for their grandchildren but avoid more serious interactions.__________
15. Grandparents who have little contact with children, except as part of holidays or other family celebrations.__________
16. Grandparents who provide information and advice to parents and child alike.__________
17. Grandparents who assume many of the normal roles and responsibilities of a parent.__________

Know the Details of Parenting

1. T F Parents influence their children, but children do not influence their parents.
2. T F Children often have low self-esteem when parents are uninvolved.
3. T F Children are more compliant when their parents are flexible and do not enforce rules consistently.
4. T F Good communication is an effective element of control.
5. T F Views of the "proper" amount of warmth and control that parents should display varies from culture to culture.
6. T F European Americans stress cooperation and collaboration rather than happiness and self-reliance in their children.
7. T F Chinese parents are warmer and less controlling than American parents.
8. T F Authoritarian parents explain rules and encourage discussion.
9. T F Indulgent-permissive parents try to minimize the amount of time spent with their children.
10. T F Children of authoritarian parents have lower self-esteem and are less skilled socially.
11. T F Children of authoritative parents are often impulsive and are easily frustrated.
12. T F Children whose parents use direct instruction and coaching tend to be more socially skilled and to have better relationships with their peers.

13. T F Learning what should not be done is called disinhibition.

14. T F Inhibition occurs when an entire class of behaviors is made less likely.

15. T F Reinforcement decreases the likelihood of a behavior that it follows.

16. T F Punishment works best when it is administered hours after an undesired behavior occurs.

17. T F Punishment teaches new behaviors to replace those that were punished.

18. T F Children often imitate physical punishment.

19. T F Time-out is effective because it interrupts the child's ongoing activity.

20. T F After time-out, parents should explain to the child why she was punished and what she should have done instead.

21. T F Fun-seeking grandparents take on many of the roles and responsibilities of a parent.

22. T F African American grandmothers who live with their daughters and grandchildren frequently adopt the surrogate-parent style of grandparenting.

23. T F African American children who live in extended families are better off than those who live in single-parent families.

24. T F Children raised by gay and lesbian parents are very different from children raised by heterosexual parents.

ANSWERS

Key Terms

1. authoritarian (293)
2. authoritative (293)
3. indulgent-permissive (293)
4. indifferent-uninvolved (293)
5. direct instruction (294)
6. counterimitation (294)
7. disinhibition (294)
8. inhibition (295)
9. reinforcement (295)
10. punishment (295)
11. negative reinforcement trap (295)
12. time-out (296)
13. formal (297)
14. fun-seeking (297)
15. distant (297)
16. dispensing-family-wisdom (298)
17. surrogate parent (298)

Know the Details

1. false (290)
2. true (291)
3. false (292)
4. true (292)
5. true (292)
6. false (292)
7. false (293)
8. false (293)
9. false (293)
10. true (293)
11. true (293)
12. true (294)
13. false (294)
14. true (295)
15. false (295)
16. false (295)
17. false (295)
18. true (296)
19. true (296)
20. true (297)
21. false (297)
22. true (298)
23. true (298)
24. false (299)

MODULE
10.3

Relationships with Siblings and Peers

- *Sibling Relationships*
- *Peer Relationships*

RELATIONSHIPS WITH SIBLINGS AND PEERS

Textbook Learning Objectives

- **How do firstborn, laterborn, and only children differ?**
- **What determines how well siblings get along?**
- **How do preschool children play together? How do parents influence their play?**

TO MASTER THESE LEARNING OBJECTIVES:

1. Know the details of sibling relationships and peer relationships

Know the Details of Sibling Relationships and Peer Relationships

1. T F Parents have more realistic expectations and are more relaxed in their discipline with laterborn children.
2. T F Firstborns are more popular with their peers and are more innovative than laterborns.
3. T F Laterborns are more likely to go to college and have higher scores on intelligence tests than firstborns.
4. T F Only children have lower levels of intelligence and are more immature than children with siblings.
5. T F Children may revert to more childish behavior when a younger sibling is born.
6. T F When siblings are born, fathers become less involved with older children.
7. T F Older siblings are a source of care and comfort for younger siblings when they are distressed or upset.
8. T F The basic pattern of sibling interactions remains fairly stable.
9. T F Sibling relationships are more harmonious between siblings of the opposite sex than between siblings of the same sex.
10. T F Sibling relationships improve as the younger sibling reaches adolescence.
11. T F Siblings get along better when they believe that their parents don't have favorites.
12. T F Sibling relationships are better when parents get along with each other.
13. T F When siblings fight, parents should not interfere and should let them work things out on their own.
14. T F Throughout the preschool years, parallel play becomes less common.
15. T F The goal of bullying is to intimidate, harass, or humiliate other children.
16. T F Throughout the preschool years make-believe play becomes more sophisticated.
17. T F Family roles and everyday activities are two favorite themes of make-believe play for European American children.

18. T F Korean American children are more polite and are more likely to strive for harmony during make-believe play than are European American children.

19. T F Children who spend more time in make-believe play tend to be more advanced in language, memory, and reasoning.

20. T F Imaginary playmates are a sign of possible developmental problems.

21. T F Children with imaginary companions have a harder time distinguishing fantasy from reality.

22. T F Wandering aimlessly is one type of unhealthy solitary play.

23. T F Parents and teachers should not be worried about preschoolers who spend much time hovering, watching other children play.

24. T F Children play less cooperatively when parents interfere in their play.

25. T F A child's relationship with his parents may provide an internal working model for all future social relationships.

ANSWERS

Know the Details

1. true (301)
2. false (301)
3. false (301)
4. false (301)
5. true (302)
6. false (302)
7. true (302)
8. true (302)
9. false (303)
10. true (303)
11. true (303)
12. true (303)
13. false (303)
14. true (304)
15. true (304)
16. true (305)
17. false (305)
18. true (305)
19. true (305)
20. false (305)
21. false (306)
22. true (306)
23. false (306)
24. false (306)
25. true (306)

MORAL DEVELOPMENT: LEARNING TO CONTROL ONE'S BEHAVIOR

MODULE
10.4

Moral Development: Learning to Control One's Behavior

- *Beginnings of Self-Control*
- *Parental Influences*
- *Temperamental Influences on Self-Control*
- *Improving Self-Control*
- *Learning About Moral Rules*

Textbook Learning Objectives

- **When does self-control begin and how does it change as children develop?**
- **What factors influence children's ability to maintain self-control?**
- **What strategies can children use to improve their self-control?**
- **When do preschoolers begin to understand that moral rules are different from other rules?**

TO MASTER THESE LEARNING OBJECTIVES:

1. Know the details of the development of self-control

Know the Details of the Development of Self-Control

1. T F Self-control is the ability to rise above immediate pressures and not give in to impulse.
2. T F Around the first birthday, infants become aware of the fact that others impose demands on them and they must react accordingly.
3. T F Children are not capable of self-regulation until about 5 years of age.
4. T F Self-control is achieved gradually throughout the elementary-school years.
5. T F Most children show no consistency across different tasks that measure self-control.
6. T F Children who showed greater self-control as 4-year-olds had more self-control, were more attentive, were better able to plan, and had higher SAT scores as 15- to 18-year-olds.
7. T F The results of Bandura and Mischel's study indicated that adult modeling of self-control does not influence children's self-control.
8. T F Children with very strict parents show more self-control than other children.
9. T F Parents who encourage their children to be independent and to make their own decisions have children with less self-control.
10. T F Emotional toddlers and preschoolers show less self-control than other children.
11. T F For fearful children, self-control is associated with a mother's gentle discipline.
12. T F Children who develop concrete ways of resisting temptation (e.g., singing, reminding oneself of the rules, etc.) are more likely to be successful at resisting temptation.
13. T F Social conventions are designed to protect people and are not arbitrary.

ANSWERS

Know the Details

1. true (308)	6. true (310)	11. true (313)
2. true (308)	7. false (311)	12. true (314)
3. false (309)	8. false (311)	13. false (314)
4. true (309)	9. false (311)	
5. false (309)	10. true (312)	

SUMMARY

MODULE 13.1: SELF

Instrumental
Expressive

Gender Roles. __________ traits describe individuals acting on the world and are usually associated with males. __________ traits describe individuals who value interpersonal relationships and are usually associated with females. By the end of the preschool years, children have begun to learn some of the traits typically associated with males and females. They tend to view gender stereotypes __________. rigidly

Gender Identity. Parents treat sons and daughters similarly, except in gender-related behavior. __________ may be particularly important in teaching about gender, because they are more likely to treat sons and daughters differently. Peers influence gender-role learning by __________ cross-gender play. Peers also influence gender roles because children play almost exclusively with same-sex peers. Television depicts men and women in a __________ fashion and children who watch television often are likely to have very stereotyped views of men and women. According to Kohlberg's theory, children gradually learn that gender is stable over time and cannot be changed according to personal wishes. After children understand gender __________, they begin to learn gender-typical behavior. According to gender-schema theory, children learn about gender by __________ to behaviors of members of their own sex and ignoring behaviors of members of the other sex. Biology influences some aspects of gender roles, a view that is supported by studies of twins and by research on females exposed to __________ during prenatal development.

Fathers
discouraging
stereotyped
constancy
paying attention
male hormones

Self-Esteem. Preschool children's self-esteem is typically assessed by asking them whether they are more like a hypothetical child (or puppet) who is, for example, popular, or more like one who is unpopular. Self-esteem is very __________ during the preschool years. high

MODULE 10.2: RELATIONSHIPS WITH PARENTS

The Family as a System. According to the systems approach, the family consists of interacting elements--parents and children __________ each other. The family itself is influenced by other social systems, such as neighborhoods and religious organizations. influence

Dimensions and Styles. One dimension of parenting is the degree of parental __________. Children clearly benefit from warm, caring parents. Another dimension is control. Neither __________ nor __________ control is desirable. Effective parental control involves setting appropriate standards and enforcing them. Combining warmth and control yields four parental styles: (a) __________ parents are controlling but uninvolved, (b) __________ parents are controlling but responsive to their children, (c) __________ parents are loving but exert little control, and (d) __________ parents are neither warm nor controlling. Authoritative parenting is usually best for children's cognitive and social development.

warmth
too much, too little
authoritarian
authoritative
indulgent-permissive
indifferent-uninvolved

Parental Behavior. Parents influence development by direct instruction and coaching. In addition, parents serve as models for their children, who sometimes imitate parents' behavior directly; sometimes children behave in ways that are similar to what they have seen (__________), and sometimes in ways that are opposite of what they've seen (counterimitation). Parents also use feedback to influence children's behavior. Sometimes parents fall into the negative reinforcement trap in which they inadvertently reinforce behaviors that they want to __________. Punishment is effective when it is prompt, __________, accompanied by an expla-

disinhibition
discourage
consistent

nation, and delivered by a person with whom the child has a warm relationship. Punishment has limited value because it suppresses behaviors but does not elimi-
Time-out nate them ,and it often has side effects. __________ is one useful form of punishment.

Children's Contributions. Parenting is influenced by characteristics of children themselves. Over time, families develop routine ways of interacting, which can be harmful if based largely on negative mutual influences.

Family Configuration. Child rearing is influenced by culture and family configu-
controlling ration. Compared to American parents, Chinese parents are more __________
and less affectionate. In African American families, grandmothers often live with
their daughters, an arrangement that eases the cost burden of housing and child
children care and benefits __________ because grandmothers can play an active role in
child rearing. Research on gay and lesbian parents suggests that they are more
similar to heterosexual parents than they are different and that their children
much like develop __________ children reared by heterosexual couples.

MODULE 10.3: RELATIONSHIPS WITH SIBLINGS AND PEERS

Firstborn, Laterborn, and Only Children. Firstborn children often are more intelligent and more likely to go to college but laterborn children are more popular and
innovative more __________. Only children are comparable to children with siblings on
achievement most dimensions and better off on some, such as __________ and autonomy.

Qualities of Sibling Relationships. The birth of a sibling can be stressful for older
children, particularly when parents ignore their older child's needs. Siblings get
same sex along better when they are of the __________, believe that parents treat them
adolescence similarly, enter __________, and have parents who get along well.

Make-believe *Peer Relationships.* __________ play is also common and, in addition to being
fun, promotes cognitive development and lets children examine frightening topics
in a nonthreatening way. Most forms of solitary play are harmless. Parents foster
mediating children's play by acting as skilled playmates, __________ disputes, and coaching
social skills.

MODULE 10.4 MORAL DEVELOPMENT: LEARNING TO CONTROL ONE'S BEHAVIOR

Beginnings of Self-Control. At 1 year, infants are first aware that others
impose demands __________ on them; by 3 years, youngsters can devise plans to regulate their
school-age behavior. During the __________ years children are better able to control their
behavior. Children differ in their self- control, but individuals are fairly consistent
consistent across tasks and these differences are moderately __________ across time.
Preschoolers with good self-control tend to become adolescents with good self-control.

Parental Influences. When children observe adults who delay gratification, they are
more __________ likely to delay gratification themselves. Similarly, when children

observe adults who show little self-control, they are likely to show __________ self-control themselves. Children who have the best self-control tend to have parents who do not use harsh punishment and who encourage their children to be __________ and make their own decisions.

little
independent

Temperamental Influences on Self-Control. Temperament helps determine how parents influence their children's self-control. With temperamentally fearful children, __________ are effective; with fearless children, parents should appeal to the __________ relationship.

gentle discipline
attachment

Improving Self-control. Children are better able to regulate their own behavior when they have plans to help them to remember the importance of the goal and to __________ them from tempting objects.

distract

Learning About Moral Rules. The roots of moral reasoning emerge in the preschool years, when children distinguish moral rules from __________, distinguish lies from mistakes, and show signs of guilt.

social conventions

CHAPTER 10 SOCIAL BEHAVIOR AND PERSONALITY IN PRESCHOOL CHILDREN

TEST YOURSELF

1. Which of the following is an instrumental trait?
  a. Independence
  b. Emotionality
  c. Kindness
  d. Awareness of others' feelings

2. Which of the following is an expressive trait?
  a. Self-confidence
  b. Mechanical aptitude
  c. Devotion to others
  d. Dominance

3. Cross-cultural studies of gender stereotypes have shown that
  a. gender stereotypes are the same in all countries.
  b. gender stereotypes are not influenced by one's culture.
  c. Americans have more extreme gender stereotypes than people in other countries.
  d. Americans have less extreme gender stereotypes than people in other countries.

4. Children
  a. have little knowledge of gender stereotypes when they enter elementary school.
  b. are more likely to ignore stereotypes when judging whether hypothetical children will play with masculine or feminine toys.

c. don't have adult-like knowledge of gender stereotypes until they are teenagers.
d. consider gender stereotypes to be binding guidelines for behavior for all boys and girls.

5. According to social learning theorists, children learn gender roles through
a. observational learning and reinforcement.
b. by understanding gender constancy.
c. by paying more attention to gender-appropriate experiences and events.
d. prenatal exposure to sex hormones.

6. Fathers and mothers differ in the socialization of gender in their children because
a. mothers are more likely to encourage gender-related play.
b. mothers are more likely to treat their children in gender-typed ways.
c. fathers are more likely to respond to the individual needs of each child.
d. fathers are more likely to push their sons and accept dependence in their daughters.

7. Children
a. are very accepting of cross-gender play.
b. choose same-sex playmates because they are pressured to do so by adults.
c. resist parents' efforts to get them to play with members of the opposite sex.
d. only show reluctance to play with members of the opposite sex in gender-typed play.

8. Which of the following is correct of boys' and girls' play?
a. Boys' play is rougher and more competitive than girls' play.
b. Girls tend to be more dominating in their interactions.
c. In boys' interactions, actions and remarks tend to support others and to sustain the interaction.
d. In girls' interactions, one partner typically tries to emerge as the victor.

9. "When you grow up, will you be a mommy or a daddy?" is a question that addresses
a. gender stability.
b. gender constancy.
c. gender labeling.
d. gender consistency.

10. According to Martin and Halverson's gender-schema theory, children learn
a. gender roles through reinforcement and punishment.
b. gender-appropriate behavior after achieving gender constancy.
c. gender-appropriate behavior by paying attention to experiences and events that are gender-appropriate.
d. gender roles through prenatal exposure to sex hormones.

11. Support for biological influences on gender differences come from the fact that
a. fraternal twins are more similar in terms of instrumental and expressive traits than identical twins.
b. females who experience prenatal exposure to male hormones prefer masculine activities.
c. females who experience prenatal exposure to male hormones prefer female playmates.

d. females who experience prenatal exposure to male hormones do not differ from other females.

12. At which age would you be most likely to find the highest levels of self-esteem?
a. Preschool years
b. Early elementary-school years
c. Late elementary-school years
d. Junior high years

13. According to the systems view of families,
a. parents influence their children, both directly and indirectly, but children do not influence their parents.
b. a family's neighborhood can affect family dynamics.
c. parents influence their children directly, but not indirectly.
d. a family's culture does not influence family dynamics.

14. Which of the following statements reflects good parenting practices?
a. Parents should exercise little control over their children.
b. Parents should be flexible and not enforce their rules consistently.
c. Parents should not explain their rules.
d. Parents should set standards that are appropriate for their child's age.

15. Parents who lay down rules for their children to follow without argument are showing which style of parenting?
a. Authoritarian
b. Authoritative
c. Indulgent-permissive
d. Indifferent-uninvolved

16. Authoritative parents
a. exert restrictive control over their children.
b. are firm but warm and responsive to their children.
c. exert very little control over their children.
d. are not involved with their children.

17. Children of authoritarian parents
a. have high grades in school.
b. have high levels of self-esteem.
c. are the most likely to be involved in misconduct at school.
d. are less skilled socially.

18. Praising a child for studying is an example of
a. punishment.
b. counterimitation.
c. reinforcement.
d. inhibition.

19. A child who sees his sister being punished for stealing a cookie from the cookie jar will be less likely to steal a cookie himself. This is an example of
a. disinhibition.
b. counterimitation.
c. reinforcement.
d. negative reinforcement trap.

20. Punishment
  a. should be administered hours after an undesired behavior occurs.
  b. teaches children new, more acceptable behaviors.
  c. often makes children angry over the punishment so that they ignore why they are being punished.
  d. is not related to greater aggression in children.

21. Which parents would you expect to show the most warmth and the least amount of control?
  a. Parents in China
  b. Parents in Taiwan
  c. European American parents
  d. Parents who emigrated from Taiwan to the United States

22. Tina's grandfather is interested in her activities but he is not interested in getting involved in her rearing. Which style of grandparenting is Tina's grandfather showing?
  a. Fun-seeking
  b. Formal
  c. Distant
  d. Dispensing-family-wisdom

23. Children of lesbian mothers
  a. have lower grades in school than children of heterosexual mothers.
  b. have more psychological problems than children of heterosexual mothers.
  c. are less likely to identify with their own gender.
  d. resemble children of heterosexual parents in many domains.

24. Which of the following is *true* of firstborn children compared to laterborn children?
  a. Firstborns have lower scores on intelligence tests.
  b. Firstborns are more willing to conform to parents' and adults' requests.
  c. Firstborns are more innovative.
  d. Firstborns are more popular with peers.

25. Compared to children with siblings, research has shown that only children
  a. have lower grades.
  b. are more immature.
  c. are more dependent upon parents.
  d. show more leadership.

26. Research on sibling relationships has found that
  a. relationships are more harmonious when siblings are of the opposite sex than when they are of the same sex.
  b. relationships become worse as the younger sibling enters adolescence.
  c. relationships are less harmonious when children believe that their parents have "favorites."
  d. conflict between siblings is not related to conflict between the parents.

27. Make-believe play
  a. is not related to the values of a child's culture.
  b. is not a common part of preschoolers' play.
  c. allows children to explore topics that frighten them.
  d. does not involve imaginary companions.

28. Preschoolers with imaginary companions
   a. have fewer real friends than other preschoolers.
   b. are more sociable than other preschoolers.
   c. cannot distinguish fantasy and reality as well as other preschoolers.
   d. have developmental problems.

29. Solitary play
   a. indicates a problem if it consists of wandering aimlessly around the room.
   b. is not a problem if children hover and watch other children play.
   c. such as drawing, assembling blocks, or solving puzzles are signs of social maladjustment.
   d. is always an indication of unhealthy peer relations.

30. Which of the following is *true* of the influence that parents have on peer relationships?
   a. Parental mediation during play leads to more cooperative play and longer play between children.
   b. The quality of the child's attachment to parents is not related to the child's quality of interaction with peers.
   c. Parents have a direct influence, but not an indirect influence, on peer interactions.
   d. Parents' use of more advanced forms of play usually does not influence their children's level of play.

31. According to Claire Kopp, the first phase in the mastery of self-control occurs when
   a. children internalize some of the external controls placed on them.
   b. children become capable of self-regulation.
   c. children realize that others impose demands on them and expect them to react accordingly.
   d. children can delay gratification.

32. In a longitudinal study of self-control, researchers found that self-control in 4-year-olds
   a. was negatively related to their self-control as teenagers (i.e., 4-year-olds with the most self-control had the least self-control as teenagers).
   b. was positively related to their self-control as teenagers (i.e., 4-year-olds with the greatest self-control had the greatest self-control as teenagers).
   c. was not related to their self-control as teenagers.
   d. was not stable over time.

33. Bandura and Mischel's study on the effects of modeling on delay of gratification in children showed that
   a. children who saw models delay gratification were influenced to delay gratification themselves.
   b. children who saw models delay gratification were less likely to delay gratification.
   c. children's observations of models affected their behavior only if the behavior of the model matched the usual behavior of the child in a similar situation.
   d. impulsive children imitated models who delayed gratification but children with self-control did not imitate the models who chose immediate gratification.

34. Which of the following statements is *true* regarding the relation of parenting and self-control?
a. Children with very strict parents have higher levels of self-control.
b. Children whose parents do not encourage independence have greater self-control.
c. Children whose parents encourage them to make their own decisions have more self-control.
d. Children whose parents "overcontrol" them have higher levels of self-control.

35. Studies of child temperament, parental discipline, and self-control indicate that
a. fearful children are more likely to be compliant when their parents use gentle discipline.
b. fearless children are more likely to be compliant when their parents use gentle discipline.
c. the type of parental discipline did not matter with fearful children because they were usually compliant.
d. child temperament is not related to compliance and self-control.

36. Children who are most likely to resist temptation
a. frequently look at the tempting object.
b. remind themselves of rules against touching the tempting object.
c. do not try to divert attention from the object of temptation.
d. do not have a concrete way of handling the temptation.

37. Which of the following would be a violation of a moral rule?
a. Stealing from someone
b. Using your fingers to eat instead of silverware
c. Not paying attention at school
d. Calling your teacher by his first name

ESSAY QUESTIONS

1. Jeannie is eight-months pregnant with her first child. She has little use for traditional gender roles and plans for her son or daughter not to view the world in gender-related terms. What can you tell Jeannie about some things that she can do to help achieve her goal and the influence of other factors in the development of gender stereotypes?

2. Your 6-year-old niece does not like to play with boys. Your brother thinks that this is okay but his wife thinks that your niece should play with both boys and girls. What can you tell your sister-in-law about gender differences in styles of interaction and how that is related to the selection of same-sex playmates?

3. You and your spouse want to use a consistent style of parenting in raising your son. Your spouse was raised in an authoritarian home where the children did as they were told without questioning. You were raised in an authoritative home in which your parents had firm rules but they could be flexible about these rules. Based on what you know about the outcomes of children from authoritarian and authoritative homes, which style of parenting would be the best for you and your spouse to choose?

4. Your sister-in-law recently announced that she is a lesbian and she is divorcing your brother. Your sister-in-law would like to have custody of their two children but your brother does not want his children raised by a lesbian. What can you tell your brother about the development of children whose parents are gay or lesbian that might make him feel better about the situation?

5. Your friend Shabrisha is concerned because her 7-year-old daughter and 5-year-old son seem to fight constantly. Shabrisha's daughter has always been temperamental and Shabrisha thinks that the fighting may be her fault. Shabrisha remembers being very close to her sister when they were children and she thinks that her own children might be unusual because they fight so much. What can you tell Shabrisha about the factors that are related to harmonious relationships between siblings?
6. You and your spouse have one wonderful daughter and you are trying to decide if you should have another child. On the one hand, you are quite content with your daughter. On the other hand, your spouse is afraid that your daughter will be selfish, spoiled, and self-centered if she is an only child. Based on what you know about only children, what would you tell your spouse?
7. Lyndon is an 8-year-old boy who wants to have everything now! He seems unable to wait for anything. For example, although his parents have encouraged him to save a small portion of his weekly allowance, Lyndon invariably spends all of it, usually on the day that he receives it. How might his parents encourage Lyndon to exercise self-control and delay gratification?

ANSWERS

Multiple Choice

1. a (281)
2. c (281)
3. c (281)
4. d (281)
5. a (283)
6. d (283)
7. c (283)
8. a (284)
9. a (285)
10. c (286)
11. b (287)
12. a (288)
13. b (290)
14. d (291)
15. a (293)
16. b (293)
17. d (293)
18. c (295)
19. b (294)
20. c (295)
21. c (293)
22. b (297)
23. d (299)
24. b (300)
25. d (301)
26. c (303)
27. c (304)
28. b (305)
29. a (306)
30. a (306)
31. c (308)
32. b (310)
33. a (311)
34. c (311)
35. a (312)
36. b (313)
37. a (314)

Essay

1. First, Jeannie should be aware of the fact that many parents encourage gender-typed play. Fathers are more likely than mothers to encourage gender-typed behavior and to treat sons and daughters differently. Jeannie and her husband will need to make a conscious effort to model chores and behaviors that are not gender-bound. Also, they should base decisions about their

child's toys and activities on the child's interests not the child's sex. Second, Jeannie also should be aware of the fact that in spite of her best efforts her child will probably adhere to some traditional gender-related behavior and stereotypes. Parental influence on gender roles is minimal because children also are affected by influences outside of the family such as their peers and television. Other children are very critical of children who engage in cross-gender play. This is particularly true of boys who engage in feminine activities. Children also tend to play with same-sex peers. In general, television's portrayal of men and women is very stereoptyped and children who watch a lot of television have more stereotyped views of men and women than children who don't watch as much television. So, Jeannie and her husband should limit the amount of exposure that their child has to gender stereotypes on TV. (282-285)

2. In many cultures, girls generally play with girls and boys play with boys. Even when parents encourage boys and girls to play with each other most children will resist. Part of this resistance comes from the fact that boys and girls have very different styles of interacting with peers. Girls' remarks and behaviors tend to provide support for each other. Boys' behavior tends to be rougher and boys try to dominate each other by using intimidation, threats, and exaggeration. When boys and girls interact, girls find that their enabling style is ineffective with boys. So, your niece is not unusual and your sister-in-law's efforts to get her to play with boys will probably not be very successful. (284)
3. The authoritative style of parenting is consistently associated with positive developmental outcomes. Children of authoritative parents have higher self-esteem, are more self-reliant, and are friendlier. In contrast, children of authoritarian parents have lower self-esteem, are less self-reliant, and are less skilled socially. Based on the research, authoritative parenting is the best style of parenting to choose. (293)
4. More than a million children in the United States have a gay or lesbian parent. Most of the studies of these children have been done with children who were born in heterosexual marriages that ended when one parent revealed his or her homosexuality. In general, the development of children of gay or lesbian parents does not differ from the development of children of heterosexual parents. Preschool children of gay or lesbian parents identify with their own gender and develop typical gender-based activities, friends, preferences, and interests. On other dimensions, children of gay and lesbian parents do not differ in terms of intelligence, social skill, moral reasoning, or self-concept. Based on the research, your brother should be assured that his children are no more likely to develop problems with a lesbian mother than with a heterosexual mother. (298-299)
5. The first factor that is related to the quality of sibling relationships is gender. Same-sex siblings tend to have better relationships than opposite sex siblings. The second factor is temperament. Siblings tend to have better relationships when neither child is emotionally temperamental. Third, if children believe that their parents do not have favorites they will have a better relationship with each other. Fourth, relationships generally improve as the younger sibling approaches adolescence. Fifth, less conflict between parents is related to less conflict between siblings. Based on these factors, Shabrisha's children already have two factors working against a harmonious relationship: they are

a mixed-sex pair and one of them is emotionally temperamental. Shabrisha also should look at her treatment of the children to see if she plays favorites and at the quality of her relationship with her husband. Even if there is nothing that she can do, the sibling relationship should improve as her son approaches adolescence. (302-303)

6. The research shows that only children are better off in many ways than children with siblings. In no case were only children worse off in comparisons of achievement, intelligence, and character. In fact, only children had higher levels of achievement, higher intelligence, greater leadership, autonomy, and maturity. Only children seemed to benefit considerably from a lifetime of exclusive parental attention. (301)

7. First, Lyndon's parents might want to examine their own behavior. Are they overly strict and controlling with Lyndon or do they encourage independence and independent decision-making? Self-control is higher in children whose parents encourage independence and independent decision-making. Children of parents who are very strict and controlling do not internalize self-control. Second, are Lyndon's parents good models of self-control? If not, they should change their behavior if they want to be good models for Lyndon. If they are modeling self-control, they should provide additional models of delay of gratification for Lyndon to observe. Third, during the waiting period while Lyndon is delaying gratification, they can help Lyndon wait by providing distractions and by helping him find ways not to think about the things that he wants to buy. (311; 312-314)

Chapter 11
Physical Development in School-Age Children

Module 11.1 *Growth of the Body*

Module 11.2 *Motor Development*

Module 11.3 *Children with Special Challenges*

This chapter examines different aspects of physical growth, growing motor skills, and different challenges to physical development that face some children.

GROWTH OF THE BODY

MODULE
11.1

Growth of the Body

- *Physical Growth*
- *Nutrition*
- *Tooth Development*
- *Vision*

Textbook Learning Objectives

- **How much do school-age children grow?**
- **What are elementary-school children's nutritional needs? What are the best ways to approach malnutrition and obesity?**
- **When do children's primary teeth begin to come in?**
- **What vision problems are common in school-age children?**

TO MASTER THESE LEARNING OBJECTIVES:

1. Know the terms associated with physical growth
2. Know the details of physical growth

Know the Terms Associated with Physical Growth: Match each definition with the correct term

Basal metabolic rate
Myopia
Malocclusion

1. The speed at which the body consumes calories. __________
2. This occurs when the upper and lower teeth don't meet properly. __________
3. This occurs when the lens of the eye projects images of distant objects in front of the retina instead of on it, which means the objects look fuzzy instead of sharp. __________

Know the Details of Physical Growth

1. T F Most of the increase in height during the elementary-school years comes from an increase in the length of the trunk.
2. T F Boys and girls are about the same size for most of the elementary-school years.
3. T F Boys are more likely to enter puberty before girls.
4. T F African American children tend to be taller than both European American and Asian American children.
5. T F Growth hormone therapy usually makes short children taller as adults.
6. T F Breakfast should provide about one-fourth of a child's daily calories.
7. T F Children who don't eat breakfast often have difficulty paying attention in school.
8. T F Children who receive free or reduced-price meals at school tend to do better in school.
9. T F Obesity usually does not affect a child's self-esteem.
10. T F Adopted children and adolescents' weights are related to the weights of their adoptive parents and not to the weights of their biological parents.
11. T F During the preschool years, internal control of eating is replaced gradually with external signals.
12. T F The most effective way for obese children to lose weight is to involve the entire family.
13. T F Long-lasting weight loss is more likely to occur when parents are involved in their children's dieting.
14. T F Children lose their first primary tooth at around 11 years.
15. T F Once they begin to lose their primary teeth, children lose about 4 teeth per year.
16. T F In the United States, very few children and adolescents are cavity-free.
17. T F Malocclusion can be caused by thumb sucking.
18. T F Myopia usually emerges between the ages of 5 and 8 years.
19. T F Identical twins are more likely than fraternal twins to be myopic.
20. T F Children who spend more time doing activities that draw upon near vision are more likely to become myopic.

ANSWERS

Key Terms

1. basal metabolic rate (324)
2. malocclusion (326)
3. myopia (327)

Know the Details

1. false (322)
2. true (322)
3. false (323)
4. true (323)
5. false (323)
6. true (324)
7. true (324)
8. true (324)
9. false (324)
10. false (324)
11. true (325)
12. true (325)
13. true (325)
14. false (325)
15. true (325)
16. false (326)
17. true (326)
18. false (327)
19. true (327)
20. true (327)

MODULE
11.2

Motor Development

- *Growth of Motor Skills*
- *Physical Fitness*
- *Participating in Sports*
- *Accidents*

MOTOR DEVELOPMENT

Textbook Learning Objectives

- **How do motor skills improve during the elementary-school years? Do boys and girls differ in their motor skills?**
- **Are American children physically fit?**
- **What are the benefits of participating in sports? What are the optimal circumstances for children to participate?**
- **What kinds of accidents are common in school-age children and how can they be prevented?**

TO MASTER THESE LEARNING OBJECTIVES:

1. Know the details of motor development

Know the Details of Motor Development

1. T F Girls tend to have better handwriting than do boys.
2. T F Boys tend to be better than girls at gross-motor tasks that involve flexibility and balance, such as tumbling.
3. T F Boys' bodies have more muscle and less fat than girls' bodies.
4. T F Girls often have fewer opportunities to practice gross-motor skills such as running, throwing, and catching.
5. T F Almost all U.S. school children can meet fitness standards on fitness tests.
6. T F Children spend nearly half of their time in physical education classes standing around rather than exercising.

7. T F Boys are more likely than girls to participate in sports because it enhances their self-esteem.

8. T F Boys are more likely than girls to gain social status by participating in sports.

9. T F Children develop better skills when their coaches emphasize winning.

10. T F The most common cause of death for school-age children in the United States is an accident involving an automobile.

11. T F By modeling behavior such as fastening one's seat belt or wearing a bike helmet, parents make their children more safety-conscious.

12. T F Parents can help prevent accidents by realistically assessing their own child's skills.

ANSWERS

Know the Details

1. true (328)	**5.** false (330)	**9.** false (332)
2. false (329)	**6.** true (331)	**10.** true (333)
3. true (329)	**7.** false (331)	**11.** true (333)
4. true (329)	**8.** true (331)	**12.** true (333)

CHILDREN WITH SPECIAL CHALLENGES

MODULE 11.3

Children with Special Challenges

- *Children with Learning Disabilities*
- *Attention Deficit Hyperactivity Disorder*
- *Children with Mental Retardation*

Textbook Learning Objectives

- **What are learning disabilities?**
- **What is attention deficit hyperactivity disorder?**
- **What are the different forms of mental retardation?**

TO MASTER THESE LEARNING OBJECTIVES

1. Know the terms associated with special children
2. Know the details associated with special children

Know the Terms Associated with Special Children: Match each definition with the correct term

Attention deficit hyperactivity disorder
Familial
Learning disability
Mental retardation
Organic

1. This occurs in someone of normal intelligence who has difficulty mastering an academic subject and whose difficulties cannot be explained by other conditions such as sensory impairment or inadequate instruction.__________
2. __________ is a condition in which a child exhibits overactivity, inattention, and/or impulsivity.
3. The condition of being substantially below average in intelligence and having problems adapting to an environment that emerges before the age of 18 years.__________

4. Mental retardation that is caused by specific biological or physical problems.__________
5. Mental retardation that simply represents the lower end of the normal distribution.__________

Know the Details Associated with Special Children

1. T F Many distinct learning disabilities exist.
2. T F Children with reading disabilities often benefit from extensive instruction on the connections between letters and their sounds.
3. T F All learning disabilities seem to have similar causes and treatments.
4. T F Diagnosing learning disability is not difficult.
5. T F More girls than boys are diagnosed with ADHD.
6. T F Children with ADHD often act before thinking.
7. T F Children with ADHD often are unusually energetic, fidgety, and unable to keep still.
8. T F All children with ADHD show the same pattern of symptoms.
9. T F Children with ADHD do not have normal levels of intelligence.
10. T F ADHD is caused by eating too much sugar.
11. T F Identical twins are more likely to both have ADHD than fraternal twins.
12. T F ADHD is often treated with stimulant drugs.
13. T F Parents of ADHD children who were trained to reinforce attention and compliance and who effectively punish inattention had children who showed fewer symptoms of ADHD.
14. T F In addition to drug treatment, children need to learn to regulate their behavior and attention.
15. T F Organic mental retardation is the most common form of retardation.
16. T F Down syndrome is the most common form of organic mental retardation.
17. T F Familial retardation usually is more severe than organic mental retardation.
18. T F The most severe forms of mental retardation make up the majority of all cases of retardation.
19. T F Moderately retarded individuals usually cannot dress or feed themselves.
20. T F Mildly retarded individuals can learn job skills and lead independent lives.

ANSWERS

Key Terms

1. learning disability (335)
2. attention deficit hyperactivity disorder (336)
3. mental retardation (338)
4. organic mental retardation (338)
5. familial mental retardation (338)

Know the Details

1. true (335)
2. true (336)
3. false (335)
4. false (336)
5. false (336)
6. true (336)
7. true (336)
8. false (336)
9. false (337)
10. false (337)
11. true (337)
12. true (338)
13. true (338)
14. true (338)
15. false (338)
16. true (338)
17. false (339)
18. false (339)
19. false (339)
20. true (339)

SUMMARY

MODULE 11.1: GROWTH OF THE BODY

Physical Growth. Elementary-school children grow at a steady pace, more so in their __________ than in their __________. Boys and girls tend to be about the __________ for much of these years, but there are large individual differences and ethnic differences. Some children receive growth hormone because their bodies do not produce enough growth hormone naturally for normal growth. Other children with adequate natural growth hormone also receive synthetic growth hormone, but this practice is __________ by scientists and health-care professionals.

legs, trunk
same size
discouraged

Nutrition. School-age children need approximately 2400 calories daily, preferably drawn from each of the five food groups. Children need to eat breakfast because this meal should provide approximately __________ of their daily calories and, without breakfast, they often have trouble __________ in school. Many children living in poverty do not eat breakfast and do not receive adequate nutrition overall. Programs for free and reduced-price meals are often available for these children but sometimes their parents do not realize that their children are eligible to participate. Many obese children are unpopular, have __________, and are at risk for medical disorders. Obesity reflects both __________ and acquired eating habits. In the most effective programs, for treating obesity in youth, both children and parents set eating and __________ goals and monitor their daily progress.

one-fourth
concentrating
low self-esteem
heredity
exercise

Tooth Development. Children start to lose their primary teeth at __________ years of age and, by age 12, have 24 of their permanent teeth. The loss of a baby tooth is celebrated in most cultures worldwide as a sign of maturity. Good dental hygiene includes frequent brushing, flossing, fluoride treatments, and regular checkups.

5 or 6

Vision. Most sensory systems change little during childhood. An exception is vision: Many children have __________, in which they can see nearby objects clearly but not distant objects. Myopia reflects heredity and __________ and is easily remedied with glasses.

myopia
experience

MODULE 11.2: MOTOR DEVELOPMENT

dexterity
balance
strength

Growth of Motor Skills. Fine and gross motor skills improve substantially over the elementary-school years, reflecting children's greater size and strength. Girls tend to excel in fine-motor skills that emphasize __________ (e.g., handwriting) as well as gross-motor skills that require flexibility and __________ (e.g., tumbling); boys tend to excel in gross-motor skills that emphasize __________ (e.g., throwing). Although some of these differences reflect differences in body makeup, they also reflect differing cultural expectations regarding motor skills for boys and girls.

often enough
activity
lifetime

Physical Fitness. Although children report spending much time being physically active, in fact, fewer than half of American school children meet all standards for physical fitness. Part of the explanation for the lack of fitness is physical education classes in elementary school: The classes are not taught __________ and involve too little __________. Television may contribute. Physical education in the schools needs to be more frequent and more oriented toward developing patterns of __________ exercise. Families can become more active, thereby encouraging children's fitness.

cooperation
overemphasize
leadership

Participating in Sports. Many school-age children participate in team sports; both boys and girls believe that sports participation enhances their self-esteem, helps them master skills and learn about __________, and is a means to stay physically fit. Adult coaches often can help children improve their skills but they sometimes __________ competition, they are so controlling that children have little opportunity to experience __________, and they overemphasize drills, strategy, and performance which turns "play" into "work."

Accidents. Because elementary-school children are more mobile and more independent, they're at greater risk for injury than preschool children. The most common cause of injury and death at this age is the automobile--children are hurt either as a passenger or as a pedestrian. Parents can help to prevent accidents by being good role models (e.g., always wear their own seat belts in a car), insisting that children wear seat belts in cars and helmet while biking, and by not overestimating their children's cognitive and motor skills. Another way to prevent accidents is through community- and school-based programs in which children learn safety behaviors and have the opportunity to practice them.

MODULE 11.3: CHILDREN WITH SPECIAL CHALLENGES

normal
sounds

Children with Learning Disabilities. Children with a learning disability have __________ intelligence but have difficulty mastering specific academic subjects. The most common is reading disability, which often can be traced to inadequate understanding and use of language __________.

impulsive
stressful
parent

Attention Deficit Hyperactivity Disorder. Children with ADHD are often overactive, inattentive, and __________. They sometimes have conduct problems and do poorly in school. ADHD is due to heredity and to environmental factors, particularly a __________ home environment. A comprehensive approach to treatment--involving medication, instruction, and __________ training--produces best results.

Children with Mental Retardation. Individuals with mental retardation have IQ scores of 70 or lower and deficits in adaptive behavior. __________ mental retardation can be linked to specific biological or physical causes; __________ mental retardation reflects the lower end of the normal distribution of intelligence. Most persons with retardation are classified as mildly or educably retarded; they attend school, __________, and have families.

Organic
familial
work

CHAPTER 11 PHYSICAL DEVELOPMENT IN SCHOOL-AGE CHILDREN

TEST YOURSELF

1. During the elementary-school years,
   a. children grow at a very rapid pace.
   b. children show more growth in their trunks than in their legs.
   c. boys are much larger than girls.
   d. girls are more likely than boys to enter puberty.

2. Based on ethnic differences in height, who would you expect to be the tallest child?
   a. Michael, who is an African American
   b. John, who is a European American
   c. Chan-ho, who is an Asian American
   d. It is impossible to tell, because there are no ethnic differences in height.

3. Growth hormone treatments
   a. are relatively inexpensive.
   b. usually make children taller as adults.
   c. may make some children more prone to infections.
   d. are recommended for use with all short children.

4. Compared to their well-nourished peers, malnourished children
   a. are more irritable.
   b. do as well in school.
   c. are as healthy.
   d. usually receive the free and reduced-price meals that are available to them at school.

5. Which of the following is *true* of obese children?
   a. They have severe behavior problems.
   b. They are viewed favorably by their peers.
   c. They are at risk for diabetes and high blood pressure.
   d. They are likely to outgrow their "baby fat" and become slim adults.

6. Obesity may be caused by
   a. one's heredity setting a low basal metabolic rate.
   b. television advertising that emphasizes the cultural ideal of thinness.
   c. parents who emphasize internal signals rather than external signals to control eating.
   d. one's heredity determining a high activity level.

7. Malocclusion
   a. is not related to problems with chewing.
   b. does not make teeth more prone to decay.
   c. may be caused by heredity.
   d. can be corrected with braces.

8. Myopia
   a. means that distant objects are seen more sharply than near objects.
   b. is more common in children who spend more time in activities that use near vision.
   c. usually emerges around age 5 or 6.
   d. does not have a hereditary cause.

9. Compared to girls, elementary-age boys have greater
   a. dexterity on fine-motor tasks like handwriting.
   b. balance.
   c. strength.
   d. flexibility.

10. In the United States, physical education classes
   a. should meet more frequently each week to promote physical fitness.
   b. usually require high levels of activity during most of the class.
   c. should emphasize team sports that are fun for the children.
   d. do not need to emphasize lifetime physical activity.

11. White and her colleagues (1998) asked both boys and girls about the purpose of sports participation. They found that
   a. boys were more likely than girls to believe that sports participation enhances their self-esteem.
   b. boys were more likely than girls to view skill mastery as an important reason for sports participation.
   c. boys were more likely than girls to believe that sports participation enhanced their social status.
   d. there were no differences between boys and girls in their reasons for participating in sports.

12. Adult coaches should
   a. criticize the players.
   b. emphasize winning over skill development.
   c. have high expectations for the children.
   d. coach positively with praise for the children.

13. Parents can help prevent accidents in their children by
   a. being realistic in assessing their children's skills.
   b. letting their children be independent.
   c. avoiding community programs that emphasize safety.
   d. giving their children the freedom to choose whether to wear a seat belt or a bike helmet.

14. Learning disabilities
   a. should be treated by specifically tailoring instruction to the individual child's needs.
   b. have virtually the same cause.
   c. do not occur together (i.e., the same child will not have both math and reading disabilities).
   d. are easy to diagnose.

15. Children with attention deficit hyperactivity disorder (ADHD)
   a. tend to think carefully before acting.
   b. are well-liked by their peers in school.
   c. often do poorly in school.
   d. usually have below normal levels of intelligence.

16. Which of the following is *true* of the cause and treatment of ADHD?
   a. The best treatment is administering stimulant drugs only.
   b. Parents should reinforce attention and compliance in their ADHD child.
   c. ADHD usually is caused by the child's diet.
   d. There is no evidence that heredity contributes to the incidence of ADHD.

17. Most causes of mental retardation are
   a. biological in nature.
   b. chromosomal in nature.
   c. familial in nature.
   d. genetic in nature.

18. Mildly or educably mentally retarded persons
   a. can learn the skills necessary for a job.
   b. can keep up with peers in school with a little extra work.
   c. usually are institutionalized.
   d. are unable to learn even the simplest self-care skills.

ESSAY QUESTIONS

1. Your friend Dorothy is upset because her adopted 10-year-old daughter is overweight. No one else in the family has a weight problem. What can you tell Dorothy about the influence of heredity and environment on one's weight? What advice can you give Dorothy about weight loss in children?

2. Your friend Jess is worried about the safety of his son Chris. Jess has heard that accidents are the most common cause of death in elementary-school children. What can you tell Jess about things that he can do to help prevent accidents where Chris might be the victim?

3. Your son has just been diagnosed with a learning disability in reading. Your spouse wonders if this means that your son is mentally retarded. What can you tell your spouse about the causes and treatments of learning disability?

4. Fred and Wilma's 6-year-old son Frank has just been diagnosed as having attention deficit hyperactivity disorder. Fred and Wilma believe that now that Frank is taking the drug Ritalin everything will be fine. What can you tell Fred and Wilma about other treatments for ADHD?

ANSWERS

Multiple Choice

1. d (322)
2. a (323)
3. c (323)
4. a (324)
5. c (324)
6. a (324)
7. d (326)
8. b (327)
9. c (328)
10. a (330)
11. c (331)
12. d (332)
13. a (333)
14. a (335)
15. c (336)
16. b (337)
17. c (339)
18. a (339)

Essay

1. Tell Dorothy that heredity plays an important role in juvenile obesity. Adopted children's weight is related to the weight of their biological parents and not to the weight of their adoptive parents. Genetic influence may contribute to obesity by determining a person's activity level and one's basal metabolic rate (the speed with which the body consumes calories). A less active person with a slower basal metabolic rate will be more likely to be overweight than someone who is active and has a faster basal metabolic rate. Dorothy may also be providing an environment that encourages her daughter to eat even when she is not hungry. For example, many parents encourage their children to clean their plates at the dinner table even though the child may be full.

   Dorothy's daughter can lose weight but she should remember that weight loss in obese children and adolescents is most successful if the whole family is involved in decreasing the number of calories consumed and increasing the amount of exercise. Parental involvement in the weight loss program seems to be related to long-term changes in diet and exercise habits. (324-325)

2. Jess can do a number of things to help protect Chris. First, Jess can be a good role model for safe behaviors such as fastening his seat belt and wearing a bike helmet. Second, Jess can insist that Chris fasten his own seat belt and wear a helmet every time that he is in the car or on his bike. Both of these behaviors should make Chris more safety conscious and less prone to take risks. Third, Jess should be realistic in assessing Chris' skills. For example, does he pay attention while riding his bike or has he had some close calls with cars even when he is with an adult. If Chris isn't very attentive to cars while riding his bike while supervised, Jess probably shouldn't let him ride his bike unsupervised. Fourth, Chris should participate in community programs that emphasize safety such as bicycle safety and fire safety programs. After participating in the program, Jess should review the safety practices with Chris. (333-334)

3. You can tell your spouse that children with learning disabilities have normal levels of intelligence, but they have difficulty mastering one or more academic subjects. This is different from mental retardation where individuals have below average intelligence. There are a number of distinct learning disabilities. One common classification scheme distinguishes disabilities in language, reading, and arithmetic. Because there are many distinct learning disabilities

there probably are multiple causes and treatments of learning disabilities. Diagnosis is difficult because of multiple causes and overlapping disabilities. However, once a learning disability is diagnosed the best treatment is to pinpoint specific cognitive and academic deficits and then tailor instruction to meet individual needs. (335-336)

4. Although Ritalin helps ADHD children calm down, it alone does not help their school performance. The use of medication should be combined with instructions that help children regulate their behavior and attention. For example, children should be taught to remind themselves to read instructions before starting assignments. Children also need to be reinforced for inhibiting impulsive behavior. Parents also need to be taught to encourage attention and goal-oriented behavior at home. If parents reinforce attention and compliance and effectively punish inattention, their children often show fewer symptoms of ADHD. (337-338)

Chapter 12
Cognitive Development in School-Age Children

Module 12.1 *Cognitive Processes*

Module 12.2 *The Nature of Intelligence*

Module 12.3 *Individual Differences in Intellectual Skills*

Module 12.4 *Academic Skills*

Module 12.5 *Effective Schools*

This chapter covers cognitive processes in school-age children, different definitions of intelligence, ways in which children differ in their intellectual abilities, academic achievement, and educational practices that foster children's learning.

COGNITIVE PROCESSES

MODULE
12.1

Cognitive Processes
- *Concrete Operational Thinking*
- *Memory Skills*

Textbook Learning Objectives

- **What are the strengths and weaknesses of concrete operational thinking?**
- **How do strategies and knowledge help school-age children to remember more effectively?**

TO MASTER THESE LEARNING OBJECTIVES:

1. Know the terms associated with concrete operational thought and memory
2. Know the details of concrete operational thought and memory

Know the Terms Associated with Concrete Operational Thought and Memory: Match each definition with the correct term

Concrete operational	Memory strategies
Mental operations	Scripts

1. The stage in which children first use mental operations. __________
2. Strategies and rules that make thinking more systematic and powerful. __________
3. Activities that improve remembering. __________
4. A memory structure used to describe the sequence in which events occur. __________

Know the Details of Concrete Operational Thought and Memory

1. T F Concrete operational children cannot reverse mental operations.
2. T F Concrete operational children can solve conservation tasks.
3. T F Concrete operational children confuse appearance with reality.
4. T F The thought of concrete operational children is centered.
5. T F Concrete operational children can think in the abstract and hypothetical.
6. T F To learn information, it must be transferred from working memory to long-term memory.
7. T F Memory strategies are activities that improve remembering.
8. T F Preschool children use simple memory strategies such as looking at or touching objects that they've been told to remember.
9. T F Rehearsal involves repetitively naming to-be-remembered information.
10. T F Typically, children begin using rehearsal when they are 12 years old.
11. T F As children grow older, they become worse at choosing appropriate memory strategies.
12. T F Monitoring what you have learned and what you have yet to learn improves gradually with age.
13. T F Students should read a text without a goal in mind.
14. T F After students skim a module in their textbooks, they should try to write an outline of the module's main topics.
15. T F Child chess experts remember fewer chess pieces than do adults who have no knowledge of chess (see figure at right).
16. T F Knowledge in a specific area helps organize and give meaning to information in that area.
17. T F A script is a memory structure that describes a sequence in which events occur.
18. T F Experience or knowledge that contradicts a script can distort one's memory for the event or knowledge.

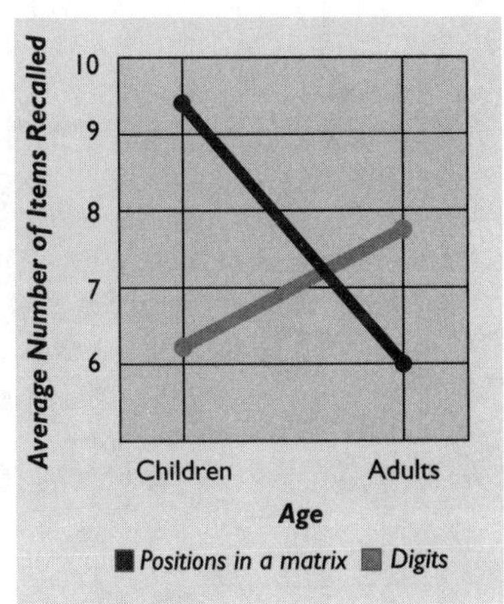

ANSWERS

Key Terms

1. concrete operational (344)
2. mental operations (344)
3. memory strategies (345)
4. script (348)

Know the Details

1. false (344)	**7.** true (345)	**13.** false (347)
2. true (345)	**8.** true (345)	**14.** true (347)
3. false (345)	**9.** true (346)	**15.** false (347)
4. false (345)	**10.** false (346)	**16.** true (347)
5. false (345)	**11.** false (346)	**17.** true (348)
6. true (345)	**12.** true (346)	**18.** true (349)

MODULE
12.2

The Nature of Intelligence
- *Psychometric Theories*
- *Gardner's Theory of Multiple Intelligences*
- *Sternberg's Triarchic Theory*

THE NATURE OF INTELLIGENCE

Textbook Learning Objectives

- **What is the psychometric view of the nature of intelligence?**
- **How does Gardner's theory of multiple intelligences differ from the psychometric approach?**
- **What are the three components of Sternberg's triarchic theory of intelligence?**

TO MASTER THESE LEARNING OBJECTIVES:

1. Know the terms associated with the different views of intelligence
2. Know the details of the different views of intelligence

Know the Terms Associated with Different Views of Intelligence: Match each definition with the correct term

Componential	Psychometricians
Components	Savants
Contextual	Social-cognitive flexibility
Experiential	Triarchic theory

1. Psychologists who specialize in the measurement of psychological characteristics such as intelligence and personality.__________
2. Individuals with mental retardation who are extremely talented in one domain.__________
3. A person's skill in solving social problems with relevant social knowledge. __________
4. Sternberg's theory of intelligence that includes three subtheories.__________
5. According to this subtheory, intelligent behavior involves skillful adaptation to the environment.__________
6. According to this subtheory, intelligence is revealed in both novel and familiar tasks.__________
7. According to this subtheory, intelligence depends on basic cognitive processes.__________
8. The basic cognitive processes that are needed to complete cognitive tasks.__________

Know the Details of the Different Views of Intelligence

1. T F Charles Spearman argued that many different intelligences exist.

2. T F Hierarchical theories of intelligence include both general and specific components of intelligence.

3. T F Gardner's theory of multiple intelligences is based on standardized intelligence test performance.

4. T F Gardner's theory of multiple intelligences does not address the developmental history of the different intelligences.

5. T F All of Gardner's intelligences are included in psychometric theories of intelligence.

6. T F According to Gardner, each intelligence is regulated by distinct regions of the brain.

7. T F People with greater social-cognitive flexibility have more interpretations of social scenarios than those who have lower social-cognitive flexibility.

8. T F Gardner believes that schools should foster all intelligences.

9. T F According to Sternberg's triarchic theory of intelligence, intelligent behavior always involves skillful adaptation to an environment.

10. T F According to the triarchic theory of intelligence, test items should be completely novel.

11. T F Sternberg's triarchic theory of intelligence identifies specific contents of intelligence.

12. T F Sternberg's triarchic theory of intelligence suggests that intelligence is associated with more efficient organization and use of components.

ANSWERS

Key Terms

1. psychometricians (350)
2. savants (353)
3. social-cognitive flexibility (353)
4. triarchic theory (353)
5. contextual (354)
6. experiential (354)
7. componential (354)
8. components (354)

Know the Details

1. false (351)
2. true (351)
3. false (352)
4. false (352)
5. false (352)
6. true (352)
7. true (353)
8. true (353)
9. true (354)
10. false (354)
11. false (354)
12. true (354)

MODULE
12.3

Individual Differences in Intellectual Skills

- *Binet and the Development of Intelligence Testing*
- *Do Tests Work?*
- *Hereditary and Environmental Factors*
- *Impact of Ethnicity and Social Class*
- *Gender Differences in Intellectual Abilities and Achievement*

INDIVIDUAL DIFFERENCES IN INTELLECTUAL SKILLS

Textbook Learning Objectives

- **Why were intelligence tests devised initially? What are modern tests like?**
- **How well do modern intelligence tests work?**
- **What are the roles of heredity and environment in determining intelligence?**
- **How do ethnicity and social class influence intelligence test scores?**

TO MASTER THESE LEARNING OBJECTIVES:

1. Know the terms associated with intelligence testing
2. Know the details of intelligence testing and the factors that influence intelligence test scores

Know the Terms Associated with Intelligence Testing: Match each definition with the correct term

Culture-fair tests	Mental age
Dynamic testing	Mental rotation
Intelligence quotient	Validity

1. The level of difficulty of the problems that children could solve correctly.__________
2. The ratio of mental age to chronological age, multiplied by 100.__________
3. The extent to which a test really measures what it claims to measure. __________
4. This measures a child's learning potential by having the child learn something new in the presence of the examiner.__________
5. Intelligence tests that include test items based on experiences common to many cultures.__________
6. The ability to imagine how an object will look after it has been moved in space. __________

Know the Details of Intelligence Testing and the Factors that Influence Intelligence Test Scores

1. T F The purpose of Binet and Simon's first intelligence test was to determine which children needed special instruction in school.
2. T F According to Binet and Simon's scoring method, a "bright" child would have the mental age of a younger child.
3. T F The Stanford-Binet provides a verbal IQ, a performance IQ, and an overall IQ.
4. T F Group intelligence tests optimize the motivation and attention of the examinee.
5. T F If the reliability of a test is high, then the test does a good job of measuring what it claims to measure.

6. T F Intelligence tests often are validated by correlating test scores with school performance.

7. T F Intelligence test scores are perfectly correlated with grades in school.

8. T F Intelligence tests are effective in predicting success in the workplace, particularly for more complex jobs.

9. T F Dynamic testing measures what a child has learned in the past.

10. T F Intelligence test scores of identical twins are more similar than test scores of fraternal twins.

11. T F In terms of IQ scores, fraternal twins develop more similarly than identical twins.

12. T F Studies of adopted children indicate that the impact of heredity on IQ decreases during childhood and adolescence.

13. T F Children whose parents are stimulating, responsive, and involved tend to have higher IQs.

14. T F For African American children, a well-organized home environment is associated with higher IQ scores.

15. T F The results of the Carolina Abecedarian Project indicate that intervention does not improve disadvantaged children's IQ scores.

16. T F The use of culture-fair intelligence tests eliminates ethnic differences in test scores.

17. T F There is considerable overlap in the IQ scores of European Americans and African Americans.

18. T F Males typically have higher levels of verbal ability than females.

19. T F Gender differences in brain maturation may lead to gender differences in verbal ability.

20. T F Mental rotation is the ability to imagine how an object will look after it has been moved in space.

21. T F A recessive gene on the X chromosome may promote spatial ability.

22. T F The right hemisphere of the brain may be more specialized for spatial processing in females than in males.

23. T F Girls are more likely than boys to participate in activities that foster spatial skill.

24. T F Initially, girls excel in math computation but later boys excel in math problem solving.

25. T F Boys get better grades in math courses in school.

26. T F Gender differences for math skill have gotten smaller since the 1970s.

ANSWERS

Know the Terms

1. mental age (357)
2. intelligence quotient (IQ) (358)
3. validity (360)
4. dynamic testing (360)
5. culture-fair tests (365)
6. mental rotation (366)

Know the Details

1. true (357)
2. false (357)
3. false (358)
4. false (359)
5. false (360)
6. true (360)
7. false (360)
8. true (360)
9. false (360)
10. true (361)
11. false (361)
12. false (362)
13. true (362)
14. true (362)
15. false (363)
16. false (365)
17. true (364)
18. false (366)
19. true (366)
20. true (366)
21. true (367)
22. false (367)
23. false (367)
24. true (367)
25. false (368)
26. false (368)

MODULE
12.4

Academic Skills
- *Reading Skills*
- *Writing Skills*
- *Math Skills*

ACADEMIC SKILLS

Textbook Learning Objectives

- **What are the components of skilled reading?**
- **As children develop, how does their writing improve?**
- **When do children understand and use quantitative skills?**

TO MASTER THESE LEARNING OBJECTIVES:

1. Know the terms associated with academic skills
2. Know the details of the development of academic skills

Know the Terms Associated with Academic Skills: Match the definition with the correct term

Comprehension
Knowledge-telling
Knowledge-transforming
Phonological awareness
Propositions
Word recognition

1. The process of identifying a unique pattern of letters.__________
2. The process of extracting meaning from a sequence of words.__________
3. Being able to hear the distinctive sounds associated with each letter.__________
4. These provide meaning to words and are the result of combining words.__________
5. The writing strategy of writing down information on a topic as it is retrieved from memory. __________
6. The writing strategy of deciding what information to include and how best to organize it for one's reader. __________

Know the Details of the Development of Academic Skills

1. T F Word recognition and comprehension are two important processes involved in reading.

2. T F Knowing one's letters is an important prereading skill.

3. T F Kindergartners who are not aware of letter sounds read as well in first grade as kindergartners who are aware of letter sounds.

4. T F Reading rhymes to children increases their phonological awareness.

5. T F "Sounding out" is not commonly used by beginning readers.

6. T F Word recognition is a one-way street in which readers first recognize letters and then recognize words.

7. T F Context does not help readers recognize letters and words.

8. T F Sentence context can speed word recognition.

9. T F Beginning readers sound out words and advanced readers directly retrieve words.

10. T F Meaning is derived by combining propositions.

11. T F An increase in the capacity of working memory contributes to improved comprehension.

12. T F Increasing knowledge of the world allows children to understand more of what they read.

13. T F Older readers are less likely than younger readers to reread passages that are difficult or confusing.

14. T F Older readers are better able to select a reading strategy that suits the material being read.

15. T F Younger children usually use a knowledge-transforming strategy when writing.

16. T F For young children, the mechanical demands of printing letters often interferes with the quality of their writing.

17. T F When young writers revise their writing, their changes usually dramatically improve their writing.

18. T F Young children usually retrieve math facts from memory rather than counting on their fingers.

19. T F Retrieval from memory is most likely for math problems that involve small addends.

20. T F American elementary school students are better at math operations and math problem solving than their peers in Japan or Taiwan.

21. T F Students in Taiwan and Japan spend less time in school than do American students.

22. T F Students in Taiwan and Japan do less homework than American students.

23. T F American parents are more likely to be satisfied with their children's school performance than are parents in Japan and Taiwan.

24. T F American parents are more likely to believe that effort is the key factor in school success.

25. T F American schools could be improved by giving teachers more free time to prepare lessons.

26. T F American schools could be improved by setting higher standards for students.

ANSWERS

Know the Terms

1. word recognition (370)
2. comprehension (370)
3. phonological awareness (371)
4. propositions (373)
5. knowledge-telling (375)
6. knowledge-transforming (375)

Know the Details

1. true (370)
2. true (371)
3. false (371)
4. true (371)
5. false (372)
6. false (372)
7. false (372)
8. true (372)
9. false (373)
10. true (373)
11. true (373)
12. true (373)
13. false (374)
14. true (374)
15. false (375)
16. true (375)
17. false (376)
18. false (377)
19. true (377)
20. false (377)
21. false (378)
22. false (378)
23. true (378)
24. false (378)
25. true (379)
26. true (379)

MODULE
12.5

Effective Schools
- *School-Based Influences on Student Achievement*
- *Teacher-Based Influences on Student Achievement*

EFFECTIVE SCHOOLS

Textbook Learning Objectives

- **What are the hallmarks of effective schools and effective teachers?**
- **How are computers used in school and what are their effects on instruction?**

TO MASTER THESE LEARNING OBJECTIVES:

1. Know the details of effective schools

Know the Details of Effective Schools

1. T F Student success in school is not related to parental involvement in the school.
2. T F Students are more likely to succeed in schools where the climate is safe and nurturant.
3. T F Students are more likely to succeed in schools where the progress of students, teachers, and programs is monitored.
4. T F The teacher's classroom management is not related to student learning.
5. T F Students learn the most when teachers assume that students are responsible for their own learning.
6. T F Good teachers use passive, rather than active, teaching methods.
7. T F Computers in classrooms can be used as tutors.
8. T F Computers can help students achieve traditional academic goals.

ANSWERS

Know the Details

1. false (380)	**4.** false (381)	**7.** true (382)
2. true (380)	**5.** false (381)	**8.** true (382)
3. true (381)	**6.** false (381)	

SUMMARY

MODULE 12.1: COGNITIVE PROCESSES

Concrete Operational Thinking. Between 7 and 11, children begin to use and can reverse operations to solve perspective-taking and __________ problems correctly. The main limit to thinking at this stage is that it is limited to the __________ and real.

conservation
concrete

Memory Skills. Beginning in the preschool years, children use strategies to help them remember. With age, children use more powerful strategies, such as __________ and outlining. Using memory strategies successfully depends, first, upon analyzing the __________ of a memory task, and, second, upon monitoring the effectiveness of the chosen strategy. Both skills are mastered gradually during childhood and adolescence. A child's knowledge of the world can be used to __________ information that is to be remembered. When several events occur in a specific order, they are remembered as a single __________. Knowledge improves memory for children and adolescents, although older individuals often reap more benefits because they have more knowledge. Knowledge can also __________ memory by causing children and adolescents to forget information that does not conform to their knowledge or to remember events that are part of their knowledge but that did not actually take place.

rehearsal
goal
organize
script
distort

MODULE 12.2: THE NATURE OF INTELLIGENCE

Psychometric Theories. Psychometric approaches to intelligence include theories that describe intelligence as a general factor as well as those that include specific factors. Hierarchical theories include both general intelligence as well as various __________ skills, such as verbal and spatial ability.

specific

Gardner's Theory of Multiple Intelligences. Gardner's theory of multiple intelligences proposes seven distinct intelligences. Three are found in psychometric theories (__________, logical-mathematical, and spatial intelligence) but four are new (musical, bodily kinesthetic, interpersonal, and __________ intelligence). Gardner's theory has stimulated research on nontraditional forms of intelligence, such as __________. The theory also has implications for education, suggesting, for example, that schools should adjust teaching to each child's unique intellectual strengths.

linguistic
intrapersonal
social-cognitive flexibility

contextual
experiential
componential

Sternberg's Triarchic Theory. Robert Sternberg's triarchic theory includes (a) the __________ subtheory, which specifies that intelligent behavior must always be considered in relation to the individual's culture, (b) the __________ subtheory, which specifies that intelligence depends on the familiarity of the task, and (c) the __________ subtheory, which specifies that intelligent behavior involves organizing basic cognitive processes into an efficient strategy for completing a task.

MODULE 12.3: INDIVIDUAL DIFFERENCES IN INTELLECTUAL SKILLS

intelligence quotient

Binet and the Development of Intelligence Testing. Binet created the first intelligence test to identify students who would have difficulty in school. Using this work, Terman created the Stanford-Binet, which introduced the concept of the __________. The WISC-III is another widely used intelligence test.

school achievement
potential

Do Tests Work? Intelligence tests are reasonably valid measures of __________. They also predict people's performance in the workplace. Dynamic tests are designed to improve validity by measuring children's __________ for future learning.

similar
well-organized

Hereditary and Environmental Factors. Evidence for the impact of heredity on IQ comes from the findings that (a) siblings' IQ scores become more alike as siblings become more __________ genetically, and (b) adopted children's IQ scores are more like their biological parents' test scores than their adoptive parents' scores. Evidence for the impact of the environment comes from the finding that children who live in responsive, __________ home environments tend to have higher IQ scores, as do children who participate in intervention projects.

lower
middle-class

Impact of Ethnicity and Social Class. The average IQ score for African Americans is __________ than the average score for European Americans, a difference attributed to the facts that more African American children live in poverty and that intelligence tests assess knowledge based on __________ experiences. IQ scores remain valid predictors of school success, because middle-class experience is often a prerequisite for school success.

verbal
Girls
boys

Differences in Intellectual Abilities and Achievement. Girls excel in __________ skills whereas boys excel in spatial ability. __________ get better grades in math; __________ get better scores on math achievement tests. This difference in math skill has remained the same over the past few decades. Differences in intellectual abilities reflect some combination of hereditary and environmental factors.

MODULE 12.4: ACADEMIC SKILLS

sounds, Word recognition
sounding out
Comprehension
increases

Reading. Information-processing psychologists divide reading into a number of component skills. Prereading skills, those that are necessary to learn to read, including knowing letters and the __________ associated with them. __________ is the process of identifying a word. Beginning readers more often accomplish this by __________ words; advanced readers more often retrieve a word from long-term memory. __________, the act of extracting meaning from text, improves with age due to several factors: working memory capacity __________, readers gain more world knowledge, and, readers are better able to monitor what they read and to match reading strategies to the goals of the reading task.

Writing. As children develop, their writing improves, reflecting several factors: They know more about the world and so they have more to say; they use more effective way of __________ their writing; they master the mechanics (e.g., handwriting, spelling) of writing; and they become more skilled at __________ their writing.

organizing
revising

Math Skills. Children first add and subtract by counting, but it is replaced by more effective strategies such as retrieving addition facts __________ from memory. In mathematics, American students __________ students in most other industrialized nations. This difference can be traced to cultural differences in the time spent in schoolwork and homework, and in parents' __________ towards school, effort, and ability.

directly
lag behind
attitudes

MODULE 12.5: EFFECTIVE SCHOOLS

School-Based Influences on Achievement. Students are most likely to achieve when their school emphasizes __________, has a safe and nurturing environment, monitors pupils' and teachers' progress, and encourages parents to be __________.

academic excellence
involved

Teacher-Based Influences on Student Achievement. Students achieve at higher levels when their teachers manage classrooms __________, take responsibility for their students' learning, teach __________ of material, pace material well, value tutoring, and show children how to __________ their own learning. Computers are used in schools as __________, to provide experiential learning, and as a multipurpose tool to achieve traditional academic goals.

effectively
mastery
monitor
tutors

CHAPTER 12 COGNITIVE DEVELOPMENT IN SCHOOL-AGE CHILDREN

TEST YOURSELF

1. According to Piaget, the concrete operational child
   a. cannot reverse mental operations.
   b. cannot solve conservation tasks.
   c. thinks in an abstract and hypothetical manner.
   d. knows that appearances can be deceiving.

2. Preschool children typically use which of the following memory strategies?
   a. They organize to-be-remembered information
   b. They use rehearsal
   c. They outline to-be-remembered information
   d. They touch objects that they are asked to remember

3. The ability to use an effective memory strategy
   a. does not change with age.
   b. involves evaluating the effectiveness of a particular strategy for the task at hand.
   c. does not influence how much one remembers.
   d. is well-developed by the time children are 7 years old.

4. Which of the following is *not* involved in successful learning and remembering?
   a. Identifying the goals of a memory problem
   b. Choosing an effective memory strategy
   c. Monitoring the effectiveness of the chosen memory strategy
   d. Using rehearsal because it is the most effective memory strategy

5. Research by Michelene Chi with child chess experts and adult chess novices has shown that
   a. knowledge within a particular area does not influence memory performance.
   b. adults' memories are better than children's even when children have expert knowledge in a particular area.
   c. knowledge in a particular area organizes and gives meaning to new information.
   d. child chess experts could not remember more chess pieces than adult chess novices.

6. Scripts of events
   a. can distort a child's memory for an event.
   b. force children to remember every individual activity that is part of an event.
   c. make remembering a specific event more difficult.
   d. do not provide information about the sequence in which events occur.

7. The psychometric approach to intelligence
   a. measures intelligence using standardized intelligence tests.
   b. equates intelligence with the existence of exceptional talent.
   c. says that intelligent behavior always involves skillful adaptation to an environment.
   d. suggests that many different intelligences exist.

8. Hierarchical theories of intelligence
   a. include only general factors of intelligence.
   b. include only specific factors of intelligence.
   c. include both general and specific factors of intelligence.
   d. is based on research and theories of cognitive development.

9. Which of the following is *not* one of the intelligences proposed by Gardner?
   a. Musical intelligence
   b. Sensory-perceptual intelligence
   c. Intrapersonal intelligence
   d. Bodily-kinesthetic intelligence

10. Gardner's theory of intelligence
    a. suggests that one general intelligence exists.
    b. does not address the issue of the development of intelligence.
    c. suggests that schools should foster only linguistic and logical/mathematical intelligences.
    d. suggests that different intelligences are regulated by different regions of the brain.

11. Sternberg's triarchic theory of intelligence
    a. identifies specific contents of intelligence.
    b. suggests that intelligence is independent of one's culture or environment.
    c. suggests that intelligence is revealed only in familiar tests.
    d. suggests that intelligence is associated with more efficient organization and use of components.

12. According to the method that Binet and Simon used to score their intelligence scale, a 7-year-old child who could correctly solve problems that the average 8-year-old could solve would have a mental age (MA) of
a. 7 years.
b. 7 years, 6 months.
c. 8 years.
d. 9 years.

13. According to the method that Terman used to score the early versions of the Stanford-Binet, a child with a chronological age of 10 years and a mental age of 12 years would have an IQ of
a. 83.
b. 100.
c. 112.
d. 120.

14. An intelligence test is valid if it
a. yields consistent scores over various time intervals.
b. measures what it claims to measure.
c. yields similar scores on equivalent forms.
d. has been standardized.

15. Which of the following statements *best* describes the predictive ability of intelligence tests?
a. Intelligence test scores are very useful in predicting success in the workplace, particularly for simple jobs.
b. Intelligence test scores almost perfectly predict school performance.
c. Intelligence test scores do a reasonable job of predicting school success.
d. Intelligence test scores are not related to school performance.

16. Dynamic tests of intelligence
a. have been used for many years and have produced well-established results.
b. measure a child's learning potential.
c. produce the same information as static tests of intelligence.
d. measure what a child already knows.

17. Which of the following statements best describes hereditary and environmental influences on intelligence?
a. Heredity determines intelligence within the normal range.
b. The environment determines intelligence within the normal range.
c. Both heredity and environment determine intelligence.
d. It is not possible to determine the effects of heredity and environment on intelligence.

18. Which of the following siblings would have the most similar IQ scores?
a. Children and their adopted siblings
b. Siblings who have the same biological parents
c. Identical twins
d. Fraternal twins

19. Studies of adopted children and both their biological and adoptive parents indicate that
  a. heredity does not influence IQ because the IQ scores of adopted children do not resemble those of their biological parents.
  b. environment does not influence IQ because the IQ scores of adopted children do not resemble those of their adoptive parents.
  c. the impact of the environment on IQ increases as children grow older.
  d. the impact of heredity on IQ increases as children grow older.

20. Higher IQ scores in children are associated with home environments
  a. that include involved parents.
  b. that include many toys.
  c. where a father is absent.
  d. where both parents work outside the home.

21. The results of the Carolina Abecedarian Project indicate that intervention programs
  a. with disadvantaged children do not improve their IQ scores.
  b. that focus only on preschoolers work as well as long-term intervention programs.
  c. that focus on the school environment work as well as programs that focus on both the school and home environments.
  d. are most successful when they last for years and they focus on both the school and home environments.

22. Which of the following statements *best* describes the relation between ethnicity and IQ?
  a. African American children tend to have higher IQs than European American children.
  b. When African American and economically disadvantaged children feel more at ease with the examiner, their test scores improve considerably.
  c. When children of comparable social class are compared, the ethnic differences in IQ disappear.
  d. When culture-fair intelligence tests are used, ethnic differences in IQ scores disappear.

23. Tests such as Raven's Progressive Matrices are designed
  a. to be culture-fair.
  b. for European American children.
  c. for African American children.
  d. for lower class children.

24. Which of the following is *true* of the differences between males and females?
  a. Females are superior to males in verbal ability only as adults.
  b. In high school and college, males excel in math problem solving.
  c. In early elementary school, males are superior to females in mathematical computational ability.
  d. At all ages, females are superior to males in spatial ability.

25. Which of the following best reflects gender differences in verbal ability?
  a. Only 10 percent of the published studies on gender differences found that females had greater verbal ability.
  b. Girls tend to be better readers than boys but boys are better writers.

c. Boys have more language-related problems.
d. The quality of speech production is lower in girls than in boys.

26. Over the last 25 years, gender differences
a. in mathematical ability have decreased and differences in verbal ability have increased.
b. in verbal ability have increased and differences in mathematical ability have decreased.
c. in mathematical ability have decreased.
d. in mathematical ability have remained the same.

27. Explanations for gender differences in spatial ability include:
a. A dominant gene on the Y chromosome may promote spatial ability.
b. The right hemisphere of the brain may be more specialized for spatial processing in males.
c. Boys' earlier maturation allows for less brain specialization.
d. Girls participate in more activities that foster the development of spatial skill.

28. Which of the following kindergartners will be most likely to learn to read more easily?
a. Erik, who cannot identify words that rhyme and words that don't rhyme.
b. Siu-lan, who does not know most of the letters of the alphabet.
c. Sholonda, whose parents read rhymes to her.
d. Justin, who cannot identify the first, middle, or last sounds found in short words.

29. Beginning readers
a. rarely use "sounding out" to identify words.
b. use sentence context to help them recognize words.
c. do not use direct retrieval of words.
d. retrieve unfamiliar words more rapidly than familiar words.

30. Which of the following is a factor that contributes to improved reading comprehension with age?
a. Children's knowledge of their world increases so they understand more of what they read.
b. Working memory capacity decreases which makes identifying propositions more difficult.
c. Younger readers are more likely to reread passages that they find confusing or difficult.
d. Younger readers are better able to select a reading strategy that fits the material being read.

31. Which of the following is *not* a reason for the improvements in writing that occur as children mature?
a. As children mature, they gain more knowledge about the world and, therefore, have more to tell others in their writing.
b. Adolescents use a knowledge-telling strategy and young children use a knowledge-transforming strategy when writing.
c. Older children need to concentrate less on the mechanical requirements (e.g., printing, spelling, punctuation) than do younger children.
d. As children develop, they have greater skill in revising and editing their writing.

32. As children receive formal instruction in arithmetic in first grade, they are more likely to solve addition problems by
a. counting mentally.
b. counting on their fingers.
c. counting aloud.
d. counting on both hands.

33. Retrieving answers to math problems from memory is more likely
a. if children are not confident that the retrieved answer is correct.
b. in younger children than older children.
c. when there is a weaker link between the addends and the sum.
d. with smaller addends than larger addends.

34. Stevenson and Lee's work comparing math achievement in the United States, Japan, and Taiwan has shown that differences in ______________________ account for the differences in math achievement.
a. IQ between children in the United States and the Asian countries
b. parental expectations and attitudes in the different countries
c. general cognitive skill between the children in the different countries
d. genetic makeup between children in the different countries

35. Compared to American students, students in Japan and Taiwan
a. spend more time on homework, but American students value homework more.
b. spend about the same amount of time on homework.
c. spend less time on homework, but they value it more than do American students.
d. spend more time on homework and they value it more than do American students.

36. Which of the following is most likely to be an effective teacher?
a. Someone who believes that the learning process should be a passive one
b. Someone who has good classroom management skills
c. Someone who presents the material at a rapid pace so students don't become bored
d. Someone who feels that students are responsible for their own learning

37. Computers in the classroom
a. decrease the number of interactions between students.
b. do not help children achieve traditional academic goals but help them achieve nontraditional goals instead.
c. can function as tutors.
d. do not allow students to explore the world in new and different ways.

ESSAY QUESTIONS

1. *Shining Time Station* is a favorite television show of your niece, Sunmi. The stories on this show revolve around the antics of more than a dozen toy trains. Each train has a name and a number. Your brother is shocked one day when Sunmi told him the name and number associated with each train on the show. Your brother is amazed because to him Thomas looks like James, he's never noticed any numbers on the trains, and Sunmi's memory in other areas does not seem extraordinary. What can you tell your brother about how knowledge influences memory that might help explain Sunmi's memory?

2. Recently, you took your nephew, Jamie, to a local fast food restaurant. When you took Jamie home, he told his mother, "We drove to Wendy's, we got out of the car, we stood in line, I got a Kid's Meal with chicken nuggets and milk, and I got a cool toy, too." Jamie's recall of the visit to Wendy's was mostly correct but Wendy's was out of milk so Jamie got a soft drink instead. What can you tell Jamie's mother about scripts and how they can influence memory that might explain Jamie's incorrect memory of his lunch?

3. Your friends Andre and Mia are both above average in intelligence and they are concerned that their new daughter Diane will be intelligent also. They want to know what they can do to shape Diane's environment to increase the chances that she will be above average in intelligence. What can you tell them about the effects of heredity and environment on intelligence?

4. Your friend Elena has been asked to supervise an intervention program that is aimed at preparing disadvantaged children for school. The program will receive enough money for a 3-year preschool intervention program but they probably won't receive more money for the second phase of the program which includes intervention with school-age children. Based on the results of the Carolina Abecedarian Project do you think that only one phase of the program is enough to help these disadvantaged children? Why or why not?

5. Your friend Gretchen is an elementary school teacher. She told you that she has noticed that the boys in her class seem to have more language problems than the girls. She's also noticed that the girls seem to have better computational skills than the boys but this doesn't seem consistent with the fact that few women are in jobs that require extensive mathematical skill. Gretchen wonders if gender differences in verbal and mathematical ability are substantiated by research or if she has unusual students. What can you tell Gretchen about gender differences in mathematical and verbal ability?

6. Your friend, Jason, is a concerned father and he would like to do all that he can to help his 4-year-old daughter, Gay, learn to read. What can you tell Jason about prereading skills that are related to more skilled reading in first grade?

7. You are having a discussion with a friend about the differences in math achievement in children in the United States and children in Asian countries. During your discussion, your friend states, "It must be genetic. Or maybe Asian kids are just smarter than American kids." What can you tell your friend about the reasons for cultural differences in math achievement that refute his statement?

8. Your friend's first-grade son, Hasani, has been writing a story every Monday in school. Your friend is concerned about Hasani's writing because she thinks that his stories aren't very good. They often have no organization and seem very incomplete. What can you tell your friend about the changes in writing ability that might make her feel better?

9. At a recent parent council meeting at your child's elementary school, a group of parents raised objections to the use of computers in the classroom. They felt that teachers used computers solely to entertain the children and that computers were a waste of instructional time. What can you tell this group of parents about the benefits of using computers in the classroom?

ANSWERS

Multiple Choice

1. d (344)
2. d (345)
3. b (346)
4. d (346)
5. c (347)
6. a (348)
7. a (350)
8. c (351)
9. b (352)
10. d (353)
11. d (354)
12. c (357)
13. d (358)
14. b (360)
15. c (360)
16. b (360)
17. c (361)
18. c (361)
19. d (362)
20. a (362)
21. d (363)
22. b (364)
23. a (365)
24. b (366)
25. c (366)
26. d (368)
27. b (367)
28. c (371)
29. b (372)
30. a (373)
31. b (374)
32. a (377)
33. d (377)
34. b (378)
35. d (378)
36. b (381)
37. c (382)

Essay

1. Tell your brother that knowledge is memory power. Greater knowledge in a particular area allows one to organize and give meaning to new information. Looking at Sunmi's recall of the trains, you notice that she remembers the names of all of the blue engines, then all of the red engines, etc. Sunmi's knowledge of the train engines makes it easier for her to learn the names and numbers of new engines but does not help her memory in other areas. To your brother, who has very little knowledge of the train engines, all of the trains probably do look alike. (347)

2. Scripts are memory structures that help describe the sequence of events. Jamie obviously has a script for going to a fast food restaurant. Jamie's script includes eating chicken nuggets and drinking milk. Scripts can simplify remembering because they eliminate the need to remember each individual activity. However, a script can distort memories that are not consistent with one's script. Drinking a soft drink for lunch at a fast food restaurant is not consistent with Jamie's script for the event so he incorrectly "remembered" information that was consistent with his script. (348-349)

3. Both heredity and environment influence intelligence. Studies of twins and adopted children provide support for the importance of heredity in influencing intelligence. In twin studies, identical twins have more similar IQ scores than do fraternal twins or other non-twin siblings. Studies comparing adopted children's IQs to those of their biological and adoptive parents have shown that as children grow older their IQs become more similar to their biological parents' IQs. The environment also is important in shaping one's intelligence. Parental behavior is an important aspect of the environment. Children with high IQ scores have parents who are responsive, stimulating, and highly involved. Also, having a variety of toys that are age-appropriate in

an organized environment is associated with higher test scores. Diane probably received genes for above average intelligence from her parents and they will probably provide a stimulating environment that nurtures Diane's intellectual development. (361-363)

4. The Carolina Abecedarian Project included both intervention with preschoolers and early-elementary school children and their parents. Some children received 5 years of preschool intervention, some received 3 years of intervention during the first 3 years of elementary school, and others received all 8 years of intervention. Four years after the school-age intervention ended, all of the children were tested. The children who received all 8 years of intervention had the highest achievement scores and those who received no intervention had the lowest scores. Will only one phase of your friend Elena's intervention help some disadvantaged children? The answer is, yes, it will, a little. The children will probably do better in school than children who receive no intervention but a 3-year program is not likely to produce large, long-lasting benefits. (363-364)

5. Research does show that females tend to have better verbal ability than males. For example, females score higher on general measures of verbal ability, they are better readers, better writers, and better spellers than males. Females also have fewer language-related problems than males. Elementary-school girls also have better math computational skills than boys but this advantage seems to reverse in high school and college. This reversal probably accounts for the small numbers of women in jobs that require a high level of mathematical skill. So, you can tell Gretchen that the students that she has seen conform to the patterns found for the average boy and girl. (366-368)

6. Kindergarten children who know most of their letters and who can easily distinguish the sounds that the different letters make are more skilled readers as first graders. Jason can help Gay master these skills by playing games with her that involve identifying the letters of the alphabet. Jason also can read books, such as Dr. Seuss or nursery rhymes, that contain rhymes that will increase her phonological awareness. Playing word games that involve identifying different letter sounds in words also will increase Gay's phonological awareness. (371-372)

7. You can tell your friend that, in fact, there are no systematic differences in general intelligence nor in general cognitive skills between children in the United States and those in Japan or Taiwan. Experiences at home and school seem to account for the differences in math achievement. In general, children in Japan and Taiwan spend more hours in school and spend a greater percentage of those hours engaged in academic pursuits. Children in Japan and Taiwan also spend more time per week doing homework and they rate homework as being more valuable than do children in the United States. Parents in Japan and Taiwan tend to have higher expectations for achievement in their children and they believe that effort and experience are critical in determining achievement. In other words, differences in achievement stem from differences in cultural attitudes and school practices. (377-379)

8. You can tell your friend that most first-graders are not very good writers. First, their stories often are very limited because their knowledge of the world is limited. As children learn more about the world, they have more interest-

ing information to incorporate into their stories. Second, young writers, like Hasani, use a knowledge-telling strategy in which they write down information on a topic as they retrieve it from memory. This often means that the writing is disorganized and disjointed. Third, as children become more proficient at the mechanical requirements of writing (e.g., spelling, punctuation, handwriting) they can devote more of their attention to the other aspects of writing that make a story more interesting. Finally, as children develop, they become better editors of their own writing. Older children are more likely to find problems and revise them. So, as Hasani matures during the elementary-school years his writing should improve and his mother shouldn't be worried about his simple-minded, unorganized stories. (374-376)

9. First, computers allow individual instruction that occurs at the student's pace. This may be particularly helpful for students who are slower or faster than the average students in the class. Second, simulation programs allow for experiential learning. These simulations allow students to experience things such as space travel without leaving the classroom. Third, graphics and word-processing programs are important tools that ease the drudgery of assignments so that students can concentrate on the creative aspects of the assignments. (440-441)

Chapter 13
Social Behavior and Personality in School-Age Children

This chapter examines children's self-esteem, their relationships with their peers, ways in which children help and hurt each other, and how children are affected by divorce and after-school care.

SELF-ESTEEM

MODULE
13.1

Self-Esteem
- *Measuring Self-Esteem*
- *Developmental Changes in Self-Esteem*
- *Sources of Self-Esteem*
- *Consequences of Low Self-Esteem*

Textbook Learning Objectives

- **How is self-esteem measured in school-age children?**
- **How does self-esteem change in the elementary-school years?**
- **What factors influence the development of self-esteem?**
- **How is children's development affected by low self-esteem?**

TO MASTER THESE LEARNING OBJECTIVES:

1. Know the details of self-esteem

Know the Details of Self-Esteem

1. T F How smart a child feels is known as scholastic competence.
2. T F How adequate a child feels about behaving the way that she is supposed to is known as social acceptance.

3. T F Children's overall self-worth is usually simply the average of their self-worth in specific areas.

4. T F During the elementary-school years, self-esteem drops as children begin to compare themselves to their peers.

5. T F Self-esteem becomes less differentiated as children become older.

6. T F During the school years, academic self-concepts become particularly well-defined.

7. T F Children are more likely to view themselves positively when their parents are affectionate with them.

8. T F Family harmony is not related to self-esteem.

9. T F High self-esteem in children is related to parents who set rules and are willing to discuss rules and discipline with their children.

10. T F Children's self-esteem is influenced by how they are viewed by other people.

11. T F Gifted children in gifted classrooms often have lower academic self-esteem than gifted children in regular classrooms.

12. T F Self-esteem is lower in children who participate in extracurricular activities.

13. T F Students' self-esteem is greater when they feel that teachers care about them.

14. T F Children with low self-esteem are less likely to have problems with peers.

15. T F Children with low self-esteem are more likely to suffer from psychological disorders such as depression.

16. T F Children with high self-esteem are more likely to do poorly in school.

17. T F Children with low self-esteem are more likely to be involved in antisocial behavior.

ANSWERS

Know the Details

1. true (388)
2. false (388)
3. false (389)
4. true (390)
5. false (390)
6. true (390)
7. true (390)
8. false (391)
9. true (391)
10. true (391)
11. true (392)
12. false (392)
13. true (392)
14. false (392)
15. true (392)
16. false (392)
17. true (392)

RELATIONSHIPS WITH PEERS

MODULE
13.2

Relationships with Peers

- *An Overview of Peer Interactions in School-Age Children*
- *Friendship*
- *Popularity and Rejection*
- *Prejudice*

Textbook Learning Objectives

- **Why do children become friends and what are the benefits of friendship?**
- **Why are some children more popular than others? What are the causes and consequences of being rejected?**
- **What are the origins of prejudice?**

TO MASTER THESE LEARNING OBJECTIVES:

1. Know the details of peer relationships

Know the Details of Peer Relationships

1. T F Elementary-school children are better able than younger children to resolve conflicts with peers.
2. T F By the elementary-school years, children realize that people's perspectives may differ because they have access to different information.
3. T F During rough and tumble play, children intend to harm each other.
4. T F Friends tend to be similar in age, race, and gender.
5. T F Interracial friendships are more likely to form in large classes.
6. T F Over time, friends become more similar in their attitudes and values.
7. T F Children with both same- and opposite-sex friendships do not differ from those who have only opposite-sex friendships.
8. T F Other than providing companionship, there are no other benefits associated with having good friends.
9. T F Controversial children are both liked and disliked by classmates.
10. T F Smarter and physically attractive children are more likely to be popular.
11. T F Popular children are less likely to cooperate and more likely to pick fights.
12. T F Rejected children often are aggressive and hostile.
13. T F The characteristics that are associated with popularity are the same across different cultures.
14. T F Children who had been rejected in elementary school did not do well in school and had low self-esteem 7 years later.
15. T F Inconsistent discipline is associated with antisocial and aggressive behavior in children.
16. T F It is not possible to teach rejected children more acceptable social behavior.
17. T F Prejudice is a typically negative view of others based on their membership in a specific group.
18. T F Kindergarten children are more likely to attribute negative traits to their own group and attribute positive traits to other groups.

19. T F Prejudice lessens as children learn that social groups are heterogeneous.
20. T F Prejudice disappears in older children.
21. T F Prejudice decreases when additional contact with individuals from other social groups occurs.

ANSWERS

Know the Details

1. true (394)	**8.** false (396)	**15.** true (399)
2. true (394)	**9.** true (397)	**16.** false (399)
3. false (395)	**10.** true (397)	**17.** true (399)
4. true (395)	**11.** false (397)	**18.** false (399)
5. false (396)	**12.** true (397)	**19.** true (399)
6. true (396)	**13.** false (398)	**20.** false (400)
7. false (396)	**14.** true (398)	**21.** true (400)

MODULE
13.3

Helping Others
- *Skills Underlying Prosocial Behavior*
- *Situational Influences*
- *Socializing Prosocial Behavior*

HELPING OTHERS

Textbook Learning Objectives

- **What skills do children need to behave prosocially?**
- **What situations influence children's prosocial behavior?**
- **How can parents foster prosocial behavior in their children?**

TO MASTER THESE LEARNING OBJECTIVES:

1. Know the terms associated with prosocial behavior
2. Know the details of prosocial behavior

Know the Terms Associated with Prosocial Behavior: Match each definition with the correct term

Altruism
Dispositional praise
Empathy
Prosocial behavior

1. Actions that benefit others.__________
2. Behavior that helps another with no direct benefit to the individual.__________
3. The ability to experience another person's emotions.__________
4. Praise that links a child's altruistic behavior to an underlying altruistic disposition.__________

Know the Details of Prosocial Behavior

1. T F Children with greater perspective-taking skills are more likely to act prosocially.

2. T F Children with lower levels of empathy are more likely to act prosocially.

3. T F Children are more likely to act altruistically when they do not feel responsible for the person in need.

4. T F Children are more likely to act altruistically when they feel they have the skills that are needed to help others.

5. T F Children are more likely to act altruistically when they are in a happy mood.

6. T F Children are more likely to act altruistically when it entails few or modest sacrifices.

7. T F Repeated exposure to reasoning during discipline seems to promote perspective-taking in children.

8. T F Modeling does not influence altruistic behavior in children.

9. T F Children who receive dispositional praise are more likely to act prosocially in the future.

ANSWERS

Key Terms

1. prosocial behavior (402)
2. altruism (402)
3. empathy (402)
4. dispositional praise (405)

Know the Details

1. true (402)
2. false (403)
3. false (403)
4. true (403)
5. true (403)
6. true (403)
7. true (404)
8. false (405)
9. true (405)

AGGRESSION

MODULE
13.4

Aggression

- *The Nature of Children's Aggressive Behavior*
- *Roots of Aggressive Behavior*
- *Victims of Aggression*

Textbook Learning Objectives

- **What forms of aggressive behavior are common during the elementary-school years?**
- **How do families, television, and the child's own thoughts contribute to aggression?**
- **Why are some children victims of aggression?**

TO MASTER THESE LEARNING OBJECTIVES:

1. Know the terms associated with aggressive behavior
2. Know the details of aggressive behavior

Know the Terms Associated with Aggressive Behavior: Match each definition with the correct term

Aggression
Instrumental aggression
Reactive aggression
Relational aggression

1. Behavior meant to harm others. __________
2. This form of aggression is used to achieve an explicit goal. __________
3. This form of aggression is caused by another child's behavior. __________
4. A common form of verbal aggression in which children try to hurt others by undermining their social relationships. __________

Know the Details of Aggressive Behavior

1. T F Aggression is behavior that is meant to harm others.
2. T F Aggressive behaviors and assertive behaviors are the same thing.
3. T F Pushing another child for no apparent reason is an example of reactive aggression.
4. T F Physical aggression is more common in girls than in boys.
5. T F Individual boys' tendencies to behave aggressively are not stable over time.
6. T F Teacher ratings of aggression in 10-year-olds are related to adult criminal behavior. (see figure below)
7. T F Children are more likely to be aggressive if their parents use physical punishment with them.
8. T F Children are more likely to be aggressive when parents are coercive and emotionally uninvested in them.
9. T F The best response to a child's aggression is to discourage the aggression and reward other forms of nonaggressive social behavior.

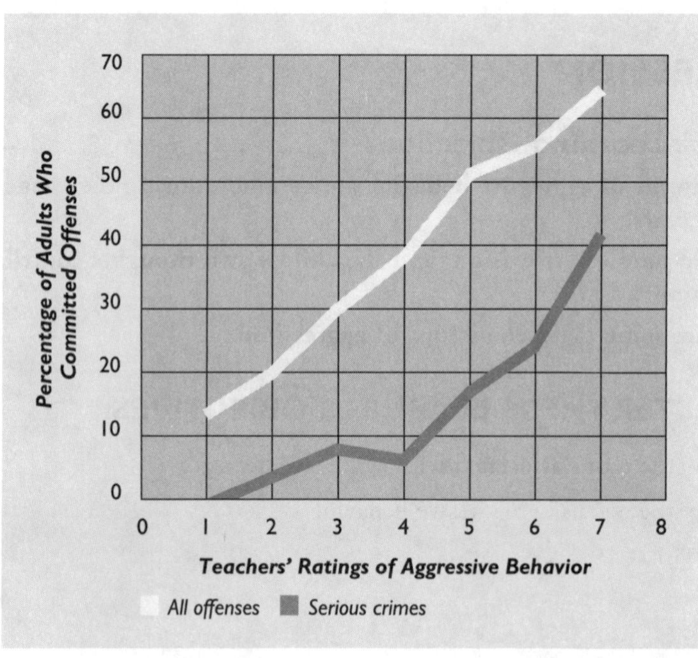

10. T F Aggressive children with good sibling relationships are more aggressive than those with conflicted sibling relationships.

11. T F Parents may foster aggression by using harsh punishment with children who are impulsive, angry, and have poor regulation of their own behavior.

12. T F Children who view many violent television programs are more accepting of interpersonal violence.

13. T F Boys who viewed more TV violence at age 8 had committed more serious criminal offenses at age 30 (see figure below)

14. T F Aggressive boys are as skilled as other children at interpreting other people's intentions.

15. T F Aggressive children cannot be trained to interpret others' intentions correctly.

16. T F In the United States and Europe, about 10 percent of school children are chronic victims of aggression.

17. T F The majority of victims of aggression are overreactive, irritable, or restless.

18. T F Victims of aggression are less tolerant of personal attacks when their self-esteem increases.

ANSWERS

Key Terms

1. aggression (407)
2. instrumental aggression (407)
3. reactive aggression (407)
4. relational aggression (408)

Know the Details

1. true (407)
2. false (407)
3. false (407)
4. false (408)
5. false (408)
6. true (408)
7. true (409)
8. true (409)
9. true (409)
10. false (409)
11. true (410)
12. true (410)
13. true (411)
14. false (411)
15. false (412)
16. true (412)
17. false (413)
18. true (413)

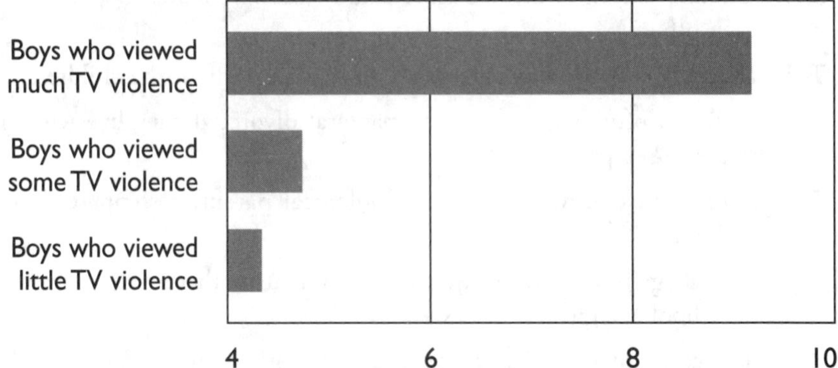

Seriousness of Criminal Activity at Age 30 (Large numbers indicate more serious offenses)

MODULE
13.5

Families at the Turn of the Century

- *After-School Care*
- *Divorce*

FAMILIES AT THE TURN OF THE CENTURY

Textbook Learning Objectives

- **How well can children care for themselves after school?**
- **What are some of the effects of divorce and remarriage on children?**

TO MASTER THESE LEARNING OBJECTIVES:

1. Know the details of after-school care and divorce

Know the Details of After-School Care and Divorce

1. T F Children who care for themselves are called latchkey children.
2. T F Latchkey children are more anxious and dependent than children who are cared for by a parent.
3. T F Children who live in safe neighborhoods and who spend much unsupervised time with peers are more likely to engage in aggressive and delinquent behavior.
4. T F When contemplating self-care for their children, parents should consider their child's age and emotional maturity.
5. T F Children who are in self-care need to know the rules for their own behavior after school (e.g., rules for using the stove or inviting friends over).
6. T F The United States has the highest divorce rate in the world.
7. T F In the first few months after divorce, mothers become more affectionate with their children.
8. T F In the first few months after divorce, mothers have a hard time controlling their children.
9. T F Two years after the divorce, mother-child relationships usually have improved.
10. T F Single mothers have more discipline problems with their daughters than with their sons.
11. T F Over the years, the negative consequences of divorce have become greater.
12. T F Children of divorce have a much greater risk of emotional disorders as adults than children from intact families.
13. T F Children adjust to divorce more readily if their parents cooperate with each other.
14. T F In joint custody, both parents retain legal custody of the children.
15. T F Children often adjust better to parental divorce if they live with the opposite-sex parent.
16. T F A blended family consists of a biological parent, a stepparent, and children.
17. T F School-age boys tend to adjust better to their mother's remarriage than do school-age girls.
18. T F The constant presence of noncustodial mothers may interfere with a stepmother's efforts to establish close relationships with her stepchildren, particularly with her stepdaughters.

ANSWERS

Know the Details

1. true (415)	**7.** false (418)	**13.** true (421)
2. false (416)	**8.** true (419)	**14.** true (421)
3. false (417)	**9.** true (419)	**15.** false (421)
4. true (418)	**10.** false (419)	**16.** true (421)
5. true (418)	**11.** false (419)	**17.** true (421)
6. true (418)	**12.** true (419)	**18.** true (422)

SUMMARY

MODULE 13.1: SELF-ESTEEM

Measuring Self-Esteem. One of the most common measure of self-esteem is Harter's Self-Perception Profile for Children (SPPC), which assesses self-esteem in five areas: scholastic competence, __________, social acceptance, __________, and physical appearance. It also measures overall self-worth.

athletic competence, behavioral conduct

Developmental Changes in Self-Esteem. During the elementary-school years, self-esteem usually __________ somewhat. Self-esteem usually becomes more __________ as children evaluate themselves on more aspects of self-esteem, including different types of academic skills.

declines
differentiated

Sources of Self-Esteem. Children's self-esteem is greater when parents are __________ and involved with them and when parents set __________ and discuss disciplinary action. Self-esteem also depends on peer comparisons. Self-esteem is usually greater when children know that others view them positively.

affectionate, rules

Consequences of Low Self-Esteem. When children have low self-esteem, they are more likely to have poor __________, suffer from psychological disorders such as depression, be involved in __________ activities, and do poorly in school. Therapy and improved skills can enhance children's self-esteem.

peer relations
antisocial

MODULE 13.2: RELATIONSHIPS WITH PEERS

An Overview of Peer Interactions in School-Age Children. Peer relations improve during the elementary-school years and emphasize talking, __________, and rough-and-tumble play.

being together

Friendship. Friendships are based on common interests and getting along well. Friends are usually similar in __________, sex, __________, and attitudes. Children with friends are usually more socially skilled and better adjusted.

age, race

Popularity and Rejection. Popular children are socially skilled. They often share, __________, and help others. They are __________ to behave antisocially (fight

cooperate, unlikely

aggressive
inconsistent

or whine). Some children are rejected by their peers, because they are too __________. These children are often unsuccessful in school and have behavioral problems. Their aggressive style of interacting can be linked to parents who are belligerent or __________ in their discipline.

declines
heterogeneous

Prejudice. Prejudice emerges in the preschool years, but __________ during elementary-school years as children's cognitive growth helps them understand that social groups are __________. However, older children and adolescents still show prejudice, which is best reduced by additional constructive exposure to individuals from other social groups.

MODULE 13.3: HELPING OTHERS

perspectives

Skills Underlying Prosocial Behavior. Children are more likely to behave prosocially when they are able to take others' __________ and are more empathic.

are able to, good

Situational Influences. Children's prosocial behavior is often influenced by situational characteristics. Children more often behave prosocially when they feel that they should and __________ help, when they are in a __________ mood, and when they believe that they have little to lose by helping.

reasoning
dispositional praise

Socializing Prosocial Behavior. Parenting approaches that promote prosocial behavior include using __________ during discipline, modeling prosocial behavior, using __________ for prosocial behavior, and having adolescents do family-oriented chores.

MODULE 13.4: AGGRESSION

less
stable

The Nature of Children's Aggressive Behavior. As children grow older, physical aggression becomes __________ common but verbal aggression becomes more common. Typical forms of aggression include instrumental and reactive aggression. Overall levels of aggression in individuals are fairly __________, which means that very aggressive young children often become involved in criminal activities as adolescents and adults.

physical punishment
interpreting

Roots of Aggressive Behavior. Children's aggressive behavior has been linked to their parents use of harsh __________. Other factors that contribute to children's aggression are excessive viewing of televised violence and lack of skill at __________ others' actions and intentions.

overreact
self-esteem

Victims of Aggression. Children who are chronic targets of aggression are often lonely and anxious. Some victims of aggression tend to __________ when provoked; others tend to withdraw and submit. Victimization can be overcome by increasing children's social skills, their __________, and their number of friends.

MODULE 13.5: FAMILIES AT THE TURN OF THE CENTURY

safe neighborhood

After-School Care. Children can care for themselves after school if they are mature enough, live in a __________, and are supervised by an adult.

Divorce. Directly after a divorce, a mother's parenting is less effective and her children behave __________. Family life typically improves, except for __________ relationships, which are often filled with conflicts. Divorce harms in many ways, ranging from school achievement to adjustment. The impact of divorce stems from __________ of children, economic hardship, and __________ between parents. Children often benefit when parents have joint custody or when they live with the __________ parent. When parents remarry, children sometimes have difficulty adjusting because stepparents may disturb existing parent-child relationships.

immaturely, mother-son

less supervision, conflict

same-sex

CHAPTER 13 SOCIAL BEHAVIOR AND PERSONALITY IN SCHOOL-AGE CHILDREN

TEST YOURSELF

1. How popular a child feels in social interactions with peers is called
   a. scholastic competence.
   b. athletic competence.
   c. social acceptance.
   d. behavioral conduct.
2. During the elementary-school years,
   a. children are less likely to compare themselves to peers than during the preschool years.
   b. self-esteem becomes more differentiated than during the preschool years.
   c. self-esteem shows large increases compared to the preschool years.
   d. girls' self-esteem drops more than boys' self-esteem.
3. Children are more likely to have higher levels of self-esteem if
   a. they do not participate in extracurricular activities.
   b. their parents do not set rules for them.
   c. the school environment is nurturing.
   d. their parents do not discuss rules and discipline with them.
4. Academic self-esteem is highest in gifted children who
   a. are in special classrooms for gifted children.
   b. are in classrooms for gifted children and who value being at the top of the class.
   c. are in classrooms for gifted children where common assignments and comparative evaluations are made.
   d. are in regular classrooms.
5. Compared to other children, children with low self-esteem
   a. are likely to have good relations with peers.
   b. are more prone to psychological disorders such as depression.
   c. are less likely to be involved in antisocial behavior.
   d. are more likely to do well in school.

6. During the elementary-school years,
   a. peer relations involve more conflicts than they did during the preschool years.
   b. friends usually spend time together participating in sports and academic activities.
   c. children spend more time with peers under direct supervision from adults than during the preschool years.
   d. peers often engage in rough-and-tumble play.

7. Elly is an African American girl who is 8 years old. Who is most likely to be her friend?
   a. John, an African American boy who is 10 years old
   b. Leah, an Asian American girl who is 8 years old
   c. Sholonda, an African American girl who is 8 years old
   d. Lafon, an African American girl who is 10 years old

8. Interracial friendships
   a. are more common when school classes are large.
   b. occur when children attend segregated schools.
   c. are more common when they are encouraged by teachers.
   d. usually are confined to school.

9. Compared to children who lack friends, children with good friends
   a. have higher self-esteem.
   b. are more likely to be depressed.
   c. are more likely to be lonely.
   d. are less willing to share and cooperate with others.

10. Popular children
   a. are not skilled at initiating social interactions.
   b. are less skillful at communicating.
   c. are unskilled at assessing and monitoring their own social impact.
   d. are better able to tailor their responses to new social situations.

11. Rejected children
   a. are less likely than other children to be aggressive.
   b. are less disruptive in school.
   c. are more likely to commit juvenile offenses.
   d. are less likely than other children to drop out of school.

12. Morison and Masten measured the long-term impact of peer relationships. In a 7-year follow-up, they found that compared to popular children, rejected children
   a. had less social skill but higher academic achievement.
   b. had less self-worth but higher social skill.
   c. had lower self-esteem and lower academic achievement.
   d. had higher self-esteem but less social skill.

13. Rejected children
   a. often have parents who model effective social skills.
   b. often have parents who are inconsistent in their discipline.
   c. often have effective social skills but are rejected for other reasons.
   d. are rejected because they are smarter than their classmates.

14. Actions that help others with no direct benefit to the individual are known as
a. empathy.
b. prosocial behavior.
c. role-taking.
d. altruism.

15. The ability to experience the feelings of another person is called
a. role-taking.
b. egocentrism.
c. empathy.
d. altruism.

16. Which child would be most likely to engage in prosocial behavior?
a. A child with high levels of perspective-taking
b. A child who uses rewards and punishments as the basis for moral judgments
c. A child who has low levels of empathy
d. A child with high levels of egocentrism

17. Which child would be most likely to act altruistically?
a. A child who does not feel responsible for the person in need
b. A child who believes that there are few costs associated with the act
c. A child who is in a bad mood
d. A child who feels that she doesn't have the skills necessary to help

18. Parents who use which of the following disciplinary practices are more likely to have children who exhibit more altruistic behavior?
a. Physical punishment
b. Reasoning
c. Time out
d. Rewarding good behavior

19. Aggression that is used to achieve an explicit goal is called
a. instrumental aggression.
b. reactive aggression.
c. relational aggression.
d. bullying.

20. Which of the following statements *best* describes the impact that parents have on aggressive behavior?
a. Parents of aggressive children do not model aggression.
b. Parents' use of harsh physical punishment is not associated with aggressive behavior in children.
c. Parental coercion and unresponsiveness are related to aggression in children.
d. Parents of aggressive children are more likely to break off aggressive exchanges so that they don't escalate.

21. According to Gerald Patterson's work with aggressive children, the *best* way to deal with aggressive children is
a. to physically punish the child for aggressive behavior.
b. to have the child be a target of aggressive behavior so that he can see how it feels.
c. discourage aggression while encouraging and rewarding nonaggressive behaviors.
d. to respond in a low-key, angry tone to the child.

22. Which of the following statements *best* reflects the relation between viewing television violence and aggressive behavior?
a. There is no relation between viewing TV violence and aggressive behavior in children.
b. Viewing TV violence is the primary cause of aggression in children.
c. Viewing TV violence and aggressive behavior are related only in laboratory settings and not in naturalistic settings.
d. Viewing TV violence makes children more accepting of interpersonal violence.

23. According to Crick and Dodge's information-processing model of aggressive children's thinking,
a. aggressive and nonaggressive children do not differ in their processing of social information.
b. aggressive children are less likely to attend to information that signals non-hostile motives.
c. aggressive and nonaggressive children both know the appropriate responses but aggressive children choose to act aggressively.
d. aggressive children are more skilled at interpreting others' behavior.

24. Chronic victims of aggression
a. are typically withdrawn and submissive.
b. are almost always overreactive, restless, and easily irritated.
c. have high levels of self-esteem.
d. tend to be boys who have controlling mothers.

25. Latchkey children
a. are likely to engage in antisocial behavior.
b. tend to show high levels of anxiety.
c. are more dependent than children who are cared for by their mothers.
d. need to be mature enough to handle the responsibility.

26. In the first few months following divorce,
a. mothers become more affectionate with their children.
b. the children regress to less mature forms of behavior.
c. mothers showed more effective parenting.
d. fathers became more strict and less indulgent.

27. Six years after a divorce,
a. mothers and daughters often have developed a very close relationship.
b. mothers report frequent conflict with their daughters.
c. mothers commonly are caught in a negative reinforcement trap with their daughters.
d. mothers are more likely to complain about their daughters than their sons.

28. Results of Amato and Keith's study of the impact of divorce indicate that
a. the overall impact of divorce is greater for girls than for boys.
b. divorce is more harmful when it occurs during the preschool and college years.
c. children whose parents are divorced do not differ from those whose parents stay married.
d. the negative effects of divorce have decreased over the past few decades.

29. Children who adjust the *best* to parental divorce
   a. have parents who have a lot of conflict.
   b. tend to interpret events more positively.
   c. suffer economic hardship following the divorce.
   d. live with the opposite-sex parent.

30. Which of the following is a special challenge for blended families that include a father, stepmother, and children?
   a. Fathers often are awarded custody of easy-going, well-adjusted children.
   b. Fathers often are awarded custody when they have a particularly close relationship with their children.
   c. Noncustodial mothers are less likely than noncustodial fathers to remain involved in their children's lives.
   d. Fathers have more unrealistic expectations for blended families.

ESSAY QUESTIONS

1. Your friends Frank and Kathie have a young son, Jessie. Frank and Kathie are concerned that Jessie will grow up feeling good about himself. They are wondering if there is anything that they can do that will increase the chances that Jessie will have high levels of self-esteem. What can you tell Frank and Kathie about the factors that influence self-esteem?

2. Senator Saveabuck thinks that research on popularity and rejection is a waste of money because children's popularity (or lack of it) has nothing to do with their later development. What can you tell the Senator about the long-term effects of popularity and rejection on later development?

3. Your friend Enrique told you that he would like his young son Joe to grow up to be a nice, helpful person. What can you tell Enrique about parental behaviors that are related to socializing prosocial behavior?

4. Your friends are the parents of an aggressive 6-year-old son. When their son behaves aggressively, they spank him to punish him for his behavior. They have not seen any improvement in his behavior and they have asked you for advice. What can you tell them about parental behavior that is related to aggression in children?

5. Your friend is an elementary school teacher who has noticed that there are a few children in his class who are very aggressive and, consequently, have been rejected by the other children in the class. Your friend would like to train these aggressive children to behave more appropriately and has come to you for advice. What elements should be included in the training program?

6. Your friends Mark and Bianca are getting an amicable divorce. They have two sons and they want to do all that they can to provide the best circumstances for the adjustment of their sons. Based on the research on the adjustment to parental divorce, what suggestions would you give Mark and Bianca?

ANSWERS

Multiple Choice

1. c (388)
2. b (390)
3. c (391)
4. d (391)
5. b (392)
6. d (394)
7. c (395)
8. d (396)
9. a (396)
10. d (397)
11. c (397)
12. c (398)
13. b (399)
14. d (402)
15. c (402)
16. a (402)
17. b (403)
18. b (404)
19. a (407)
20. c (408)
21. c (409)
22. d (410)
23. b (411)
24. a (413)
25. d (415)
26. b (418)
27. a (419)
28. d (419)
29. b (420)
30. b (422)

Essay

1. Many aspects of parenting are related to children's self-esteem. Children have higher levels of self-esteem when their parents are affectionate with them, are involved with them, set rules for them, and discuss rules and discipline with them. The school environment also influences self-esteem. Children who work hard in school, who get along with their peers, who avoid disciplinary problems, and who participate in extracurricular activities have higher levels of self-esteem. Also, a nurturing school environment enhances self-esteem. In other words, Frank and Kathie can contribute to Jessie's self-esteem by practicing the type of parenting that is associated with high self-esteem, by encouraging Jessie to work hard and avoid problems at school, by encouraging Jessie to participate in extracurricular activities, and by choosing a school that provides a nurturing environment. (390-391)
2. Senator Saveabuck should know that in the long run the lack of research on and intervention with rejected children will cost society more. First, rejected children are more likely to drop out of school than their more popular peers. These dropouts are less likely to be productive members of society and are more likely to collect unemployment. Second, rejected children are more likely to commit juvenile offenses and have criminal records thus costing society the expenses associated with the legal system. Third, rejected children are more likely to suffer from psychopathology. However, rejected children can be helped. Studies have shown that they can be taught how to initiate interactions appropriately, how to communicate clearly, how to act friendly, and how to avoid behaviors that others dislike. Rejected children who learn these skills are more likely to be accepted by peers and avoid the long-term negative effects associated with rejection. (398-399)
3. Research has found four parental behaviors that are related to socializing prosocial behavior in children. First, parents who use reasoning in their disciplinary style tend to have children who are more altruistic. These parents emphasize the consequences for others when their children misbehave. Repeated exposure to reasoning during discipline seems to promote children's ability to take the perspective of other people. Second, parents whose children

are more altruistic model altruistic behavior for their children. Third, dispositional praise (praising the child for helping and linking the helping to the child's helpful disposition) is related to greater altruistic behavior on the part of the child. So, by using reasoning in discipline, modeling altruistic behavior, and using dispositional praise Enrique will increase the likelihood that Joe will engage in altruistic behavior. (404-406)

4. Your friends should examine their behavior because parents and siblings play a large role in cultivating aggressive behavior in children. First, your friends should stop spanking their son because physical punishment only suppresses aggression in the short term and it provides the child with a model that aggression does work to control others. Other parental behaviors such as coercion, unresponsiveness, and little emotional investment are related to greater aggression in children. Second, your friends should discourage aggression (by punishing it or ignoring it) while encouraging and rewarding other nonaggressive behaviors. (408-410)

5. First, these aggressive children need to be taught that aggression is painful and does not solve problems. Second, the children need to be taught to interpret others' intentions accurately. For example, they need to be taught to pay attention to cues that signal non-hostile intent on the part of others. Third, the children need to be taught effective, prosocial ways to solve interpersonal disputes. (411-412)

6. Fortunately, Mark and Bianca get along and they are concerned about their sons' adjustment to the divorce. Mark and Bianca's sons will adjust better if a) they both stay involved in the boys' lives, b) there is little change in their financial situation, c) Mark and Bianca have as little conflict as possible, d) Mark and Bianca agree on the discipline of the children, e) they have joint custody of the children, and e) the boys live with Mark because children tend to fare better when they live with same-sex parents. (420-421)

Chapter 14 Physical Growth in Adolescents

Module 14.1 *Pubertal Changes*

Module 14.2 *Sexuality*

Module 14.3 *Health*

This chapter covers physical growth during adolescence, adolescent sexual behavior, and important influences on health growth during adolescence.

PUBERTAL CHANGES

MODULE
14.1

Pubertal Changes
- *Signs of Physical Maturation*
- *Mechanisms of Maturation*
- *Psychological Impact of Puberty*

Textbook Learning Objectives

- **What physical changes occur in adolescence that mark the transition to a mature young adult?**
- **What factors cause the physical changes associated with puberty?**
- **How do physical changes affect adolescents' psychological development?**

TO MASTER THESE LEARNING OBJECTIVES:

1. Know the terms associated with pubertal changes
2. Know the details of pubertal changes

Know the Terms Associated with Pubertal Changes: Match each definition with the correct term

Menarche
Osteoporosis
Primary sex characteristics
Puberty
Rites of passage
Secondary sex characteristics
Spermarche

1. Physical changes that mark the transition from childhood to young adulthood.__________
2. A disease in which a person's bones become thin and brittle. __________
3. The bodily organs that are directly involved in reproduction. __________
4. Physical signs of maturity that are not linked directly to the reproductive organs. __________
5. The beginning of menstruation that typically occurs around age 13.__________
6. The first spontaneous ejaculation of sperm-laden fluid. __________
7. Rituals that mark the transition into adulthood. __________

Know the Details of Pubertal Changes

1. T F Early adolescence is a period of rapid growth.
2. T F Boys reach their mature stature about 2 years before girls do.
3. T F Muscle growth during puberty is more pronounced in girls than in boys.
4. T F During adolescence, body fat increases more rapidly in boys than in girls.
5. T F Most people with osteoporosis are women.
6. T F Bones acquire most of their mass during childhood and adolescence.
7. T F For girls, the growth of breasts occurs after the appearance of pubic hair. (see figure below)
8. T F Early menstrual cycles are usually irregular and without ovulation.
9. T F For boys, the growth of the testes and scrotum occurs before the appearance of pubic hair. (see figure below)

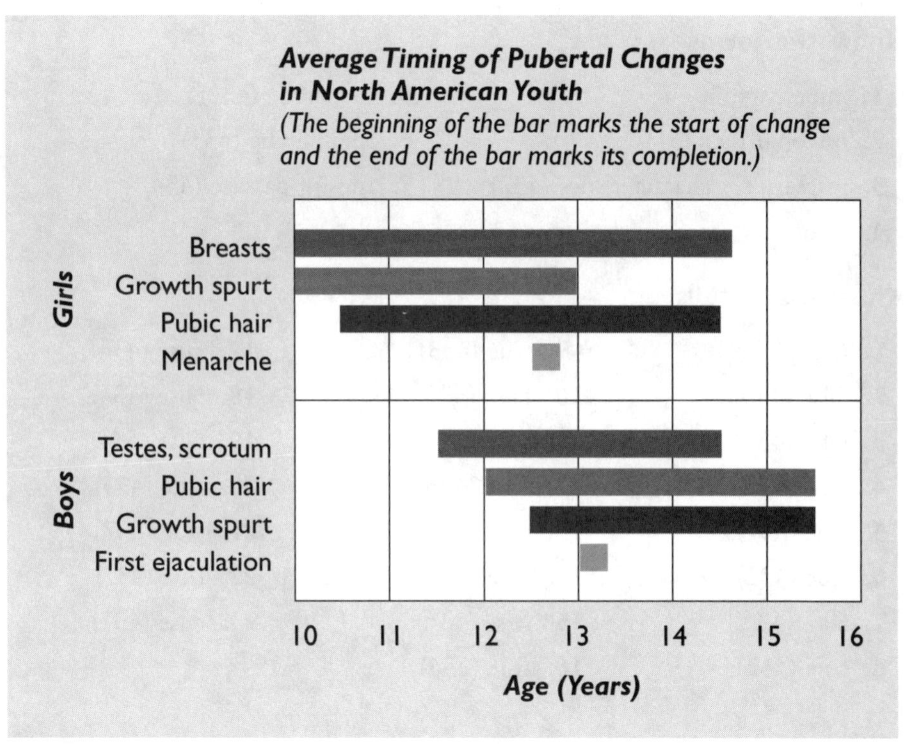

10. T F Initial ejaculations usually contain enough sperm to fertilize an egg.

11. T F The pituitary gland signals other glands to secrete hormones that stimulate pubertal changes in the body.

12. T F Estrogen is present only in females' bodies.

13. T F Both heredity and environment influence the timing of puberty.

14. T F Menarche occurs earlier in countries where nutrition and health care are adequate.

15. T F The age of menarche is still dropping in industrialized countries.

16. T F Menarche occurs earlier in girls who experience much family conflict or depression.

17. T F Adolescent boys are more likely than girls to be worried about and dissatisfied with their appearance.

18. T F Most girls rarely tell their mothers when they have their first menstrual period.

19. T F Boys usually tell their parents and friends about their spermarche.

20. T F Most teenagers' mood shifts are associated with changes in activities and social settings.

21. T F Boys who mature early tend to be more independent, self-confident, and popular with peers.

22. T F Early maturation in girls may lead them to associate with older adolescents who encourage them to engage in age-inappropriate activities.

23. T F The effects associated with the timing of puberty continue into adulthood.

ANSWERS

Know the Terms

1. puberty (430)
2. osteoporosis (431)
3. primary sex characteristics (432)
4. secondary sex characteristics (432)
5. menarche (432)
6. spermarche (433)
7. rites of passage (434)

Know the Details

1. true (430)
2. false (430)
3. false (431)
4. false (431)
5. true (431)
6. true (432)
7. false (432)
8. true (432)
9. true (433)
10. false (433)
11. true (433)
12. false (433)
13. true (433)
14. true (433)
15. false (434)
16. true (434)
17. false (434)
18. false (434)
19. false (434)
20. true (435)
21. true (437)
22. true (437)
23. false (437)

MODULE
14.2

Sexuality

- *Sexual Behavior*
- *Sexual Orientation*
- *Sexual Coercion*
- *A Final Remark*

SEXUALITY

Textbook Learning Objectives

- **Why are some adolescents sexually active? Why do so few use contraceptives?**
- **What determines an adolescent's sexual orientation?**
- **What circumstances make date rape especially likely?**

TO MASTER THESE LEARNING OBJECTIVES:

1. Know the details of adolescent sexuality

Know the Details of Adolescent Sexuality

1. T F Self-stimulation of the genitals is called masturbation.
2. T F Teenage girls are more likely than teenage boys to masturbate.
3. T F By the end of adolescence, most American boys and girls have had intercourse at least once.
4. T F Adolescent premarital sex has become much more common since the 1970s.
5. T F Asian American adolescents begin sexual activity at a younger age than adolescents from other racial groups.
6. T F Teens living in suburbs are more sexually active than their peers who live in rural and inner city areas.
7. T F Girls are more likely than boys to describe their first sexual partner as "someone they love."
8. T F Boys' peers are more likely than girls' peers to express disapproval of their sexual experiences.
9. T F When parents and friends have more positive attitudes about sexuality, adolescents are more likely to have sexual intercourse.
10. T F Adolescents tend to be less sexually active when their parents monitor their behavior and communicate with them effectively.
11. T F Young adults with AIDS usually contracted the disease during adolescence.
12. T F Chlamydia, syphilis, and gonorrhea are sexually transmitted diseases that cannot be cured.
13. T F Adolescents are especially susceptible to AIDS because they are more likely than adults to engage in unprotected sex and to use intravenous drugs.
14. T F Asian American adolescents are the more likely to become teenage mothers than Hispanic American or African American teens.
15. T F Most sexually active teens consistently use effective birth control methods.
16. T F Most adolescents know the facts of conception.
17. T F Most adolescent girls do not believe that pregnancy could happen to them.

18. T F Some teens do not know where to obtain contraceptives.

19. T F Teens who participate in programs that involve role-playing about sexual situations are more likely to abstain from intercourse or use contraceptives when they do have intercourse.

20. T F Sons become gay when they are raised by a domineering mother and a weak father.

21. T F Children raised by homosexual parents become homosexual themselves.

22. T F Biology probably plays an important role in the development of one's sexual orientation.

23. T F Homosexuality is considered to be a psychological disorder by the American Psychological Association.

24. T F Drinking alcohol increases the risk of date rape.

25. T F If a couple has had sex previously, a male is more likely to dismiss his partner's protests which can lead to date rape.

26. T F Date rape workshops emphasize the need for females to be clear and consistent in expressing their sexual intent.

ANSWERS

Know the Details

1. true (438)
2. false (438)
3. true (439)
4. true (439)
5. false (439)
6. false (439)
7. true (439)
8. false (439)
9. true (439)
10. true (440)
11. true (441)
12. true (441)
13. true (441)
14. false (441)
15. false (441)
16. false (441)
17. true (441)
18. true (442)
19. true (442)
20. false (443)
21. false (443)
22. true (443)
23. false (443)
24. true (444)
25. true (444)
26. true (444)

MODULE 14.3

Health

- *Nutrition*
- *Physical Fitness*
- *Threats to Adolescent Well-Being*

HEALTH

Textbook Learning Objectives

- **What are the elements of a healthy diet for adolescents? Why do some adolescents suffer from eating disorders?**
- **Do adolescents get enough exercise? What are the pros and cons of participating in sports in high school?**
- **What are common obstacles to healthy growth in adolescence?**

TO MASTER THESE LEARNING OBJECTIVES

1. Know the causes and effects of eating disorders
2. Know the details of adolescent health

Know the Causes and Effects of Eating Disorders: Match each statement with the correct problem of physical growth

Anorexia nervosa   Bulimia nervosa

1. A persistent refusal to eat that is accompanied by an irrational fear of being overweight.__________
2. Individuals with this alternate between binge eating and purging through self-induced vomiting or with laxatives.__________
3. This can lead to heart damage.__________
4. This is more likely to occur when parents are autocratic and controlling.__________

Know the Details of Adolescent Health

1. T F Most teenagers do not consume enough calories each day.
2. T F Teenagers need calcium for growth.
3. T F Both boys and girls need iron to make extra hemoglobin.
4. T F Teens who do not consume enough iron are often listless and moody.
5. T F Teens who eat too many fast-food meals have diets that are low in fat and sodium.
6. T F Adolescents with anorexia and bulimia tend to be well-behaved, conscientious, good students, and from middle-class homes.
7. T F People with bulimia nervosa may purge food from their bodies by taking laxatives.
8. T F The adolescent "fat spurt" may contribute to the incidence of anorexia.
9. T F A girl whose mother is preoccupied with her own weight is more likely to become anorexic.
10. T F Cultural emphasis on thinness is not related to the incidence of anorexia.
11. T F Twin and family studies indicate an inherited predisposition for anorexia and bulimia.
12. T F In the United States, most adolescents get enough exercise.
13. T F The most popular sport for boys is basketball.
14. T F Sports participation often enhances self-esteem.
15. T F Steroid use can damage the liver, skeletal, cardiovascular, and reproductive systems.
16. T F Steroid use is associated with mood swings and depression.
17. T F The most common cause of death among African American adolescent boys is motor vehicle accidents.
18. T F Most accidental deaths of adolescents are not preventable.
19. T F Adolescents are more likely than adults to emphasize social consequences when making decisions.
20. T F Adolescents and adults use very different decision-making processes.

ANSWERS

Causes and Effects

1. anorexia nervosa (446)
2. bulimia nervosa (447)
3. anorexia nervosa (446)
4. anorexia nervosa (447)

Know the Details

1. false (446)
2. true (446)
3. true (446)
4. true (446)
5. false (446)
6. true (447)
7. true (447)
8. true (447)
9. true (447)
10. false (448)
11. true (448)
12. false (448)
13. false (448)
14. true (448)
15. true (449)
16. true (449)
17. false (449)
18. false (449)
19. true (450)
20. false (450)

SUMMARY

MODULE 14.1: PUBERTAL CHANGES

height less fat predictable

Signs of Physical Maturation. Puberty includes bodily changes in __________ and weight as well as sexual maturation. Girls typically begin the growth spurt earlier than boys, who acquire more muscle, __________, and greater heart and lung capacity. Sexual maturation, which includes primary and secondary sex characteristics, occurs in __________ sequences for boys and girls.

testes nutrition depression

Mechanisms of Maturation. Pubertal changes take place when the pituitary gland signals the adrenal gland, ovaries, and __________ to secrete hormones that initiate physical changes. The timing of puberty is influenced strongly by health and __________. In addition, the timing of puberty is influenced by the social environment, coming earlier when girls experience family conflict or __________.

appearance moodier

Psychological Impact of Puberty. Pubertal changes affect adolescents' psychological functioning. Teens, particularly girls, become particularly concerned about their __________. When forewarned, adolescents respond positively to menarche and spermarche. Adolescents are __________ than children and adults, primarily because their mood shifts in response to frequent changes in activities and social setting. Early maturation tends to be harmful to girls but beneficial to boys.

MODULE 14.2: SEXUALITY

recreational approve

Sexual Behavior. By the end of adolescence, most American boys and girls have had sexual intercourse, which boys view as __________ but girls see as romantic. Adolescents are more likely to be sexually active if they believe that their parents and peers __________ of sex. Sexually transmitted diseases and pregnancy are common consequences of adolescent sexual behavior because sexually active adolescents use contraceptives __________. infrequently

Sexual Orientation. A small percentage of adolescents are attracted to members of their own sex. Sexual orientation probably has its roots in __________. Gay and lesbian youth may face many special challenges and consequently suffer from __________ problems. biology mental-health

Sexual Coercion. Adolescent and young adult females are sometimes forced into sex against their will, typically because males __________ or disregard females' intentions. Sexual coercion is particularly likely when either partner has been __________ or when the couple has had __________ previously. Date-rape workshops strive to improve __________ between males and females. misinterpret drinking alcohol, sex communication

MODULE 14.3: HEALTH

Nutrition. For proper growth, teenagers need to consume adequate calories, calcium, and iron. Unfortunately, many teenagers do not eat properly and do not receive adequate nutrition. Anorexia and bulimia are eating disorders that typically affects adolescent girls. They are characterized by an irrational fear of being __________. Several factors contribute to anorexia, including cultural standards for thinness, a need for __________ within an autocratic family, and heredity. overweight control

Physical Fitness. Individuals who work out at least 3 times weekly often have improved physical and __________ health. Unfortunately, many high school students do not get enough exercise. Millions of American boys and girls participate in sports. Football and __________ are the most popular sports for boys and girls, respectively. The benefits of participating in sports include improved physical fitness, enhanced __________, and understanding teamwork. The potential costs include __________ and abuse of performance-enhancing drugs. mental basketball self-esteem injury

Threats to Adolescent Well-Being. Accidents involving automobiles or __________ are the most common cause of death in American teenagers. Many of these deaths could be prevented if, for example, adolescents did not drive recklessly (e.g., too fast and without wearing seat belts). Adolescents and adults often make decisions similarly, considering the __________ available, the consequences of each alternative, and the desirability and __________ of these consequences. The outcomes of decision making sometimes differ because adolescents are more likely to emphasize the __________ consequences of actions. firearms alternatives likelihood social

CHAPTER 14 PHYSICAL GROWTH IN ADOLESCENTS

TEST YOURSELF

1. The adolescent growth spurt
   a. usually begins earlier for girls than for boys.
   b. usually ends earlier for boys than for girls.
   c. is a time when girls gain more muscle than boys.
   d. is a time when boys gain more fat than girls.

2. Research on osteoporosis has shown that
   a. most people with osteoporosis are men.
   b. most bone mass is formed during adulthood.
   c. swimming is a good weight-bearing exercise that strengthens bones.
   d. most adolescents don't get enough calcium or exercise of healthy bone growth.

3. For girls, puberty typically begins with
   a. appearance of pubic hair.
   b. growth of the breasts.
   c. menarche.
   d. the growth spurt.

4. For boys, puberty typically begins with
   a. appearance of pubic hair.
   b. growth of the testes and scrotum.
   c. growth of the penis.
   d. the growth spurt.

5. Which of the following girls would you expect to enter puberty first?
   a. Shalicia, whose mother entered puberty at a young age
   b. Chara, who is malnourished and does not receive adequate health care
   c. Anita, who has a chronic illness
   d. Jane, who lived in Europe in 1840

6. Which of the following statements is *true*?
   a. Adolescent boys are more likely than adolescent girls to be dissatisfied with their appearance.
   b. Most adolescent girls do not know about menstruation before it happens.
   c. Most adolescent boys learn about spermarche from their parents.
   d. Girls usually tell their mothers about menarche right away.

7. Adolescent moodiness
   a. is a myth that is not supported by research.
   b. is strongly related to adolescent hormonal surges.
   c. is related to adolescents' changes in social settings or activities.
   d. is similar to the degree of moodiness found in adults and younger children.

8. Early maturing boys
   a. are less popular with peers than late-maturing boys.
   b. are less likely to be given adultlike responsibilities than late-maturing boys.
   c. have less self-confidence than late-maturing boys.
   d. are more independent than late-maturing boys.

9. Early maturing girls
   a. have more negative feelings about their physical development than other girls.
   b. are more self-confident than other girls.
   c. are more poised and socially competent than other girls.
   d. are more popular with peers than other girls.

10. Which of the following statements *best* describes teenage sexual behavior?
   a. By the end of adolescence, most American teens have had intercourse at least once.
   b. Most American adolescents have never had intercourse.
   c. Asian American teens are more likely than African American or Hispanic American teens to become pregnant.
   d. Suburban teens are more likely to be sexually active than rural and inner city teens.

11. Among sexually active adolescents
   a. girls are more likely than boys to view sexual intercourse as a recreational activity.
   b. boys are more likely than girls to report feelings of love for their first sexual partner.
   c. girls' peers typically express some disapproval of sexual experience.
   d. boys tend to have feelings of fear and guilt after their first sexual experience.

12. Adolescents are more likely to have intercourse
   a. if their parents and peers have positive attitudes about sexuality.
   b. if they feel guilty about having intercourse.
   c. if they are concerned about getting pregnant.
   d. if they are afraid of getting a sexually transmitted disease.

13. A study of African American and Hispanic American adolescents examined the factors that are related to frequency of intercourse and number of sexual partners among adolescents. The researchers found that adolescents were less active sexually when
   a. parents talked to them about various sex-related topics.
   b. parents communicated openly with their teens.
   c. parents did not monitor their activities.
   d. parents approved of teen sexual behavior.

14. Which of the following is *not* one of the reasons teens give for failing to use effective birth control?
   a. Teens say that they cannot afford contraceptives.
   b. Teens often don't know the facts regarding conception.
   c. Teens may feel awkward buying contraceptives.
   d. Teens often believe that pregnancy "can't happen to them."

15. Which of the following probably has a role in the development of a homosexual sexual orientation?
   a. Sons become gay when they have a domineering mother and a weak father.
   b. Heredity and hormones seems to influence sexual orientation.
   c. Girls are more likely to become lesbians if their fathers are their primary role models.
   d. Children who are raised by gay and lesbian parents usually become homosexual.

16. Date rape is least likely to occur when
   a. a male assumes that when a female says no, she really means yes.
   b. one or both of the partners have been drinking alcohol.
   c. a female dresses provocatively.
   d. the couple has not had sex previously.

17. The diet of the average teenager in the United States
   a. does not contain enough calories per day.
   b. contains enough calcium and iron.
   c. contains too much sodium and fat.
   d. is usually well-balanced with foods from all of the basic food groups.

18. Anorexia and bulimia are more likely to occur in girls who are
   a. good students.
   b. in elementary school.
   c. "trouble makers."
   d. irresponsible.

19. Adolescent girls are more likely to develop anorexia when
   a. they perceive themselves to be of normal weight.
   b. their mothers are satisfied with their own weights.
   c. their parents are autocratic.
   d. they ignore the cultural ideals of the female body.

20. The use of anabolic steroids by high school athletes
   a. does not seem to have any positive benefits.
   b. can increase blood pressure and cholesterol levels.
   c. actually causes a decrease in muscle size and strength.
   d. does not seem to have any harmful consequences.

21. The leading cause of death
   a. among adolescents is the same for both genders and across various ethnic groups.
   b. for European American boys is firearm accidents.
   c. for African American boys is motor vehicle accidents.
   d. for European American girls is motor vehicle accidents.

ESSAY QUESTIONS

1. You have an 11-year-old daughter and your best friend has an 11-year-old son. Your friend thinks that your daughter has entered puberty and is wondering when his son will begin puberty and what physical events will occur during puberty. What can you tell your friend about puberty in general and the differences in onset of puberty in boys and girls?

2. At a recent parent council meeting at your daughter's high school, a group of parents proposed that the school store should sell low-priced condoms to slow down the increasing number of teenage pregnancies in the school. These parents suggested that many students do not use contraceptives because they are too expensive or they don't know how to obtain them. These parents also said that parents can't stop teens from having sex so the teens might as well have contraceptives readily available to them. What can you tell the parent council about programs that are effective in delaying sexual intercourse and increasing the use of contraceptives by teens?

3. Your friend Enrique has a co-worker that he thinks is gay. Enrique said that he thought that his coworker was gay because the coworker's mother must have been domineering, and his coworker could become heterosexual if he really wanted. What can you tell Enrique about the myths surrounding the causes of homosexuality and the role of biology in determining sexual orientation?

4. Your friend, Felicia, is the mother of a 13-year-old daughter, Yvonne. Felicia is concerned that Yvonne is anorexic because she "eats like a bird." What can you tell Felicia about the causes and symptoms of anorexia that will help her identify if Yvonne is anorexic?

5. Recently you and a friend were at a ski resort. You both noticed a group of teenagers who were engaged in very reckless behavior on the slopes. Your friend said to you, "Teenagers are so stupid and they make so many irrational decisions. Obviously, their decision-making processes are completely different from adults' processes." What can you tell your friend about similarities and differences in the decision-making processes of adolescents and adults?

ANSWERS

Multiple Choice

1. a (430)
2. d (431)
3. b (432)
4. b (433)
5. a (433)
6. d (434)
7. c (435)
8. d (437)
9. a (437)
10. a (438)
11. c (439)
12. a (439)
13. b (440)
14. a (441)
15. b (443)
16. d (444)
17. c (446)
18. a (447)
19. c (447)
20. b (449)
21. d (449)

Essay

1. Puberty is characterized by many physical changes which usually begin at age 11 in girls and at about age 13 in boys. The adolescent growth spurt is a period of very rapid growth when adolescents put on both height and weight. This growth spurt usually lasts about 4 years. In girls puberty begins with the growth of the breasts, then the start of the adolescent growth spurt, the emergence of pubic hair, and finally the onset of menstruation, or menarche, which usually occurs around age 13. For boys, puberty usually begins with the growth of the testes and scrotum, followed by the appearance of pubic hair, the start of the growth spurt, and growth of the penis. Because girls tend to begin puberty at earlier ages than do boys, it is quite likely that your daughter has entered puberty and that your friend's son has not. Tell your friend not to worry because his son has not yet reached the average age at which boys enter puberty. (430-431)

2. You can tell the parent council that while it is true that some teens do not use contraceptives because they do not know how to obtain them, there are many other factors that are related to sexual activity and the use of contraceptives. For example, teens are more likely to show more frequent and more intense sexual behavior if their friends and parents have positive attitudes about intercourse. Adolescents may not use contraceptives because they are ignorant of many of the true facts about conception. Programs such as "Postponing Sexual Involvement" are effective in delaying sexual activity and increasing the use of contraceptives when sexual activity does occur. In this program, older, trained adolescents discuss the pressures to become sexually active and strategies for resisting these pressures. Students discuss these pressures and practice refusal strategies in role-playing sessions. The adolescents who participate in this program are less likely to have intercourse; when they do have intercourse, they are more likely to use contraceptives. (98-99)

3. Enrique should know that research has shown that a number of the myths that people have about sexual orientation are wrong. The myths include the belief that sons become gay when they are reared by a domineering mother and a weak father, that girls become lesbians because their fathers are their primary role models, that children who are reared by homosexual parents usually become homosexual themselves, and that homosexual adults were seduced by an older, same-sex person when they were children. In fact, many scientists now believe that there is an inherited biological component that influences sexual orientation. One idea is that genes and hormones lead to temperaments that affect children's preference for same- and opposite-sex activities. Children who do not enjoy gender typical activities may develop a different gender identity. In other words, Enrique's coworker probably won't be able to change his sexual orientation by simply "wanting to" any more than he could change the color of his eyes. (443)

4. Tell Felicia that the typical anorexic is an adolescent female like Yvonne. Anorexics often are well-behaved, conscientious, and good students. Their homes often have autocratic parents who do not give their children much control. The mothers in these homes may be preoccupied with their own weights. Even if Yvonne and her family match this description, she may not be anorexic. An anorexic will limit food intake to such a great extent that she will become painfully thin but will perceive herself as being overweight. If Yvonne shows any of these signs, she should seek medical treatment right away. If left untreated, anorexia can lead to death. (446-447)

5. You can tell your friend that, in fact, adolescents and adults follow very similar processes when making decisions. Typically, both adolescents and adults determine 1) the alternative courses of action available to them, 2) the consequences of each action, and the desirability and likelihood of these consequences. The main difference between adolescents and adults is that adolescents are more likely to consider the social consequences (e.g., I'll make my friends mad or my friends will think I'm a wimp if I don't participate) and less likely to consider the health consequences (e.g., I might be hurt or hurt someone else with my reckless behavior) when making decisions. (449-451)

Chapter 15
Cognitive Processes in Adolescents

This chapter covers the basic properties of adolescent cognition, adolescents' reasoning about moral issues, and adolescents' ideas about work and careers.

MODULE
15.1

Cognition

- *Piaget's Stage of Formal Operational Reasoning*
- *Information Processing During Adolescence*

COGNITION

Textbook Learning Objectives

- **What are the distinguishing characteristics of formal operational thought?**
- **How does information processing become more efficient during adolescence?**

TO MASTER THESE LEARNING OBJECTIVES:

1. Know the details of cognitive development in adolescents

Know the Details of the Cognitive Development in Adolescents

1. T F Formal operational adolescents understand that reality is not the only possibility.
2. T F Formal operational thinkers cannot use hypothetical reasoning.
3. T F Adolescents cannot create hypotheses and then test them.
4. T F Formal operational thinkers use deductive reasoning.

5. T F Adolescents who are in the formal operational stage do not revert to concrete operational thinking.

6. T F Adolescents show more sophisticated reasoning when the problems are relevant to them.

7. T F Adolescents use more sophisticated reasoning to dismiss the results of studies that threaten their beliefs.

8. T F Adolescence represents a distinct, qualitatively different stage to information-processing theorists.

9. T F According to information processing, the cognitive changes that take place during adolescence are much larger than those seen in childhood.

10. T F Adolescents and adults have approximately the same working memory capacity.

11. T F Adults' processing speed is much faster than adolescents'.

12. T F Adolescents' increased knowledge helps them learn, understand, and remember more of new experiences.

13. T F Adolescents are much better than children at identifying appropriate learning strategies and monitoring the chosen strategy.

14. T F Adolescents are more likely to outline and highlight information in a text.

15. T F Adolescents rarely have a master study plan.

ANSWERS

Know the Details

1. true (456)
2. false (456)
3. false (457)
4. true (457)
5. false (458)
6. true (458)
7. true (459)
8. false (460)
9. false (460)
10. true (460)
11. false (460)
12. true (461)
13. true (461)
14. true (461)
15. false (461)

MODULE
15.2

Reasoning about Moral Issues
- *Kohlberg's Theory*
- *Beyond Kohlberg's Theory: Gilligan's Ethic of Caring*
- *Promoting Moral Reasoning*

REASONING ABOUT MORAL ISSUES

Textbook Learning Objectives

- **How do adolescents reason about moral issues?**
- **How do concern for justice and caring for other people contribute to moral reasoning?**
- **What factors help promote more sophisticated reasoning about moral issues?**

TO MASTER THESE LEARNING OBJECTIVES:

1. Know the terms associated with moral reasoning
2. Know the details of moral reasoning

Know the Terms Associated with Moral Reasoning: Match each definition with the correct term

Conventional Preconventional
Postconventional

1. Kohlberg's level of moral reasoning in which reasoning is controlled by obedience to authority and by rewards and punishments.__________
2. Kohlberg's level of moral reasoning in which moral decision making is based on social norms--what is expected by others.__________
3. Kohlberg's level of moral reasoning in which moral decisions are based on personal, moral principles.__________

Know the Details of Moral Reasoning

1. T F A person in Kohlberg's preconventional level of moral reasoning stresses the need for conformity to the existing social norms.
2. T F A person who reasons at Kohlberg's conventional level would emphasize personal, moral principles.
3. T F Kohlberg's stages of moral reasoning occur in an invariant sequence which means that the stages occur in only one order.
4. T F Results from longitudinal studies support Kohlberg's invariant sequence of stages.
5. T F Longitudinal studies show that over time individuals regress to lower levels of moral reasoning. (see figure below)

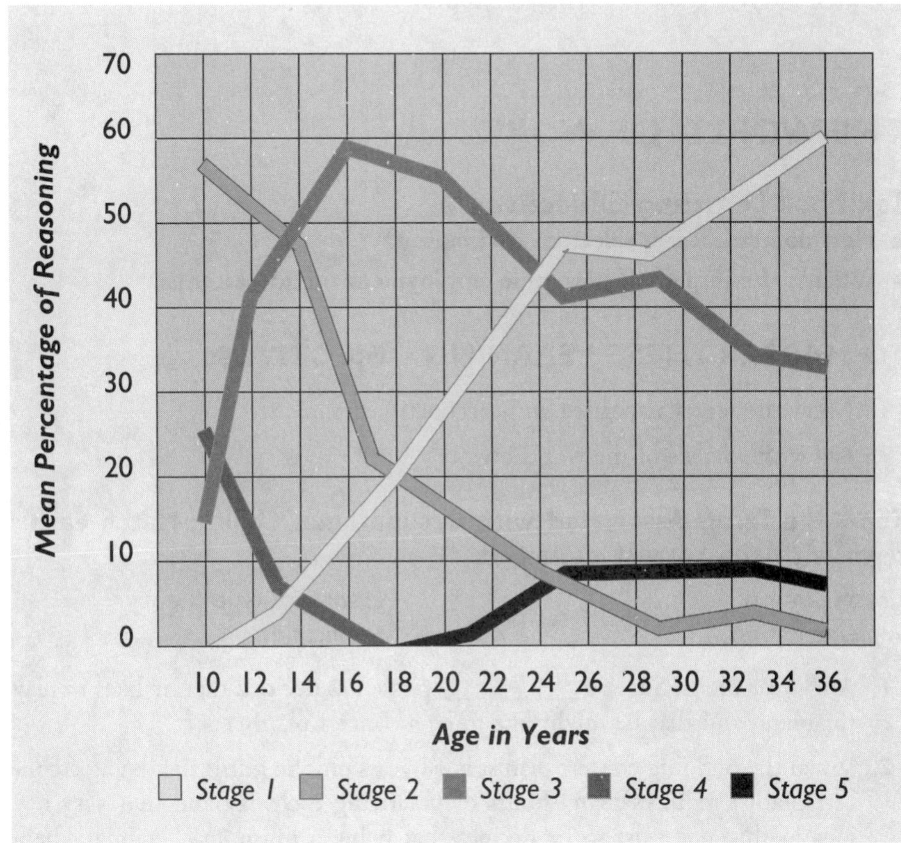

6. T F Research has shown that moral reasoning is not related to moral behavior.

7. T F Moral reasoning does not reflect one's culture.

8. T F Carol Gilligan believes that moral reasoning becomes more sophisticated but that care and responsibility is the basis for moral reasoning, especially for women.

9. T F Research has shown that both men and women use caring for others and justice as bases for moral reasoning.

10. T F Moral discussions with individuals who reason at higher levels usually improve the reasoning of those who reason at lower levels.

11. T F Teachers in Just Communities set the school policies without input from the students.

ANSWERS

Key Terms

1. preconventional (463)
2. conventional (464)
3. postconventional (464)

Know the Details

1. false (463)
2. false (464)
3. true (465)
4. true (465)
5. false (465)
6. false (465)
7. false (466)
8. true (467)
9. true (467)
10. true (468)
11. false (468)

MODULE
15.3

The World of Work

- *Career Development*
- *Part-Time Employment*

THE WORLD OF WORK

Textbook Learning Objectives

- **How do adolescents select occupation?**
- **What is the impact of part-time employment on adolescents?**

TO MASTER THESE LEARNING OBJECTIVES:

1. Know the terms associated with occupational choice
2. Know the details of the world ofwork

Know the Terms Associated with Occupational Choice: Match each term with the correct definition

Crystallization
Implementation
Personality-type theory
Specification

1. A 13-year-old in Super's __________ phase has decided that he likes to play the piano and that he might like to be a concert pianist.
2. When the budding concert pianist is 18 years old, he learns that being a concert pianist requires many hours of practicing each day and that very few jobs in this area exist so he decides that being a music teacher might be a better job for him. He is in Super's __________ phase.

3. A 23-year-old who has just graduated from college with a degree in music education and has begun a job as a high school music teacher would be in Super's __________ phase.
4. According to Holland's __________, people find their work fulfilling when the important features of a job or profession fit the workers' personalities.

Know the Details of the World of Work

1. T F According to Super, identity is the primary force in an adolescent's career choice.
2. T F During Super's crystallization phase, adolescents start to obtain the training required for a specific job.
3. T F During Super's specification phase, adolescents use their ideas about their own talents and skills to limit potential career prospects.
4. T F During Super's implementation phase, individuals enter the work force and learn firsthand about jobs.
5. T F Economic conditions and opportunities do not shape career development.
6. T F According to Holland, a person finds her job more fulfilling when an important feature of the job fits her personality.
7. T F Most people match one of Holland's personality types exactly or very closely.
8. T F Holland's personality-type theory is only useful for males.
9. T F Someone with an enterprising personality would be well-suited for a job as a scientist or technical writer.
10. T F A person with an artistic personality would be happy as a poet, musician, or actor.
11. T F People who have jobs that match their personality type are more productive.
12. T F High school girls usually have jobs that pay less than the jobs that boys have.
13. T F High school students in Western Europe and Asia are more likely than students in the U.S. to hold a part-time job.
14. T F High school students who work more than 15 hours per week are more likely to have lower grades than their peers.
15. T F Adolescents who work more than 15 or 20 hours a week are more likely to experience anxiety and depression.
16. T F Extensive part-time work is associated with less substance abuse.
17. T F Most working teens save some of their income for long-term goals like college or a car.
18. T F Jobs that allow teens to use existing skills or learn new ones are the most beneficial.

ANSWERS

Key Terms

1. crystallization (470)
2. specification (470)
3. implementation (470)
4. personality-type theory (470)

Know the Details

1. true (470)	**7.** false (471)	**13.** false (474)
2. false (470)	**8.** false (471)	**14.** true (474)
3. false (470)	**9.** false (472)	**15.** true (474)
4. true (470)	**10.** true (472)	**16.** false (474)
5. false (471)	**11.** true (471)	**17.** false (474)
6. true (471)	**12.** true (473)	**18.** true (475)

SUMMARY

MODULE 15.1: COGNITION

Piaget's Stage of Formal Operational Reasoning. With the onset of the formal oper-
abstractly ational stage, adolescents can think hypothetically and reason __________. In
logic deductive reasoning, they understand that conclusions are based on __________,
not necessarily on experience. Adolescent's reasoning is not always as sophisticated
beliefs as expected by Piaget's theory. For example, adolescents' __________ sometimes
interfere with their reasoning.

Information Processing During Adolescence. According to information-processing
gradual theorists, adolescence is a time of __________ cognitive change. Working memory
processing speed and __________ achieve adult-like levels; content knowledge increases, to expert-
metacognitive like levels in some domains; and strategies and __________ skills become much
more sophisticated.

MODULE 15.2: REASONING ABOUT MORAL ISSUES

Kohlberg's Theory. Kohlberg proposed that moral reasoning includes preconventional, conventional, and postconventional levels. Each level has two stages, creat-
rewards and punishments, ing a 6-stage developmental sequence. In the early stages, moral reasoning is based
personal on __________; in the latter stages, on __________ moral codes. As predicted by
do not the theory, people progress through the stages in sequence, __________ regress,
and morally advanced reasoning is associated with more frequent moral behavior.
However, few people attain the most advanced levels of reasoning and
cultures __________ differ in the bases for moral reasoning.

Beyond Kohlberg's Theory: Gilligan's Ethic of Caring. Gilligan proposed that females'
responsibility for others moral reasoning is often based on caring and __________, not justice. Research
does not support consistent sex differences in moral reasoning but has found that

males and females both consider caring as well as __________ in their moral judgments, depending upon the situation. justice

Promoting Moral Reasoning. Many factors can promote more sophisticated moral reasoning, including (a) noticing that one's current thinking is __________ (is contradictory or does not lead to clear actions), (b) observing others reason at more __________ levels, and (c) __________ moral issues with peers, teachers, and parents. inadequate; advanced, discussing

MODULE 15.3: THE WORLD OF WORK

Career Development. In his theory of vocational choice, Super proposes three phases of vocational development during adolescence and young adulthood: __________ in which basic interests are identified, specification in which jobs associated with interests are identified, and __________ which marks entry into the work force. Holland proposed six different work-related __________ types: realistic, investigative, social, conventional, enterprising, and artistic. Each is uniquely suited to certain jobs. People are __________ when their personalities fit their jobs and unhappy when they do not. crystallization; implementation; personality; happier

Part-Time Work. Most adolescents in the United States have part-time jobs. Adolescents who are employed more than __________ hours per week during the school year typically do poorly in school, often have lowered __________ and increased anxiety, and have problems interacting with others. Employed adolescents save relatively __________ of their income and, instead, they spend most of it on clothing, food, and entertainment for themselves, which can give misleading expectations about how to allocate income. Part-time employment can be beneficial if adolescents work relatively few hours, if the work allows them to use existing __________ or to acquire new ones, and if teens __________ some of their earnings. Summer employment, because it does not conflict with the demands of school, can also be beneficial. 15; self-esteem; little; skills, save

CHAPTER 15 COGNITIVE PROCESSES IN ADOLESCENTS

TEST YOURSELF

1. Which of the following is characteristic of formal operational thought?
   a. Animism
   b. Centration
   c. Deductive reasoning
   d. Reasoning that is limited to the tangible and real

2. When concrete operational and formal operational thinkers are asked to combine a number of clear liquids to produce a blue liquid,
   a. neither the concrete operational child nor the formal operational adolescent test the combinations of liquids in a systematic manner.

b. only the concrete operational child tests the combinations of liquids in a systematic manner.
c. only the formal operational child tests the combinations of liquids in a systematic manner.
d. both the concrete operational child and the formal operational adolescent test the combinations of liquids in a systematic manner.

3. When adolescents are presented with information that is either consistent or inconsistent with their beliefs,
a. they accept the inconsistent information.
b. they find more flaws with the studies that led to the inconsistent information.
c. they find more flaws with the studies that led to the consistent.
d. they find an equal number of flaws in the studies that led to both the consistent and inconsistent information.

4. Which of the following is *true* of cognition in adolescents?
a. Adolescents working memory capacity is much smaller than adults'.
b. Adolescents process information much more slowly than do adults.
c. Adolescents are not any better than children at choosing and monitoring memory strategies.
d. Adolescents' knowledge allows them to learn, understand, and remember more of their experiences.

5. A child who judges whether an act is good in terms of the physical consequences of reward and punishment is reasoning at which of Kohlberg's levels?
a. Preconventional level
b. Conventional level
c. Postconventional level
d. Empathic level

6. Moral decision making based on social norms is characteristic of which of Kohlberg's levels of moral reasoning?
a. Preconventional level
b. Conventional level
c. Postconventional level
d. Empathic level

7. At which level of Kohlberg's moral reasoning is reasoning governed by personal, moral principles?
a. Preconventional level
b. Conventional level
c. Postconventional level
d. Empathic level

8. A child who reasons at the preconventional level would help another person because
a. she might get a reward for helping.
b. she is afraid that others would disapprove of her if she didn't help.
c. helping is a good behavior that is valued by society.
d. she has a moral principle of responsibility for others.

9. Longitudinal studies measuring individuals' level of moral reasoning over time found that
a. many individuals skipped at least one of Kohlberg's stages.

b. it was common for individuals to revert to lower levels of reasoning.
c. most individuals progress to the highest levels of reasoning.
d. higher levels of moral reasoning are more common in adolescents and adults.

10. Individuals who are reared with traditional Hindu beliefs
a. base their moral reasoning on principles of individual rights and justice.
b. do not differ in their moral reasoning from those who are reared with Judeo-Christian beliefs.
c. base their moral reasoning on principles of duty and responsibility to others.
d. support Kohlberg's claim that the bases of moral reasoning are universal.

11. Which of the following does Carol Gilligan believe forms the basis of moral reasoning in women?
a. Justice
b. Responsibility and care
c. The need to find rewards and avoid guilt
d. The need to mature

12. Like Kohlberg, Gilligan believes that moral reasoning
a. is the same for men and women.
b. is based on justice and individual rights.
c. includes preconventional, conventional, and postconventional levels.
d. becomes qualitatively more sophisticated as individuals develop.

13. In Super's theory of career choice, adolescents are in a process of __________, in which they use their identities as a source of ideas about careers.
a. consolidation
b. crystallization
c. implementation
d. specification

14. Limiting career possibilities by learning more about specific lines of work and starting to obtain the required training for a job is called __________ by Super.
a. consolidation
b. crystallization
c. implementation
d. specification

15. Entering the work force and learning first hand about a job is called __________ by Super.
a. consolidation
b. crystallization
c. implementation
d. specification

16. Super's theory of career choice
a. takes into account economic factors that influence the job market.
b. suggests that individuals find jobs most satisfying when the distinguishing characteristics of the job fit their personalities.
c. includes six personality types that should be considered when choosing a career.
d. links career choice to the development of one's identity.

17. According to Holland's theory,
a. personality and job satisfaction are not related.
b. career development progresses through five different stages.
c. measures of vocational interest are useless in helping a person choose a career.
d. six prototypic personalities are important when people select a career.

18. Maxine likes to work in an environment that is structured and in which she has a supervisor who assigns her tasks. She used to be a payroll clerk, but now she enjoys her job as a bank teller. According to Holland, Maxine has a (n) __________ personality.
a. investigative
b. artistic
c. conventional
d. realistic

19. Research on adolescents and part-time work has found that
a. the number of adolescents with part-time jobs has decreased since the 1970s.
b. teens in the United States are more likely to hold part-time jobs than teens in Asia or Western Europe.
c. girls' jobs are more likely to pay more than boys' jobs.
d. a very small percentage of high school seniors work part-time.

20. The effects to teens who work more than 15-20 hours per week
a. include increased substance abuse.
b. are limited to poor academic performance.
c. include increased self-esteem.
d. include a greater sense of financial responsibility.

21. What do most adolescents do with the money that they earn from part-time jobs?
a. They save it for a long-term goal such as college tuition.
b. They help pay family living expenses.
c. They spend it on themselves.
d. They use it to help others.

ESSAY QUESTIONS

1. Recently your friend Martha took her sons to a hands-on children's museum. Martha noticed that her 8-year-old son and her 13-year-old son interacted with some of the displays in very different ways. One display involved opening doors to safes by determining the correct combination. Each safe had 3, 4, or 5 buttons that had to be pressed in a particular order to open the door. Martha's 8-year-old son randomly pushed the buttons and never found the correct combinations to any of the safes. Martha's 12-year-old son approached the task in a very systematic manner--trying all possible combinations of buttons until the doors opened. Now Martha is concerned that there is something wrong with her younger son. What can you tell Martha about the differences in concrete operational and formal operational thought that might explain her sons' behavior?

2. You and three of your friends were talking about Kohlberg's Heinz Dilemma. One of your friends said that Heinz should not steal the drug for his wife because it is illegal and laws are in place to protect people and property. Your other friend, who is a Hindu, said that Heinz should steal the drug because it is a husband's responsibility to care for his wife. After these two friends left, your third friend commented on the differences between the two answers. What can you tell your friend about cultural differences in moral reasoning?
3. Your 16-year-old son wants to get a part-time job at the local fast food restaurant. This job would involve working about 20 hours per week during the school year. Your spouse thinks that this is a great idea and that a part-time job will make your son more responsible and it will teach him the value of money. You, however, have read this textbook and don't think that the part-time job during the school year is a good idea. What can you tell your spouse about part-time employment during the school year for teens and the negative effects associated with it?
4. Your artistic, unconventional teenage daughter has told you that she would like to be a research scientist and discover the cure for heart disease when she grows up. You are not so sure that this is a good idea. What can you tell her about Holland's personality-type theory of occupational choice that might change her mind?

ANSWERS

Multiple Choice

1. c (457)	**8.** a (463)	**15.** c (470)
2. c (457)	**9.** d (465)	**16.** d (470)
3. b (459)	**10.** c (466)	**17.** d (471)
4. d (460)	**11.** b (467)	**18.** c (472)
5. a (463)	**12.** d (467)	**19.** b (473)
6. b (464)	**13.** b (470)	**20.** a (474)
7. c (464)	**14.** d (470)	**21.** c (474)

Essay

1. The behavior of Martha's sons fits Piaget's description of formal operational and concrete operational thought very well. According to Piaget, children who are 13 years old would be in the period of formal operations. Formal operational children use more sophisticated, logical, deductive reasoning to solve problems like the safe problem. However, concrete operational children (such as the 8-year old) use haphazard trial-and-error and often do not solve successfully problems like the safe problem. Concrete operational children are more likely to try to solve problems like this by randomly pushing buttons but formal operational children can think deductively about the possible, logical combinations before attempting the button pushing. In time, Martha's younger son also will use deductive reasoning and will solve the safe problem like his older brother. (456-457)

2. Cross-cultural research has shown that children and adolescents in North America reason at Stages 2 and 3 which is similar to findings in other cultures. However, adults in many non-Western cultures do not emphasize justice in moral reasoning. The emphasis on justice is apparent in cultures where the rights of the individual are emphasized. In cultures where the primary religion emphasizes different values, principles other than justice are used in moral reasoning. For example, the Hindu religion emphasizes duties and responsibilities toward others. In fact, research has shown that those reared with traditional Hindu beliefs do emphasize care and responsibility to others in moral reasoning. So, what you and your friend observed was a cultural difference in moral reasoning. (466-467)

3. Tell your spouse that part-time employment of over 15 hours during the school year for teens is associated with a number of negative outcomes. First, school performance drops because teens who are employed part-time don't seem to use their free time efficiently to do their homework. Second, teens who work over 15 hours per week during the school year are more likely to be depressed and suffer from anxiety. Even though many part-time jobs are boring and repetitive they may be very stressful during busy times which may lead to anxiety. This anxiety may also be related to increased substance abuse and problem behavior that is seen in teens who work many hours per week. Third, these part-time jobs rarely teach teens the value of money. Teens rarely save their money for college or help their parents pay for necessary items. Instead teens tend to spend most of their money on entertainment and personal items such as cosmetics or CDs. Because such a large percentage of their pay checks goes toward "fun" items, teens develop very unrealistic expectations about finances and budgeting. (474)

4. According to Holland's personality-type theory of vocational choice, one's personality should be a major factor in choosing a vocation. Holland suggested that people will feel more satisfied with their jobs if they choose jobs that fit their personality characteristics. Holland suggested six personality types. The first type is the realistic person who likes physical labor and likes to solve concrete problems. The second type is the investigative person who is task-oriented and enjoys thinking abstractly. The artistic person likes to express himself through unstructured tasks. The enterprising person likes to use verbal skill in positions of power or leadership. Finally, the social person is skilled verbally and socially and likes to use those skills to solve problems. Your daughter fits the artistic personality but the job of scientist fits the investigative personality. According to Holland, if your daughter would become a scientist she may not enjoy the job. (471-472)

Chapter 16
Social and Personality Development in Adolescents

Module 16.1 *Identity and Self-Esteem*

Module 16.2 *Relationships with Parents and Peers*

Module 16.3 *The Dark Side*

This chapter covers the adolescent identity and self-esteem, teens' relationships with their parents and peers, and problems that affect some adolescents.

IDENTITY AND SELF-ESTEEM

MODULE
16.1

Using This Book

- *The Search for Identity*
- *Ethnic Identity*
- *Self-Esteem in Adolescence*

Textbook Learning Objectives

- **How do adolescents achieve an identity?**
- **What is an ethnic identity? What are the stages in acquiring an ethnic identity?**
- **How does self-esteem change in adolescence?**

TO MASTER THESE LEARNING OBJECTIVES:

1. Know the terms associated with the adolescent sense of identity
2. Know the details associated with identity and self-esteem

Know the Terms Associated with the Sense of Identity: Match each definition with the correct term

Achievement
Adolescent egocentrism
Ethnic identity
Diffusion
Foreclosure
Illusion of invulnerability
Imaginary audience
Moratorium
Personal fable

1. Marcia's identity status in which individuals are confused or overwhelmed by the task of achieving an identity and they are doing little to achieve one.__________
2. Marcia's identity status in which individuals have an identity that is largely determined by adults, rather than from personal exploration of alternatives.__________
3. Marcia's identity status in which individuals are still examining different alternatives and have yet to find a satisfactory identity.__________
4. Marcia's identity status in which individuals have explored alternatives and have deliberately chosen a specific identity.__________
5. The self-absorption that marks the teen-age search for identity.__________
6. The feeling that many adolescents have that their behavior is constantly being watched by their peers.__________
7. Teenagers' tendency to believe that their experiences and feelings are unique and have never been experienced by anyone else before.__________
8. Adolescents' belief that misfortune only happens to others.__________
9. Feeling a part of an ethnic group and learning the special customs and traditions of their group's culture and heritage. __________

Know the Details Associated with the Development of a Sense of Self

1. T F Adolescents use their hypothetical reasoning skills to imagine themselves in different roles.
2. T F Adolescents experiment with religious and political beliefs.
3. T F According to Marcia, during the moratorium status individuals are overwhelmed by the task of achieving an identity and are doing little to achieve one.
4. T F According to Marcia, during the achievement status individuals have explored alternatives and have deliberately chosen a specific identity.
5. T F Achievement and moratorium statuses are more common in young adolescents.
6. T F Achievement status is attained for all aspects of identity at the same time.
7. T F Once an identity is achieved in adolescence it does not change during adulthood.
8. T F Adolescents' belief that others are constantly watching behavior is called the personal fable.
9. T F Adolescents' belief that their experiences and feelings are unique is called the illusion of invulnerability.
10. T F Children of parents who encourage discussion and recognize their children's autonomy are more likely to have children who reach the achievement status.
11. T F In the first phase of achieving an ethnic identity, adolescents begin to explore the personal impact of their ethnic heritage.

12. T F Adolescents are more likely to achieve an ethnic identity when their parents encourage them to explore alternatives rather than pressuring them to adopt a particular identity.
13. T F Adolescents who have achieved an ethnic identity have lower self-esteem.
14. T F African American children adopted by European Americans were better adjusted if they did not identify with either African or European Americans.
15. T F In general, self-esteem is highest during adolescence.
16. T F During the elementary-school years, self-esteem drops as children begin to compare themselves to their peers.
17. T F Sometimes self-esteem drops during the transition to junior high.
18. T F The drop in self-esteem associated with the transition to middle school or junior high lasts throughout adolescence.

ANSWERS

Key Terms

1. diffusion (481)
2. foreclosure (481)
3. moratorium (481)
4. achievement (481)
5. adolescent egocentrism (482)
6. imaginary audience (482)
7. personal fable (482)
8. illusion of invulnerability (483)
9. ethnic identity (484)

Know the Details

1. true (480)
2. true (480)
3. false (481)
4. true (481)
5. false (481)
6. false (481)
7. false (482)
8. false (482)
9. false (482)
10. true (483)
11. false (484)
12. true (484)
13. false (484)
14. false (486)
15. false (486)
16. true (486)
17. true (487)
18. false (487)

MODULE

16.2

Relationships with Parents and Peers

- *Parent-Child Relationships in Adolescence*
- *Relationships with Peers*

RELATIONSHIPS WITH PARENTS AND PEERS

Textbook Learning Objectives

- **How do parent-child relationships change in adolescence?**
- **What are the important features of groups in adolescence? How do groups influence adolescents?**
- **What are the important features of adolescents' friendships?**

TO MASTER THESE LEARNING OBJECTIVES:

1. Know the terms associated with peer relationships
2. Know the details of parent and peer relationships

Know the Terms Associated with Peer Relationships: Match each definition with the correct term

Clique
Crowd
Dominance hierarchy

1. A group of four to six individuals who are good friends and tend to be similar in age, sex, race, and interests.__________
2. A group of more than six older adolescents that have similar values, attitudes, and are known by a common label.__________
3. A characteristic of a group in which there is a leader to whom all other group members defer.__________

Know the Details of Parent and Peer Relationships

1. T F Teens fare best when their parents use authoritarian parenting.
2. T F Mothers of adolescent sons are particularly vulnerable to falling into the negative reinforcement trap.
3. T F Adolescents' relationships with their parents become more egalitarian.
4. T F Research supports the idea that adolescence is a time of storm and stress.
5. T F The results of cross-cultural studies indicate that most adolescents report that they usually are happy and that they do not try to avoid their homes (see figure below).

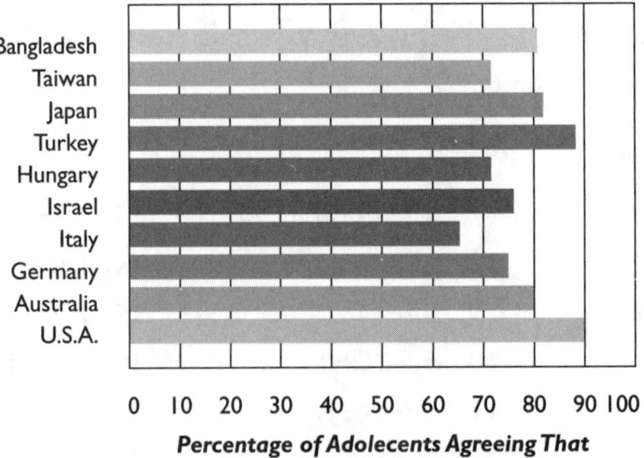

Percentage of Adolecents Agreeing That "Most of the Time, I Am Happy"

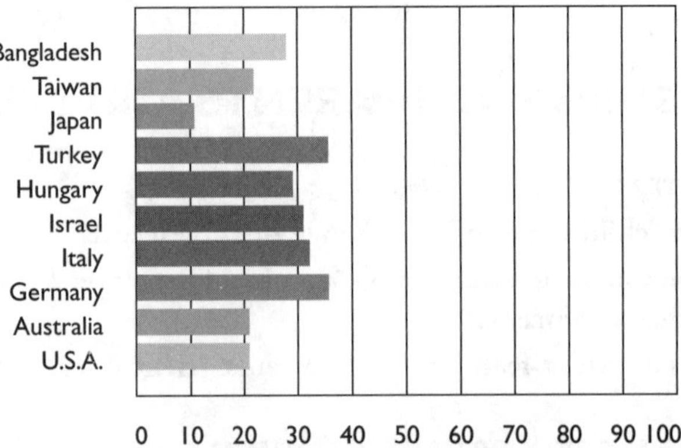

Percentage of Adolecents Agreeing That "I Try to Stay Away From Home Most of the Time"

Source: Offer et al., 1988.

6. T F In the Robbers Cave Study, hostility between the Eagles and Rattlers disappeared when the groups participated in enjoyable, noncompetitive activities like watching a movie together.

7. T F When groups of children are brought together, a group structure emerges with individuals having specific roles.

8. T F When groups compete for scarce resources, they cooperate more with other groups.

9. T F Cliques are often part of a larger group that is called a crowd.

10. T F Youth from high-status crowds tend to have lower self-esteem than those from low-status crowds.

11. T F When parents emphasize achievement and monitor their children, their children are more likely to be in the druggie crowd.

12. T F Dominance hierarchies are uncommon in children's groups.

13. T F Among girls, physical power typically is the basis for one's position in the dominance hierarchy.

14. T F Most adolescents give in to peer pressure to behave in ways that are clearly antisocial.

15. T F Peer pressure is most powerful when the standards for appropriate behavior are not clear-cut.

16. T F Adolescents believe that loyalty, trust, and intimacy are important ingredients of friendship.

17. T F Intimacy is more common in boys' friendships than in girls' friendships.

18. T F Adolescents are more likely to turn to friends than family members for support.

19. T F Adolescents with friends who have prosocietal attitudes tend to be happier and have more satisfying relationships when they are in their 30s.

20. T F Early dating experiences involve well-defined couples.

21. T F Hispanic American and Asian American teens begin dating at an earlier age and date more frequently once they begin.

22. T F As adolescents mature, dating is seen as a way to fulfill intimacy and companionship needs.

ANSWERS

Key Terms

1. clique (491)

2. crowd (491)

3. dominance hierarchy (492)

Know the Details

1. false (488)
2. true (488)
3. true (488)
4. false (489)
5. true (489)
6. false (490)
7. true (491)
8. false (491)
9. true (491)
10. false (491)
11. false (491)
12. false (492)
13. false (492)
14. false (492)
15. true (492)
16. true (493)
17. false (494)
18. true (494)
19. true (494)
20. false (494)
21. false (495)
22. true (495)

MODULE
16.3

The Dark Side
- *Drug Use*
- *Depression*
- *Delinquency*

THE DARK SIDE

Textbook Learning Objectives

- **Why do teenagers drink?**
- **What leads some adolescents to become depressed? How can depression be treated?**
- **What are the causes of juvenile delinquency?**

TO MASTER THESE LEARNING OBJECTIVES:

1. Know the terms associated with problems affecting adolescents
2. Know the details of problems that can affect adolescents

Know the Terms Associated with Problems Affecting Adolescents: Match each definition with the correct term

Adolescent-limited
Depression
Index offenses
Juvenile delinquency
Learned helplessness
Life-course persistent
Norepinephrine
Serotonin
Status offenses

1. Pervasive feelings of sadness, irritability, and low self-esteem are characteristic of __________.
2. The feeling that one is always at the mercy of external events and that one does not have any control over one's own destiny is called __________.
3. __________ is a neurotransmitter that helps control brain centers that allow people to experience and are related to depression.
4. __________ is a neurotransmitter that helps control brain centers that allow people to experience and are related to depression.
5. __________ consists of adolescents committing illegal acts that are destructive toward themselves or others.
6. __________ are acts that are not crimes if they are committed by an adult. This would include truancy and running away from home.

7. Acts that are illegal regardless of the age of the perpetrator are called __________.
8. Antisocial behavior that emerges at an early age and continues throughout life is called __________.
9. __________ antisocial behavior involves youth who engage in relatively minor criminal acts and aren't consistently antisocial.

Know the Details of Problems That Can Affect Adolescents

1. T F A majority of high school seniors use marijuana.
2. T F Teens often drink to escape a harsh and unpleasant world.
3. T F Teens are more likely to drink when drinking is an important part of their parents' social lives.
4. T F Many adolescents drink because of peer pressure.
5. T F Adolescent boys experience depression more often than do adolescent girls.
6. T F Depressed adolescents often believe that family members, friends, and classmates are not friendly toward them.
7. T F Depression often begins with an event in which an adolescent feels in control of the outcome.
8. T F There is no evidence for a hereditary or biological cause of depression.
9. T F Antidepressant drugs work by correcting the imbalance in the levels of neurotransmitters.
10. T F Suicide is more common among adolescent girls than boys.
11. T F Suicide is more common among older adolescents than among children.
12. T F Native American adolescents have the highest suicide rates of any ethnic group in the United States.
13. T F Suicide is usually spontaneous with no warning signals.
14. T F Index offenses are not crimes if they are committed by an adult.
15. T F Adolescents are responsible for many of the index offenses committed in the United States.
16. T F Life-course persistent antisocial behavior is the most common form of antisocial behavior seen in adolescents.
17. T F Adolescent crime is more common in youth from lower social classes.
18. T F Delinquent behavior is more common in adolescents who have little parental supervision.
19. T F Delinquent adolescents tend to have more self-control than nondelinquent peers.
20. T F Programs that teach self-control to aggressive and impulsive youth are not successful.

ANSWERS

Key Terms

1. depression (497)
2. learned helplessness (498)
3. norepinephrine (498)
4. serotonin (498)
5. juvenile delinquency (499)
6. status offenses (499)
7. index offenses (499)
8. life-course persistent (500)
9. adolescent-limited (500)

Know the Details

1. false (496)
2. true (496)
3. true (497)
4. true (497)
5. false (497)
6. true (497)
7. false (498)
8. false (498)
9. true (498)
10. false (499)
11. true (499)
12. true (499)
13. false (499)
14. false (499)
15. true (499)
16. false (500)
17. true (500)
18. true (501)
19. false (501)
20. false (501)

SUMMARY

MODULE 16.1: IDENTITY AND SELF-ESTEEM

foreclosure achievement watching felt discussion	*The Search for Identity.* The task for adolescents is to find an identity. The search for identity typically involves four statuses. Diffusion and __________ are more common in early adolescence; moratorium and __________ are more common in late adolescence and young adulthood. As they seek identity, adolescents often believe that others are always __________ them and that no one else has __________ as they do. Adolescents are most likely to achieve an identity when parents encourage __________ and recognize their autonomy; they are least likely to achieve an identity when parents set rules and enforce them without explanation.
exploration higher	*Ethnic Identity.* Adolescents from ethnic groups often progress through three phases in acquiring an ethnic identity: initial disinterest, __________, and identity achievement. Achieving an ethnic identity usually results in __________ self-esteem but is not consistently related to the strength of one's identification with mainstream culture.
comparisons declines responsibilities	*Self-Esteem in Adolescence.* Social __________ begin anew when children move from elementary school to middle or junior high school, and, consequently, self-esteem usually __________ somewhat during the transition. However, self-esteem begins to rise in middle and late adolescence as teenagers see themselves acquiring more adult skills and __________.

MODULE 16.2: RELATIONSHIPS

Parent-Child Relationships in Adolescence. As was true for parent-child relationships in childhood, adolescents benefit from __________ parenting and often face the challenges of their parents' divorce or remarriage. The parent-child relationship becomes more __________ during the adolescent years, reflecting adolescents' growing independence. Contrary to myth, adolescence is not usually a period of __________. Most adolescents love their parents, feel __________ by them, rely upon them for advice, and adopt their __________.

authoritative
egalitarian
storm and stress, loved
values

Relationships with Peers. Adolescents often form __________ --small groups of like-minded individuals--that become part of a crowd. Some crowds have higher status than others and members of higher-status crowds often have __________ self-esteem than members of lower-status crowds. Most groups have a dominance hierarchy, a well-defined structure with a leader at the top. Physical power often determines the dominance hierarchy, particularly among younger __________. However, with older children and adolescents, dominance hierarchies are more often based on __________ that are important to the group. Peer pressure is greatest where standards of behavior are __________, such as tastes in music or clothing, or concerning drinking, using drugs, and sex. Compared to friendships in childhood, adolescent friendships emphasize loyalty and __________. Intimacy is more common in girls' friendships than boys', which makes girls more concerned about friends being faithful. When they need help, teenagers turn to friends more often than to parents. Boys and girls begin to date in mid-adolescence. Dating often begins with the meeting of same-sex groups and progresses to __________. For younger adolescents, dating is for both recreation and __________; for older adolescents, it is a source of intimacy and __________.

cliques
higher
boys
skills
unclear
intimacy
well-defined couples
status, companionship

MODULE 16.3: THE DARK SIDE

Drug Use. Today, many adolescents drink alcohol regularly. Adolescents are attracted to alcohol and other drugs by their need for experimentation, for __________, for escape, and for feelings of exhilaration. The primary factors that influence whether adolescents drink are encouragement from parents and peers and stress.

relaxation

Depression. Depressed adolescents have little enthusiasm for life, believe that others are __________, and wish to be left alone. Depression can be triggered by an event that deprives them of rewarding experiences, by an event in which they felt unable to __________ their own destiny, or by an imbalance in neurotransmitters such as norepinephrine and serotonin. Treatment of depression relies upon medications that correct the levels of __________ and therapy designed to improve social skills and restructure adolescents' __________ of events.

unfriendly
control
neurotransmitters
interpretation

Delinquency. Many youth engage in antisocial behavior briefly during adolescence. In contrast, the small percentage of adolescents who engage in life-course persistent anti-social behavior are involved in one-fourth to one-half of the serious crimes committed in the United States. Life-course persistent antisocial behavior has been linked to social class, __________, lack of __________, and heredity. Efforts to reduce adolescent criminal activity must take aim at all of these variables.

family processes, self-control

CHAPTER 16 SOCIAL AND PERSONALITY DEVELOPMENT IN ADOLESCENTS

TEST YOURSELF

1. In Marcia's theory, __________ describes individuals who have identities that are determined largely by adults, rather than from personal exploration.
a. diffusion
b. foreclosure
c. moratorium
d. achievement

2. In Marcia's theory, __________ describes individuals who are still examining different alternative identities.
a. diffusion
b. foreclosure
c. moratorium
d. achievement

3. Marcia's achievement identity status
a. occurs more in younger than in older adolescents.
b. occurs more in older than in younger adolescents.
c. is not related to age.
d. is achieved in all aspects of identity at the same time.

4. Sixteen-year-old Ingrid discovered a spot on her blouse after she arrived at school. Ingrid is afraid that everyone will notice the spot and think that she is stupid. Which of the following terms best describes Ingrid's beliefs?
a. Adolescent egocentrism
b. Imaginary audience
c. Personal fable
d. Illusion of invulnerability

5. Michael, 15, was just dumped by his girlfriend, Lisa. Michael's dad told him that he knew how Michael feels but that in time he will feel better. Michael is convinced that his dad does not know how it feels to be dumped by a girlfriend and that his dad does not know what he is talking about. Which of the following terms best describes Michael's beliefs?
a. Adolescent egocentrism
b. Imaginary audience
c. Personal fable
d. Illusion of invulnerability

6. Adolescents are more likely to reach achievement status when their parents
a. recognize their children's autonomy.
b. discourage discussion.
c. discourage personal experimentation.
d. simply tell them what identity to adopt.

7. Recently, Ramiro has become interested in his ethnic heritage. He has attended some Mexican American festivals and has read some books on the role that Mexican Americans have played in the history of the United States. Ramiro is in which stage of achieving an ethnic identity?
   a. First stage
   b. Second stage
   c. Third stage
   d. Fourth stage

8. Adolescents who have achieved a strong ethnic identity
   a. have lower self-esteem.
   b. find interactions with family and friends less satisfying.
   c. do poorly in school.
   d. have parents who encouraged them to explore alternative identities.

9. In a study of racial identity in African American children who were adopted by European American parents, the investigators found that
   a. most of the children identified more strongly as European Americans than African Americans.
   b. most of the children identified more strongly as African Americans than European Americans.
   c. the children who identified more strongly as African Americans were much better adjusted than those who identified as European Americans.
   d. the children who identified themselves as neither African American nor European American were better adjusted than those who identified themselves as European American.

10. At which age would you be most likely to find the highest levels of self-esteem?
   a. Preschool years
   b. Early elementary-school years
   c. Late elementary-school years
   d. Middle school/Junior high years

11. Most adolescents report that they
   a. do not love their parents.
   b. do not ask their parents for advice.
   c. embrace many of their parents' values.
   d. feel unloved by their parents.

12. According to cross-cultural research, most adolescents
   a. try to avoid home most of the time.
   b. are more affectionate with their parents than they were as children.
   c. experience much conflict with parents and emotional turmoil.
   d. report that they are happy most of the time.

13. The Robbers Cave Study demonstrated that
   a. adults usually need to intervene to establish a group structure.
   b. when groups compete for scarce resources a friendly competition between the groups arises.
   c. when common goals require cooperation, hostility between groups increases.
   d. competition for scarce resources leads to increased group identification and group support.

14. Adolescents are more likely to be in a "druggie" crowd when their parents
a. emphasize academic achievement.
b. use the authoritative style of parenting.
c. fail to monitor their out-of-school behavior.
d. when parents include their children in joint decision making.

15. When dominance hierarchies form in girls' groups, the girls at the top of the hierarchy
a. are the smartest.
b. have the skills that are the most valuable to the group.
c. are the most intimidating physically.
d. are the friendliest.

16. Peer groups are most likely to exert influence
a. when the appropriate behavior is clear and well-defined.
b. in subjective areas such as preferences in music and clothing.
c. on clearly antisocial behaviors such as stealing.
d. in unambiguous situations.

17. Friendships during adolescence
a. are characterized by intimacy and trust.
b. are not as important as friendships in younger children.
c. do not place an emphasis on loyalty.
d. are not different from those of younger children.

18. Which teen is most likely to begin dating at an earlier age?
a. Young-shin who is an Asian American
b. Marta who is a Cuban American
c. Lupe who is Mexican American
d. Jane who is European American

19. Which of the following functions of dating would you expect 19-year-old Ted to seek from dating?
a. Mate selection
b. Companionship
c. Status with his peers
d. Recreation and entertainment

20. Which is the most commonly used drug among adolescents in the United States?
a. Alcohol
b. Cocaine
c. Marijuana
d. Heroin

21. Teens are less likely to drink when
a. drinking is an important part of the ir parents' social lives.
b. they experience much conflict at home with their parents.
c. their parents limit their drinking to small quantities with meals.
d. they receive pressure to drink from their peers.

22. Depression
  a. does not seem to be influenced by heredity.
  b. is related to increased levels of neurotransmitters.
  c. may be triggered by events that the adolescent feels that s/he can control.
  d. may be treated by drugs that change the levels of serotonin.

23. Suicide is more common among
  a. older adolescents than children.
  b. African American adolescents than Native American adolescents.
  c. girls than boys.
  d. nondepressed than depressed adolescents.

24. Which of the following is an index offense?
  a. Running away from home
  b. Skipping school
  c. Sexual promiscuity
  d. Burning down an abandoned building

25. Which of the following teens is most at risk for becoming a juvenile delinquent?
  a. Frank, who has lots of parental supervision
  b. Joe, who has lots of self-control and often delays gratification
  c. Chet, who is impulsive and aggressive
  d. Fenton, who is from a middle-class home

ESSAY QUESTIONS

1. Your friends think that there is something wrong with their 16-year-old son. One week he says that he wants to be a rock star and the next he says that he wants to be a pediatrician. Your friends don't think that a normal adolescent can change identities so rapidly. Based on what you know about achieving an identity in adolescence what can you tell your friends to make them feel better?

2. Another friend is having trouble with her teenage daughter. She thinks that her daughter must feel unloved and has rejected all of her parents' values because they argue all the time about her daughter's choice of music and clothes. What can you tell your friend about adolescents to make her feel better?

3. You are a teacher in school that doesn't have much money. Unfortunately, the lack of money means that many resources such as computers and other classroom equipment are scarce. Recently, you have noticed that the children have formed groups and these groups are competing for the school's scarce resources. This competition has led to much hostility, name-calling, and fighting between the groups. Based on your knowledge of the Robbers Cave Study, what can you do to decrease the hostility and increase the positive interactions between the groups?

4. Your friend Jevan is concerned that his teenage daughter Antigone might be drinking. What can you tell Jevan about the factors associated with teenage alcohol abuse that might help him and his daughter?

5. Your brother is worried that his daughter Yolanda might be depressed and suicidal. What can you tell your brother about the signs of suicide and the course of action if these signs are present that could help him and your niece?

ANSWERS

Multiple Choice

1. b (481)
2. c (481)
3. b (481)
4. b (482)
5. c (482)
6. a (483)
7. b (484)
8. d (484)
9. a (486)
10. a (486)
11. c (489)
12. d (489)
13. d (491)
14. c (491)
15. b (492)
16. b (492)
17. a (493)
18. d (495)
19. b (495)
20. a (496)
21. c (497)
22. d (498)
23. a (499)
24. d (499)
25. c (500)

Essay

1. During early adolescence, most teens either have no identity (diffusion status) or have chosen an identity that is based on advice from adults (foreclosure status). As teens progress through adolescence they begin to "try-on" different identities to see how each one fits (moratorium status). These different identities may be as diverse as rock star and pediatrician. Eventually, during later adolescence or early adulthood, after trying many different identities, one finds an identity that "fits" (achievement status). In other words, your friends' son is acting like other teens his age and he probably won't settle on an identity for a few years yet. (481-482)
2. Research findings do not support the view that adolescence is a time of storm and stress. In fact, most adolescents love their parents, turn to their parents for advice, accept many of their parents' values, feel loved by their parents, and report that they are happy most of the time. However, as teens become more independent they may seem as if they do not love their parents as much, because they spend less time with them and are less affectionate with them. Teens also are more likely to argue with their parents over more trivial topics such as music, clothes, and curfews. (488-489)
3. Based on the Robbers Cave Study, when groups compete for scarce resources group cohesiveness increases and hostility toward other groups increases. One way to alleviate the hostility would be to provide more equipment but the school district probably won't suddenly have more money. Another way to deal with the situation is to create situations that require the groups to cooperate and collaborate to achieve a common goal. This should lead to less hostility and more positive interactions between groups. For example, the amount of time allowed for free time would be directly related to the ability to complete a classroom project in a cooperative (and thus, quicker) manner. Because the resources are scarce at your school, you should make an effort to eliminate as many situations as possible in which competition for the school's resources could occur. (490-491)

4. You can tell Jevan that adolescents often drink because their peers do and they pressure them to join them. However, the family atmosphere and the example that parents set for drinking behavior are also important. If parents set the example that drinking is a pleasurable activity, then teens are more likely to drink. In contrast, when parents limit their drinking to small quantities of alcohol to complement meals, their teens are less likely to drink. Also, teens who have more problems with parents or peers are more likely to drink and to drink more often. Jevan can help his daughter by reducing stress and conflict at home, and setting a good example of responsible drinking behavior. (496-497)

5. If Yolanda has been depressed or if she has engaged in substance abuse, your brother should be worried because these are two common precursors of suicide. Some other warning signs include the person threatening to commit suicide, being preoccupied with death, changing her eating or sleeping habits, losing interest in activities that used to be important, exhibiting marked changes in personality, expressing persistent feelings of gloom and helplessness, and giving away valued possessions. If Yolanda shows any of these signs, your brother should NOT ignore them but should ask Yolanda if she is planning to hurt herself. Your brother should remain calm and supportive. If Yolanda appears to have made preparations to commit suicide, she shouldn't be left alone. Your brother should also insist that Yolanda seek professional help to treat her feelings of depression and hopelessness that may be leading to the suicidal thoughts. (499)